THE BOYS OF WINTER

THE BOYS OF WINTER

ENGLAND'S 2003 RUGBY WORLD CUP WIN, AS TOLD BY THE TEAM

LAWRENCE DALLAGLIO

AND OWEN SLOT

BLINK

bringing you closer

First published in the UK by Blink Publishing
An imprint of The Zaffre Publishing Group
A Bonnier Books UK company
4th Floor, Victoria House,
Bloomsbury Square,
London, WC1B 4DA

Owned by Bonnier Books
Sveavägen 56, Stockholm, Sweden

Hardback – 9781788706568
Trade Paperback – 9781788706551
Ebook – 9781788706544
Audio Digital Download – 9781788706537

A CIP catalogue of this book is available from the British Library.

Designed by Envy Design Ltd
Printed and bound by Clays Ltd, Elcograf S.p.A.

1 3 5 7 9 10 8 6 4 2

Blink Publishing is an imprint of Bonnier Books UK
www.bonnierbooks.co.uk

This book is dedicated to the many people who made winning the 2003 World Cup possible, we all shared an incredible journey; to each and every England RWC squad player and to those players who didn't make the plane to Australia but who helped make us the team that became number one in the world and ultimately lifted the William Webb Ellis Cup; to our visionary leader and disruptor Clive Woodward, without whom England would simply never have won; to the entire England management team and staff who inspired and lifted us to new heights; to the RFU team, led by Francis Baron, who despite our differences were able to find and support us in a way that very few teams have matched since; to all the Premiership clubs, coaches and players who, without realising it, played a bigger role than you can ever imagine; and finally, to the legions of England supporters who grew up with us and stayed with us through the highs and lows. We reached the top of the mountain all together and it was the greatest feeling in the world!

CONTENTS

ENGLAND 2003 RUGBY WORLD CUP SQUAD

BACKS

Stuart Abbott: Age 25. England caps 2. Centre, Wasps

Iain Balshaw: Age 24. Caps 16. Wing/full-back, Bath

Kyran Bracken: Age 31. Caps 47. Scrum-half, Saracens

Mike Catt: Age 32. Caps 61. Centre, Bath

Ben Cohen: Age 25. Caps 29. Wing, Northampton Saints

Matt Dawson: Age 30. Caps 57. Scrum-half, Northampton
Saints

Andy Gomarsall: Age 29. Caps 13. Scrum-half, Gloucester

Paul Grayson: Age 32. Caps 27. Fly-half, Northampton Saints

Will Greenwood: Age 30. Caps 41. Centre, Harlequins

Josh Lewsey: Age 26. Caps 13. Wing/full-back, Wasps

Dan Luger: Age 28. Caps 34. Wing, Perpignan

Jason Robinson: Age 29. Caps 21. Wing/full-back, Sale Sharks

Mike Tindall: Age 24. Caps 27. Centre, Bath

Jonny Wilkinson: Age 24. Caps 46. Fly-half, Newcastle Falcons

FORWARDS

Neil Back: Age 34. Caps 60. Back row, Leicester Tigers

Martin Corry: Age 29. Caps 28. Back row, Leicester Tigers

Lawrence Dallaglio: Age 31. Caps 58. Back row, Wasps

Danny Grewcock: Age 30. Caps 42. Second row, Bath

Richard Hill: Age 30. Caps 60. Back row, Saracens

Martin Johnson (captain): Age 33. Caps 77. Second row, Leicester Tigers

Ben Kay: Age 27. Caps 22. Second row, Leicester Tigers

Jason Leonard: Age 35. Caps 106. Prop, Harlequins

Lewis Moody: Age 25. Caps 17. Back row, Leicester Tigers

Mark Regan: Age 31. Caps 26. Hooker, Leeds Tykes

Simon Shaw:* Age 30. Caps 23. Second row, Wasps

Steve Thompson: Age 25. Caps 18. Hooker, Northampton Saints

Phil Vickery: Age 27. Caps 31. Prop, Gloucester

Dorian West: Age 36. Caps 19. Hooker, Leicester Tigers

Julian White: Age 30. Caps 17. Prop, Leicester Tigers

Trevor Woodman: Age 27. Caps 10. Prop, Gloucester

Joe Worsley: Age 26. Caps 27. Back row, Wasps

*Injury replacement for Grewcock, mid-tournament

SENIOR COACHING STAFF

Dave Alred. Age 55, Kicking Coach

Phil Keith-Roach. Age 58, Scrum Coach

Phil Larder. Age 58, Defence Coach

Dave Reddin. Age 33, Fitness Coach

Andy Robinson. Age 39, Forwards Coach

Clive Woodward. Age 47, Head Coach

PROLOGUE

Inside the stadium, every eye is on the scrum-half. We recognise the unfolding gameplay. We watch the fly-half composing himself. He is in the pocket. Those words alone tell the story. The fly-half is in the pocket.

Lawrence is watching too. Can you remember where you were when the scrum-half was standing over the ball, when the time clock told us that this was the last chance in the game and the fly-half was in the pocket? This is a 'where were you?' moment and the answer for Lawrence is that he was out in the midfield, closer to the wing than the scrum-half and the breakdown, not that that is an error, but it is about the only place in the story when you won't find him at the centre of the action. Yet he, too, is watching, the choreography clear, the next orchestrated move the most scripted in the England playbook. We just don't know yet how it finishes.

The narrative of the story is taking place outside the stadium too. There are ticket-holders who have vacated their seats; they have crossed the world for this team, to watch a squad of Englishmen who have allowed a rare hope to rise in their souls, but they are now pacing up and down following not the action but the noise, jittery hands trying to light damp cigarettes. This is England, this is British sport, which means that there is an inevitability that somehow it won't work out, that they will find a way to render the dance move incomplete. So for some, it's safer to endure it outside, eyes on the tarmac rather than the scrum-half.

The scrum-half positions himself over the ball, crouched, sideways on. He puts his hands to the ground and we think this is it. But so does everyone, even the opposition, who shift forward nervously, greyhounds in the traps, ready to go.

Is that OK? With his hands, he gestures to the referee. Are you going to let them wander offside? This is what Lawrence specifically remembers: there are two or three of them offside. Is the referee going to give that? The referee's not giving anything.

How many are in the stadium? Officially just under 83,000. But how many have actually said: 'I was there, I was inside, I saw it happen.' It is two decades past now, but still, every week, it seems, someone will tell Lawrence, 'I was there,' or 'I couldn't take it any more; I was outside,' or 'I remember that moment because the world stood still.' So, more than 83,000 then.

How does it feel to be the fly-half, at that moment, when the world is standing still for you? He doesn't actually know. Somehow he has switched off the wiring of his mind, anxieties have become suspended, and he is in a strange, fleeting bliss where he has only focus for the scrum-half, his eyes intent on the movements of the other man's hands. 'If I'd had any conscious thought process around that moment,' he says, 'I'd probably have fallen on the floor and just fainted.'

So the opposition retreat, only by inches but this is the

perfect moment. This is the end of the dance. The scrum-half unleashes the pass, the fly-half takes it, he is completely in the moment, he unleashes a drop kick off his right foot and the ball sets off, spinning, a perfect parabola stretching gloriously through the sky.

PART ONE

CHAPTER 1

ON THE ROAD

Lawrence is fiddling with his iPhone, his thumbs setting Google Maps with the coordinates to put us on the road to Martin Johnson. It is 20 years since that drop goal and we are outside Lawrence's house in Richmond, sitting in his car, plotting the first leg of a long journey. First stop: Johnno.

It may now be two decades past, yet still, most days, someone – anyone, and it's usually someone he's not met before – will ask Lawrence about the World Cup or the drop goal. On this occasion, though, it is Lawrence setting out on a quest for a truth of his own. What did it mean, that night of the drop goal, two decades ago? How did we do it? And what did it do to us? 'No one's ever tried to answer that,' says Lawrence, checking his phone as Google Maps reveals the route to Martin Johnson and the start of the answer.

So this is the plan. We start in Richmond, and our first stop is Leicester: Martin Johnson and his old Leicester Tigers teammates. Second stop: Jason Robinson at the Landmark Hotel, Marylebone. Third stop: Kyran Bracken's house in

3

north London. And so it will go. This is a voyage around the England squad of 2003.

We certainly don't know what we are going to find. Lawrence says he feels three things: 'intrigued, excited and daunted' and he explains: 'Reuniting with a group of very special people is quite an exciting prospect, but quite daunting also.' They may have been an extraordinary team and they may also have achieved extraordinary things, but that doesn't necessarily mean that they're best buddies who see each other every week. 'Our lives have significantly moved on,' he says. 'How we saw people then is not how we see them now.' Indeed, and the drop goal of 20 years ago looks different now too.

There are some snags along the way. We struggle to pin down Matt Dawson because he's so busy. What do we do about Mike Catt in Ireland and Dan Luger in Monaco? (Well, Zoom them, of course.) And then there are the admin and logistical problems: why is Lawrence's phone charger so crap? In which case, when his battery's died and he can't get Google Maps, who's going to navigate? And how's he going to get his bets on in Ascot week?

The answer is his co-pilot. That's me, his co-author. I was also there on that unforgettable night in 2003, privileged to have a seat in the press tribune, physically spent from eight weeks of following his England team around Australia and reporting every day for *The Times*, and eventually staggered, thrilled and also somewhat apprehensive about the scale of the story that unfolded on that incredible final night.

In the car with Lawrence, there is a conversation that goes round and round without conclusion, our recurring theme: how did England win that World Cup, because if the answer was so clear, why have they never won it since? And no, the barren 20 years that followed do not make Lawrence happy. You want to poke a bear? You ask Lawrence what's wrong with England rugby. No road is long enough for that.

Yet we find answers along the way. We also find a story warped by the 20 years of its retelling. There were 31 players in that squad and a large coaching staff too; that makes for over 30 different versions. So 2003 isn't one story; it is over 30 different perspectives. So, for Lawrence, the questions start to change because, with hindsight, the picture changes too. It's not just: how did we do it? It's also: what did it take out of us? And: what was left of us after it had been and gone and the roars of acclaim were heard for the last time?

'No one really knows why we won,' says Lawrence. 'And no one knows the collateral damage of winning either. Success is complicated.'

We are also driving out of Lawrence's comfort zone here. 'Part of your make-up as a sportsman,' he says, 'is not to dwell too much on the past. You don't like to look back – you always look ahead.' So here begins an unlikely assignment for him: a journey of retrospection.

When we meet Jason Robinson, who scored England's try in that World Cup final, Robinson says exactly this – that 'it seems quite strange, actually, sitting here, talking about it. With another player. Because we've only come together once as a group in nearly 20 years.'

Part of that is cultural. It might be frustratingly rare in English sport that a national team wins a world title, but one thing is for sure: when they do, they don't feel comfortable shouting about it. 'You're taught not to sit back and talk about all your great successes,' Lawrence says.

Josh Lewsey sees it similarly, yet slightly differently; he always did. Twenty years on that hasn't changed. That group of players, he says, were like 'silverback gorillas. When your time is done, everyone just goes off to the woods to be by themselves, to find their own little corner they can call home, where perhaps they don't have to be quite as alpha. That's kind of what's happened.'

Indeed. And here we are, 20 years on, setting off into many of those far-flung corners.

There is mild disappointment, then, that due to timing and rescheduling, Monte Carlo isn't one of them; that is why we miss out on a trip to see Luger. So we meet him instead over Zoom, and even online we are left somewhat jaw-dropped at how he has mastered the lifestyle thing: working on the financial markets in the week, snowboarding at the weekend in Verbier where his girlfriend works, and spending his spare time at a private Monaco gym club with Sascha Zverev, the German tennis player, 'the F1 boys' and 'all the INEOS [cycling] boys' whom he will sometimes ride out with when the ski stations are closed.

There is a genuine joy in almost all these isolated reunions, whether on Zoom or in person. These men may have shared a unique piece of England rugby history, but they don't live in each other's pockets. As Johnson says to Lawrence, when we arrive in Leicester, 'I've not seen you since I don't know when.'

Johnson still has some old World Cup teammates – Ben Kay, Martin Corry and Julian White – living reasonably close yet, as he says, 'Blokes never meet for a coffee.' The modern way for ex-rugby players to socialise is on their road bikes. 'Actually,' Johnson says, 'when you ride a bike, you do end up having a coffee and a bit of a chat. But Cozza [Corry] is too busy for cycling now.'

So Johnson is pretty happy to meet Lawrence instead. And without road bikes. Actually, he is so happy that he is still talking

6

after an hour and a half when White joins us, and another whole hour later when Kay joins us too. So soon there are four old teammates sitting back, rewinding World Cup stories and mocking each other as though the 20 years had never passed.

White didn't play in that Sydney final, so he says that he still sometimes feels that he's not really part of the group and that 'the players who were playing have been very generous to a lot of us who weren't.' To which Johnson, dry and lightning-fast, replies: 'We haven't, Whitey. We've been slating you.'

Johnson then picks up on the theme. Sir Clive Woodward, the head coach, always made a point of saying that they weren't a team of 15, or a matchday squad of 22, but a whole World Cup squad of 30: 'At the end of everything, he'd say: "Well done to the guys not playing." Did we have a name for them, Lawrence?' Johnson smiles and then delivers the punchline: 'Those shite guys over there.'

Probably no one is more delighted to see Lawrence and talk 2003 than Phil Keith-Roach, the old scrum coach. There is also probably no one with more pride and reverence for this team. When we arrive at his apartment, near Lord's, he has his beloved jazz on loud and immediately declares that we are going out to The Summerhouse, round the corner, for dinner. 'Cheers, Phil – not quite what we expected,' says Lawrence. 'Have you tried the white wine?' he replies. 'Do you feel at home?'

Probably no one has more trophies on display than Mark Regan. He gives us a Zoom tour of his walls which involves an impromptu introduction to his cleaner.

Definitely no one has a longer driveway than Mike Tindall. Though maybe, as the only member of the royal family, that is only appropriate.

Maybe no one surprises Lawrence as much as Danny

Grewcock, who now works as a tutor and a rugby coach in the grand setting of Clifton School in Bristol. It was with his old school, Clifton, in mind that the poet Henry Newbolt wrote 'Vitai Lampada', with its famous line 'Play up! Play up! and play the game', a poem which starts with the 'breathless hush in the Close tonight' and it is in the pavilion in front of the cricket ground, with the poem's 'bumping pitch' and 'blinding light', that Grewcock discusses being an educationalist and the value of sport in education.

Lawrence asks him if, when he tells his players never to strike an opponent, they ever ask him if he himself used to practise what he preaches. 'Oh, man,' Grewcock replies. 'They've all watched YouTube and they'll be like, "Sir, I've just been watching your game against Ulster." I tell them that the game was different in those days.'

'This is a man,' says Lawrence, 'who got 70-plus caps between weeks and weeks of disciplinary bans.' Yet by the time we leave, he is hugely impressed. 'Classy and quite genteel,' he says of him.

From Bristol, we head to dinner in Cheltenham to eat at No.3, the new(ish) restaurant owned by Phil Vickery. Very good, highly recommended. We are treated to a world-class steak plus, just in one brief flash, a glimmer of what these men were probably like 20 years ago.

No.3 opened during Covid and Vickery talks about 'resilience, determination, fight, passion, will and drive' – all the attributes he needed to keep the restaurant alive and all of which, he says, were nurtured by Woodward on the rugby field. Suddenly he locks your forearm in the huge mitt of his hand, holds your eye unswervingly and explains exactly what he means: 'If you come up against me and we are exactly the same – same stats, data, same weight, power ratio, push ratio, whatever – I'd fucking have you. I'd fucking have you, sunshine.'

And Lawrence? He is loving this process of throwing a new light on it all, not that those events of 2003 could ever find themselves in the shadows.

'It's nice to see people who want to share everything with you,' he says. 'If you've played together, you have a unique and special bond. And when people bring you into their own environment, there's a trust there. There is an honesty too – which I would expect because that is what we were about as a group. Yet we're not the same; we were all just dedicated to the same cause for a period of time and we are all wired differently, and that is as clear now as it was then. At the time, because you were so focused on your job, you only saw it from your own perspective. But when you see it and hear it from other people's perspectives, you realise that we were all coming at it from a different angle.

'I get asked a lot: "Who were the best players you played against and with?" And I say: "The South Africans were the hardest and the Kiwis, in terms of their rugby intelligence, were the most challenging team on the planet. But the best individuals were all English and I am very proud to say that – the Wilkinsons, the Robinsons, the Johnsons, the Leonards, the Richard Hills, the Neil Backs." In 50 years from now, people across the world will look back and go: those were some of the best players to ever play the game. I feel very proud to have been part of that team. And it feels a bit of a privilege now, to be driving round, seeing them again, 20 years on, to reflect with honesty and insight about what really happened.'

CHAPTER 2

CHUCKING JELLY AT THE WALLS

We start with a photograph of Lawrence somewhere near where it all began.

Dave Reddin has the picture; it is Lawrence at Twickenham in 1997. At that point, Reddin was young, but he was one of the first to see that rugby fitness was becoming a new science and that there might be a living to be made as a rugby fitness coach. He was also ahead of the game because he was already doing bits and pieces helping out England. He mentions the picture, he says, because he thinks Lawrence looks back then like the Sevens player that he once was. 'You were lean,' he says. 'Not that big.'

'I can tell you exactly what I was,' Lawrence replies. 'I was 102 kilos.' Lawrence has got pretty good recall generally, but on matters of his physical development, it's all still crystal clear. The point here is that by the 2003 World Cup, he was 112kg. 'When I was 112kg,' he says, 'I knew I was right.'

In other words, in 1997, when Lawrence was already in his third season of international rugby, he was still 10kg off his optimum fighting weight. That means that there was still 9 per cent of him missing. That sounds like quite a long way from being ready to win a World Cup.

This is the story of the 2003 team: six years earlier, they were indeed probably about 9 per cent short of what it took. They weren't a lot closer by the time the 1999 World Cup came round. In 1999, they got dumped out by South Africa in a quarter-final played in Paris. Late into that night, they drowned their sorrows in a bar on the Champs-Élysées, had an altercation with a fan who told them that their problem was that they lacked passion (only one person loses that altercation) and poured Martin Johnson into a taxi before regrouping for a Eurostar home the next day which, Lawrence says, 'was a bit of a morgue' with Jonny Wilkinson turned green and jostling with various teammates for emergency bolts to the toilet. A lot would change in the next four years.

England, really, were still wrestling with the same challenge facing every other major rugby nation at the time: working out what professionalism in rugby was really all about. Rugby had become a professional sport in 1995 and, at the point of the announcement, some countries were in the starting blocks, primed and ready to go (South Africa). Others were pretty much there already (New Zealand). And England were just trundling along, scratching their head, wondering what all this would mean.

'At the start of it all,' says Martin Johnson, 'we didn't know how to do anything or what to do with the time we had. We were experimenting with everything. We didn't have a clue.'

'The mindset,' says Reddin, 'was to try and do everything differently and better. But I think, in every respect, we were all guilty of just chucking jelly at the wall.'

For the 1997 autumn internationals, Phil Larder, who was soon to become England's defence coach, was asked to come into camp as an observer. Larder had just finished a long career in rugby league that had taken him to the position of Great Britain head coach, so he knew exactly what professionalism looked like – and it looked nothing like this. 'I thought some of the coaching was terrible,' he says, 'and I couldn't believe how poor the squad were defensively.'

When he was introduced to the players, he started talking to them about defence, 'and three or four of them – Richard Hill was one of the first – came over and said, "Look, Phil, I've never ever done any work with a coach on tackling technique and defence." I then asked the whole squad and the only one who'd had coaching on defence was Neil Back.'

But it wasn't all bad, was it? 'The one thing that was clear,' he says, 'is that I was joining an absolutely special group of people.' He might not have stayed otherwise.

'When you look back,' says Reddin, 'you sort of cringe.' At what? He then recalls the days of having the players do 3km time trials around a running track in Teddington. Very old-school.

'They were fitness tests for the sake of it,' says Lawrence.

'Not completely,' says Reddin. 'Part of the reason we did them was I'd managed to get some fitness results from the All Blacks – at the time, they'd done some 3km runs too.'

Actually, Reddin had got his hands on quite a lot of fitness data from the All Blacks. He presented this one evening to the squad at their Petersham Hotel base in Richmond. 'I put a slide up saying: "This is where the All Blacks are at the moment and this is where we are." It was a big gap. And you could see the players going, "Oh fuck!"'

For a while, when some of this comparative data was reaching

Twickenham, 'there was a narrative going round,' Reddin says, 'that was doing my head in. People were saying that genetically we were never going to be able to compete with New Zealand because of the Islanders.'

'Bollocks,' says Lawrence. Astutely.

Meanwhile, some of the players felt that, in terms of their understanding of elite athletic performance, they were ahead of their coaches. For instance, Dan Luger, a winger, who was interested in sprinting. 'With a lot of clubs,' he says, 'I used to walk off the field having barneys with the fitness trainers all the time because I just thought we could be better.'

In some clubs, it was assumed that being full-time professionals meant more hours in the day and that therefore meant the same training but in greater quantities. Luger: 'It was the old-school, fuck you up, run until you're battered. Apparently that will make you good. I had a lot of injuries and bad knees. I probably sacrificed a lot of my career because of what they did to us physically. And while certain players love to go and bash each other during the week and believe it makes them better on the Saturday, for me, it didn't – so let me do that bit on a Saturday. I loved playing the game but I hated the bullshit that went with it.'

Lawrence felt that, at Wasps, he was a lucky exception to much of this. 'I was consulted and asked, "What do you think we should do? What does professional rugby actually mean?" I said, "I think it means you've got to win on Saturday, doesn't it? I think that's probably the most important day of the week, so everything has to be geared up to that. There's no point otherwise." But some people made some really stupid mistakes. Even at Leicester Tigers, it was: "Let's get them in at 8am and they can stay here until about six in the evening."'

Luger: 'I'm not even saying it was the fault of the coaches or the trainers. It was the timing. It was the period rugby was going through. I suppose with England at the 1999 World Cup we saw that, how we did so terribly. We trained very poorly in terms of how we were physically looked after.'

By 1999, Reddin was fully on board, but he himself doesn't disagree with Luger's assessment: 'We just went: whack, let's do as much as we possibly can. When you look back on it, I think we did too much. There was a huge amount of stuff that was getting thrown at players and staff in that period of time. And it wasn't without thought, but in hindsight, there was just too much going on for it to assimilate.'

Yet his point is the same: 'We were still in the very early stages of professionalism.'

All of this was abundantly clear to Clive Woodward. He was appointed late in the summer of 1997. When he clocked on at Twickenham for his first day, he spent the morning working from a chair in reception because no one had even considered that the England coach might need a desk or even an office, perhaps. What he found was a set-up sadly reminiscent of what he had experienced when he was an England player a decade and a half earlier.

'Lawrence wouldn't know this,' he says, 'but I did play for England all those years ago.' He is teasing Lawrence here, a gentle reminder that he did know a little of what he was talking about. 'I just found my England playing career hugely frustrating. I was working at the time for Xerox, a very professional organisation. I was on a graduate training pro-gramme, so my day job, the day life, was very, very professional. Then we went to the England camp and I just found it very disorganised, very fingers crossed, and we weren't overly successful. I'd say it was a great privilege and gave me great pride to play. But we never set the world on fire. I was playing in the backs and we played a very forward-oriented game. We'd just kick the ball all the time. So, when I got the job as England coach, my approach was, "Well, I've just got to put up or shut up now. I really want to take this to a whole new level." And I wanted the players' experience to be different to my experience, so when they looked back at it, they'd go, "Wow, that was a great time.'"

So this was a new era, unknown territory; England were fumbling around for answers and the 1999 World Cup demonstrated clearly that they weren't always finding them. The following four years became a race out of the amateur era. Who could get to the 2003 World Cup having worked out how to best apply what professionalism could bring?

'It's one thing,' says Lawrence, 'to talk about taking it to a whole new level, as Clive put it. But who could really do it?'

CHAPTER 3

LAWRENCE AND FRANCESCA

You think that Lawrence was pursuing the dream but actually, Lawrence himself says, this wasn't his dream at all. 'I didn't grow up wanting to be a rugby player,' he says. 'People probably don't understand that. You look at professional rugby players these days and you see people for whom that was all they ever wanted. But I didn't want that. I didn't think about it, really. And until I was 23, it wasn't a job you could do anyway.'

So why did you play rugby? 'Well, not because of my love of rugby. I was driven to it because of the community around rugby, because it gave me a sense of belonging. Or really, because of the opportunity to be part of a family. I really needed those things.'

And why did you need those things? Pause. 'Because of the death of my sister.'

Lawrence was 17 years old when, on 19 August 1989, he was supposed to attend a party on the *Marchioness*, a party boat on the Thames. He decided not to go at the last minute because he wasn't feeling well. He long wondered how it was that fate played such a decision for him. However, Francesca, his older sister, did attend the party on that tragic night. In the early hours of 20 August, the *Marchioness* collided with another vessel, a disaster which would take 51 lives. Francesca's was one of them. She was a ballet dancer, his only sibling and two years his senior; there was a sweet tightness in their bond. In his words, 'She was caring, sensible, responsible and incredibly beautiful.' And he feels that, of the pair of them, she was the one with a genuine calling: 'One of the many differences between us was that Francesca was born to dance whereas I don't believe I was born to play rugby.'

Her death would shape the rest of Lawrence's life. 'Anything negative that ever happened after I lost my sister was a minor irritation. When someone's life is so cruelly taken away, there's not much more that the gods up there can do to hurt you really. I use it as a constant reference point. Because what could ever come closer to blowing your whole world apart than waking up to the news that you've lost your sister?'

One of the more immediate impacts it had on him was his decision to drop out of school a year before his A-levels. What did you do instead? 'Well, for two years I had quite a chaotic time.' That sounds like Lawrence understatement. 'I was really struggling and I was making some terrible decisions and I was getting myself in and out of trouble. I was wandering through life going, "What the fuck's it all about?" What I needed was a sense of purpose, something that was going to give me a bit more stability; I needed a family. I had a family already, a really close-knit family, that was blown apart because I lost my sister. But after two years, I thought: "I've got to do something to get myself back on track," and so I joined a rugby club, not because I loved rugby, but because I felt like I needed to do something. And I was quite good at it, so why don't I join a rugby club?

'I joined Wasps literally because they were one of the closest teams to me. I opened the newspaper, saw that they were at the top of the table and thought, "I'll go there." I got off the Tube and was pointed towards some sort of housing estate. I thought, "No, it can't be down there." I'm not sure what I was expecting; there were two pitches that looked like they were in a state of disrepair. And then I walked in there and no one really asked me about rugby, and I liked that; it was a bit of a working men's club, really. I immediately felt at home because it gave me a family, a purpose, a community, a sense of belonging. All the things I needed. That was how it happened. That was how rugby became my life. And then I threw absolutely everything into it. It became my obsession. It was a way of me being able to honour my sister's memory.'

If the *Marchioness* hadn't happened, do you think you would have become a rugby player?

'I don't know. I can't answer that question. What I do know is that I used the memory of my sister to drive my emotions to win. I was always driven by a much higher purpose than just playing the game of rugby and that can make you quite dangerous when you're on the pitch. Technically I wasn't as gifted as many other players but where I could add a lot more value was on the emotional side and being able to really use that effectively. I learned very quickly, right from an early age, that there are lots of things that make up a very successful sports person. Obviously you've got to learn your craft but fundamentally there is also the bit that people can't really measure and that's the belief. Believing that you could win is the most important thing and a lot of people would say about me, "I tell you what, that guy's got more belief than anyone." Now, this is something that I wrestle with in my mind all the time: I know that the memory of my sister would drive me on the rugby field, but did I use what happened to her as a way of driving and fuelling me or did it do that on its own? Did I create that situation? Did I use her death as a way of inspiring myself? Or did that just happen naturally? I mean the answer is probably a bit of both, but there's nothing wrong with that, is there?'

No one should judge you on how you responded to losing your sister. But you certainly appeared to be a player brimming with belief, who didn't seem to feel self-doubt.

'Well, you have to lie to yourself quite a lot that everything's OK. The person who goes out there on the field is not the person who's in every other day of your life. It's like showing weakness, isn't it? The whole point of being a rugby player, a big tough invincible rugby player, is that you're not vulnerable. I never wanted to show any vulnerability ever, at all, at any stage, even if I was in agony or whatever. It's a bit like a heroes and villains comic-book movie. For me personally, I couldn't be that person every day of the week. I mean you can't be the person all the time that you are on a Saturday for 80 minutes. We all have self-doubt in our lives when we go individually, "Am I really up to the job?" and then collectively we go, "Are we good enough to win this game?" Then you look around the room and you can see everyone else is not sure either. But it's OK not to believe on Monday; that's OK because the game's not till Saturday. Then, as each day goes on and hour by hour the game approaches, you get there, and by the time we walk out, you've created this sense of purpose and belief that anything's possible and you're thinking: "There's no way we can lose this game." There are mechanisms I would use to try and create that, a lot of which would be twisting the truth to my own advantage to shortcut myself into believing whatever I needed to believe to get the best out of myself. My sister was definitely part of that.'

So the Dallaglio fearless superhero figure was actually an identity or a suit of armour that you'd put on for a game? It's like you went out of your way to create a personality. When you shut your door behind you when you got home, would you say to Alice, 'I'm actually not sure about this?'

'Yeah, I would do, but I would only confide in her and very few other people, but that's OK. And Alice hated rugby. Well, she didn't hate rugby but she definitely didn't like it. I think that helped as well, because she's not a wife who was obsessed with the game or whether we won or not or anything like that. I'd get home and she would literally go, "How d'you get on today? Did you win?" And I'd go, "Yeah," and she'd be studying a new set of stitches in my forehead or how my nose had been spread across my face and go, "It doesn't look like you won," and then she'd hand me my baby daughter.'

*　*　*

Lawrence's rugby wasn't just a form of therapy for himself. In those horrible numb years after Francesca died, when he was trying to find some direction in his life, his parents found that the rugby worked for them too.

'After my sister died, my mum was in a mess, my dad was in a mess. My dad had had a heart attack and they were drifting apart. They were arguing because they'd just buried their daughter two or three years previously. And then I joined the rugby club and what rugby did is it gave me a blanket, a community, a family to put its arm around me when I needed it most. And what it also did is it united and bonded my mum, my dad, our family. They started to come and watch me on a Saturday, and it brought a lot of happiness and joy back to their lives. So, the game became a way of me being able to rehabilitate myself but also to be able to do something that my parents could feel very proud of and that would honour my sister's memory. I actually never saw them as much as I did when I played rugby because then I'd see them every single weekend, and hopefully smiling most of the time. I know that my rugby career, particularly when it was close to home, had an enormous impact on my parents' lives and brought a happiness to them that you can't even begin to measure.'

This bond that the game presented was felt by others too. Lawrence's parents became friends, for instance, with Dan Luger's parents. Luger's parents are both Eastern European: his father is Croatian and his mother is Czech. When we talk to Luger, he also says how the game gave his family a sense of belonging.

'I think my parents are more English than anyone I know,' he says. 'They love the country, especially my mum.' This is interesting because Luger's search for what he might call home took him back the other way to Croatia, where he lived for a year, and he now lives in Monaco. But it was England and the game that made his parents feel that they knew where home was. 'My mum was so proud and passionate about England rugby. She loved you, Lawrence; she thought you were what rugby and England was all about. All our parents – they had such an amazing time. Rugby, I think, gave my parents everything.'

* * *

The community that Lawrence found within the England group was one that felt fortified by other players and their experiences of loss. They had to deal with a sequence of big disappointments on the field – but what athletes don't go through that? There were other bereavements too, though. Three years before the World Cup, Ben Cohen's father was assaulted outside a Northampton nightclub when trying to protect someone else and, a month later, he died of those injuries. The year before the World Cup, Martin Johnson lost his mother to cancer and Will Greenwood lost a son, born prematurely, less than an hour into his short life. In the February of World Cup year, Nick Duncombe, a young, popular Harlequins scrum-half who had two caps and, it seemed, a bright international future ahead of him, died suddenly after contracting meningitis.

In Greenwood's words, 'There was an extraordinary amount of scar tissue.'

And did that impact how this team would perform in 2003? 'You can't ever know for sure, but I'm pretty certain it did,' says Lawrence. 'It's not rocket science but the more time you spend together as a group, the more likely you are to be successful. When you see people grow up along the way, inevitably there are going to be a few setbacks on the field collectively, but also off it. We all had our bumps in the road. Mine was the reason why my rugby career started and I found that when you are driven by something far bigger than the sport itself, that can be very powerful indeed. But then if you can find the right emotional connections between a group of men, if you can speak very openly and honestly from the heart about your own experiences, that can be even more powerful again – and I felt we did that as a group.

When you see and live and breathe each other's experiences off the field, when you go through things together and you share each other's pain, it makes you very united and that makes you very strong.'

CHAPTER 4

THE DISRUPTOR

The day we are due to see Clive Woodward is one of those airless, baking days in mid-July 2022 when you can barely move, let alone travel. So we agree to meet by Zoom and, while we are waiting, Lawrence gives a typically firm opinion on Sir Clive.

Lawrence: 'If Clive hadn't been with the team, I don't think we would ever have won the World Cup.'

Really? Even though the cynical take is to look at the talent pool, the depth and quality of that England squad and say: 'With a generation like that, surely *anyone* could have done it?'

Lawrence: 'No, that's terrible. I mean, it's just wrong, wholeheartedly wrong. Ever since the World Cup started in 1987, we've had a whole load of decent players and we've still managed to screw it up royally. The 1991 team had an incredible group and they didn't win it. So, I disagree with that. The reality was that Clive completely redefined rugby in a way that people probably don't recognise.'

And at that point, on our laptops, the Woodwards' Zoom

starts to connect. It is not just Clive, it is Jayne, his wife, too, which Clive had requested and, actually, seems only appropriate. All these years on, it would be easy to forget how much of a presence Jayne had been and how influential around the edges. It was Jayne who saw it as her duty to get to know the wives and girlfriends of the players and ensure that they felt part of the community too.

'Hi, love,' she greets Lawrence. 'How are you?' She asks after Alice and their children. This is another interview that starts like a family reunion.

Lawrence recalls one of Clive's first podium addresses to the squad, back in 1997. 'You asked us, "What do you want to achieve in your England careers?" and everyone sort of looked fairly blank and no one really said very much. You said: "Well, come on. I need to hear it from you. Do you want to be the best team in the world? Or do you just want to be the best team in Europe? Because the last time we all looked at the World Cup, I don't think there was any team in Europe who'd had their name engraved on it."'

Clive chuckles at his old self. 'There's no doubt about that,' he says. 'I just saw the enemy as the southern hemisphere. I didn't see the enemy as the Five Nations. I saw it as the All Blacks, South Africa, Australia: that's what we had to measure ourselves against and that's what I made very, very clear. They were the games I wanted us to peak for. Especially playing away from home. Can we go down there and do this? This is what I think you'd not heard before. We'd always set so much stall on Grand Slams and Five Nations, then Six Nations, but that wasn't the benchmark. Every time we got to a World Cup, we got smashed. So we had to change the mindset.

'I was England's first full-time professional coach so, as I saw it, we had no excuses. It was just a great opportunity for me. In the business world and everything I've done, I like to disrupt. That's a positive term. You're trying to take things to a new level. In rugby, to be a disruptor – even moving hotels – was seen as a real kind of no-no. You don't do that sort of thing. But that's what I was able to do.'

Maybe it was exactly because of this – rugby's historical conservatism – that 'a disruptor' to some was a 'crazy professor' to others. 'Yes,' Clive says, and he's not wholly amused by it either. 'I did read somewhere that I was called a crazy professor. I mean, if they'd called me a disruptor, I would've thought it was a compliment. My big thing was: I don't think I'm a mad professor, I analyse things really carefully before we do anything, and if I think it's going to work, we are going to try it.'

For example, when Woodward was appointed, he spent a fortnight in the United States, mainly with the Denver Broncos, to see what another proper professional sport looked like. Every top coach goes on these kinds of fact-finding, information-sharing missions these days, but back then? In rugby? No one. And when he was with the Broncos, he saw how a team of different coaches operated together but all with different specialisations. In rugby union, this was unheard of. Woodward, however, got the message loud and clear. One of the first things he did when he returned from that trip was to appoint Phil Larder as England's defence coach. At that point, no other team in international rugby had one of those.

Jayne: 'There was all the noise in the media area about: "How many backroom staff does he need!?"'

Clive: 'Yes. "Who are these people? What are all their jobs?" Everything I did made total sense to me, so we had to try it.

So, I don't think I was a mad professor at all. I think I was a disruptor, and I like to think the end result justified the means. And yeah, I did have a few fall-outs with those people in the RFU on the way.'

You wonder what this might have been like to live with, but Jayne was not the personality to back off from the front line.

Jayne: 'When you get this once-in-a-lifetime opportunity, you don't then say: oh, what if it goes wrong? Or: what about the mortgage? You just say: go for it. Do it. But from that moment on, it had to be done Clive's way or the highway; you can't afford to be derailed by tradition and stodgy thinkers at the RFU. If you think that something's going to make a difference, something that you're going to change, you've just got to do it. Hand on heart, there were, for me, some unbelievably uncomfortable moments. Living with a disruptor or, as someone else called him, an agent of change – I thought that was about the nicest way of putting it – is edgy. It's edgy. He's edgy, and we're dealing with a lot of edgy people like the other person on the screen here – Lawrence. These people are not easy to live with. Ask Alice. They're different. But you can't say no. You just go for it. And it was the best ride of our lives. It was the most fantastic. Yes, there were loads of times when it was really hard. Sometimes, if there was a big loss, even though I knew what he was trying to do, you then had to suck that up as well and deal with it. But if you're going to really live life, then you've got to grasp these things with both hands and get on with it. What are you going to do? Stay at home and worry and think: oh my God, what's he doing now? Or do you actually get out there and get involved and enjoy every single aspect of it?'

The way Lawrence sees it is that pre-Clive and also in the

early Clive era, England were playing catch-up: 'It was the Kiwis who usually innovated and moved the game on. There was a firm understanding amongst us that if we wanted to achieve anything, we were going to have to stop trying to copy what other teams were doing and start to innovate. Lead rather than follow. Because if you do that, the other teams start to look over their shoulders at what you're doing, rather than the other way around.'

Clive: 'The big thing for me was always: how quick can you play the game? How quickly can you play from the set phases of play? Can we get the ball in, out, gone? Because if we can run teams off their feet, we're going to win. It was a very simple philosophy. And it wasn't aping the All Blacks, it was saying: can we play quicker than the All Blacks? We can certainly play quicker than South Africa and Australia, but can we play quicker than New Zealand? Can we play a game that's different to anything that's been done before? Back to disrupting, I was trying to disrupt the way England had always played – because if we kept playing that way, we weren't going to beat anybody.'

CHAPTER 5

JOHNNO

On the road with Lawrence, one aspect that quickly becomes clear is the height of the regard in which he is held by his old teammates. In a tribe of alphas, Lawrence stands tall, even if he is somewhat loath to recognise it.

'What a human, what a man!' says Dan Luger, to his face. Lawrence brushes the comments aside, slightly uncomfortable.

The Lawrence phenomenon was all wrapped up in his self-belief, says Will Greenwood: 'You could put Loll into an invitation team put together in Acton, give him a week and he would still think he could win the World Cup with it.'

When we talk to Luger, he recounts a conversation with Ross Beattie, the former Scotland international, who runs the gym in Monaco that he goes to. When Luger told Beattie that he was going to be catching up with Lawrence over a Zoom call, Beattie had asked if Lawrence's chin would fit inside the screen. He then sent Luger a photo of Lawrence on the rugby field in one of his familiar chin-out, no-backwards-step-taken poses with

29

the message: 'Incredible male. Always camera ready. Look at the prowess!'

Lawrence laughs dismissively. This teasing admiration – he's not really sure how to deal with it.

This friendly reverence for him is clearly in abundance. The only time the tone is notably different is when we get to Leicester for our meeting with Martin Johnson. Here, it seems, are the two ultimate silverbacks, the team's two senior leaders sharing a towering mutual respect. Yet if there was, or still is, any pecking order, Johnson remains forever the captain and Lawrence seems to acknowledge that.

It is not as if there was ever a shortage of leaders in this team. Clive Woodward used to talk about 'the godfathers' – the heavyweights who would sit in the front row of team meetings, sceptical eyes fixed on him as he addressed them. That was invariably Jason Leonard, Neil Back and often Mike Catt but always Johnson and Dallaglio.

On the road to Leicester to see Johnson, the first thing that Lawrence says about him is: 'I always thought it was nice to have a couple of teammates that look like they've murdered their own children. And Johnno was definitely one of those.'

The second is that he and Johnson took a while to break down barriers. They first toured together with England in 1994 and though they roomed together, there were not a lot of words exchanged. Back then, Johnson was a clerk at Midland Bank, dealing with customers over the counter. As Lawrence says: 'You'd rather be paying in than withdrawing.'

'He was a guy whose respect you had to win and vice versa,' he says. Plus, there was a fierce rivalry between Lawrence's Wasps and Johnson's Leicester Tigers, 'so we always viewed each other with a bit of scepticism.'

Johnson is happy to confirm this a little later: 'The Leicester boys,' he says, 'were perceived as a forward-dominated group of Neanderthals. But we were happy with that.'

The two groups only really became one after the 1999 World Cup, says Lawrence: 'That was really when a feeling of respect grew between all of us.'

Yet the two leaders remained extremely different: Lawrence who would never use one word when two were available, and Johnson who would rather grunt than say one.

'It's not my natural thing to want to always be talking,' Johnson says. 'I don't like too much talk at all.' The product of that was whenever he did open his mouth, everyone would listen.

They also had differing competitive brains. Lawrence was like an opera, his emotional highs crescendoing inevitably to the big occasions. Johnson didn't have highs and lows, just one relentless determination to come out ahead.

'Johnno would perform exactly the same for England every time,' Greenwood recounts. 'I've been on a football pitch with him in Sardinia in a five-a-side game on a summer holiday and he's nearly killed a bloke. It's a game of five-a-side! I don't believe you can treat every game like that.'

'I definitely can't be like that,' says Lawrence. Yet somehow it all worked out. 'He was a lot of fun, Johnno,' says Lawrence, 'it was just that people didn't see that.' Indeed they didn't, but that was part of the Johnson persona. He always appeared intimidating, even if his teammates eventually came to see what was beneath the exterior.

Here in Leicester, we get to see that too. Johnson, the man who was loath to talk, cannot now stop. We talk World Cup and that is a subject he loves. He also has an incredibly detailed memory of it.

We are talking drop goals – which are at the heart of this story – and he goes off on one of his tangents. 'We probably got a bit obsessed with them,' he says, and then recalls Neil Back – the cool-headed, uber-experienced openside – trying a drop goal in one of the World Cup group games. And opensides should never be trying drop goals. 'I mean, what? Yeah, whoa, whoa, Backy, whoa, whoa, whoa! Come on!'

And thus, do we overrun. We have arranged to see him for 90 minutes; three hours later he is still reminiscing, still sprinkling common sense over every magical memory, and reining in the hyperbole over every story that has grown legs over the last 20 years. Yet while there was a sense back then that he never seemed to enjoy it – at least that was how it looked front of house – he now seems to revel in it all. Twenty years on, the captain appears as at peace with himself and his achievements as any of his teammates. Maybe more so.

This is certainly the impression that he leaves on Lawrence. He also leaves Lawrence with an open invitation to go and stay at his Devon holiday cottage. That's how close they are now. 'And just so you know,' Johnson says. 'I've got my camera in place now. So I can at least keep an eye on you.'

Some hours later, when we are finally on the road home, Lawrence says, 'I've never heard that man talk so much in my life.' He then pauses for thought before shifting the subject, as though there is something that we have missed altogether: 'Everyone talks about Martin Johnson as a captain, but no one talks about Martin Johnson as a player and he was one of the greatest players that's ever lived. The greatest England player and the greatest captain.'

What he combined was an ability to deliver performances that were both world class in quality and highly passionate in their emotional content and yet simultaneously retain enough of a cool head to be able to read the game as it was passing and know what was required to lead his teammates and deal with a referee.

This was a typical comment, from Dorian West, who shared a decade on the field with him for Leicester and England: 'There's a certain number of people that we played with in that period whose knowledge of the game was top drawer. Johnno used to amaze me because we'd be playing matches and we'd be scrummaging and you've got your head up each other's arses and you're grafting, you're brawling, mauling, whatever you do. And then to be able to come in at half-time and analyse the game and give an appraisal of what we've done and what we need to do – from that position where you can't see half of it because you've got your head in a scrum or a ruck – his knowledge, his analysis, he used to absolutely amaze me.'

CHAPTER 6

THE WOODWARD DEMOCRACY

'Clive would come up with a million ideas,' says Lawrence. 'With these ideas, you'd sometimes go: "Really?" Sometimes you just couldn't fathom them. Some of them you'd consider and two or three really had legs.'

What was the craziest? 'He had one where you'd put a pillowcase on a player's head, then whip it off and they had to react immediately to the game situation in front of them. I can promise you, that was one that definitely didn't happen.'

To the same question, Martin Johnson has a different answer: 'The Israeli fighter pilot computer game. We went down to north London and he was: "I've got this software that the Israelis use to determine who's got it to be a fighter pilot." It was basically a computer program game. It could probably weed out people who had no coordination. So of course, all our young lads who'd grown up in the gaming world were fantastic. The coaches who'd never grown up with the joysticks were just horrendous. So that didn't last long.'

The relationship between Woodward and the team leaders is fascinating and it was clearly crucial. As the seasons progressed, they learned increasingly how to manage each other. 'It was never dull with Clive,' says Johnson. 'There was always stuff going on.'

The team book that was given to all the players was an example of Woodward's energy and zeal.

Johnson: 'We got this big Filofax full of all these rules. Honestly, it was a telephone directory of everything; there was loads of stuff. They were beautiful; I've still got mine at home, in the box, unread. I remember the meeting when he gave them to us. He says: "I've done all this, now you guys have got to take them away and read through them." You're sitting there trying not to bite your hand. He says: "We'll sign off on it tomorrow." And that was a big old document, right? But no one had to read it because the guys had already learned what was important. We'd created an environment where, if you'd got anything about you as a player, you'd go: "These guys are winners. If I want to be here, I've got to be right on top of my game in every sense." So, the next day, when we had to sign it off, I knew no one had read the book. The important thing was everyone was doing what they needed to do, on and off the field. And that might sound very regimented and very rigid but actually it was the opposite because when you can trust everyone, that they'll do the important things, then you can relax.'

One point the squad had drilled into them was their timekeeping. It was known as 'Lombardi time' – named after the famous American football coach Vince Lombardi and his quote: 'If you are five minutes early, you are already ten minutes late.'

Lawrence: 'Clive's words were: "How can you trust somebody who doesn't turn up on time?"'

Johnson: 'He would always hammer away at us: we're on time for everything, bam bam bam, Lombardi time. But ultimately, when you do it and you do it and you do it, it becomes a point of pride within the team.'

Those rare occasions when players messed up on their timing are thus widely remembered. Julian White recalls vividly arriving on his motorbike for the meeting on the first day of a camp and failing to make Lombardi time: 'You are hoping you might see someone else who is late also legging it in with their team book under their arm. But nothing. Then, as you walk down the hall, you hear Clive's voice. I was still in my bloody motorbike leathers. I walked in and Ronnie [Mark Regan] said: "Who ordered a pizza?"'

Part of the challenge for Woodward, clearly, was having to manage a very strong-minded group of players.

Johnson: 'After a while, he realised that he had to trust us, that we weren't there to be told what to do and, ultimately, on the back of all that, I think we came out stronger as a group. I can remember sitting there after we'd beaten South Africa in the last of the November games in 2002 and Woody's going: "Have a great break over Christmas now and then we'll get ready for the Six Nations." And I'm thinking: "I know you're going skiing. That's fine, but don't rub it in. I'm having a beer with the lads tonight, get home tomorrow and I'll be lifting weights back at Leicester on Monday. And then playing: bang bang bang." By the Six Nations, we've fully played eight or nine more games including European fixtures and midweek over Christmas. So you then come back into camp in January. I can see it now – we'd all go into that room and Woody would give the big address: "Right. All the coaches have had a lot of thinking time." All that blue sky thinking. "We're doing this, we're gonna do that." I'll be looking at you, Lawrence, at Jason [Leonard], Vicks [Phil Vickery], Backy [Neil Back]. Oh for fuck's sake. Then, it's: "Clive, can we have a senior players' meeting?"'

Lawrence: 'It wasn't that they were the wrong ideas. The coaches just had so much enthusiasm and they hadn't recently played eight games.'

Johnson: 'Plus, they hadn't coached for two months. So, we'd get the senior players meeting with him and say: "Clive, we don't need to do this bit or that bit. We just need to maximise our time. Can we do only what we need to do to get ready for this game?" Because you haven't got the energy at this point in the season to go out and do massive three-hour training sessions. The thing is: by that point, he's very receptive to us. He loved feedback. Clive could do a 180. He'd then say: "I've spoken to the senior players; they don't want to do that. Brilliant, love the feedback. So we're going to do this instead." He had that trust in us.'

It was clearly a strength of Woodward's that he wasn't interested in being an autocratic leader. This is scrum-half Matt Dawson: 'Clive used to love a little motivational note, didn't he? I was clearing out the house the other day and I found a couple of little cards from him. One of them said: "I really appreciate the fact that you tell me exactly how it is. Don't stop telling me how it is." The irony was the next game I told him how it was and he dropped me.'

This is Will Greenwood, talking specifically about how there was a certain democracy to team tactics too: 'We were always tweaking and changing and trialling until we came up with something. Some coaches don't like you to change and tweak, and some players are terrified to do it. But I always felt that we were given an enormous amount of flexibility to change ideas that we were given.'

This is Johnson on that autumn series in 2002 when they beat the All Blacks, then Australia and then South Africa on three successive Saturdays. 'The pressure to win the All Blacks game was immense. We beat them and then it was: "OK, now you've got to back it up." And Australia really came to play. We beat them and then it was: "You've got to back that one up too." After Australia, we had a senior players' meeting with the coaches. I said: "The preparation has got to change next week because you're going through the same week of training and it's just repetitive, it's dull, it's not inspiring." I remember this distinctly because they went: "No, no, no, Johnno. We've shown that if we do the week's training this way, we win." And Will Greenwood went: "Do we have to lose one before you change?" There was just silence. And they did then change the week's training.'

Lawrence: 'What we had developed into was a group who wanted to take responsibility off the pitch but could also take responsibility on it.'

The case in point was the game away in Melbourne in the summer of 2003, the final game in a long, arduous season. 'I've never been so flat in a week before a Test match,' is how Johnson recalls it. 'I was just knackered. The coaches said to us before the game: "Everyone's a bit jaded, so we'll take them on up front, a tight game, possession, territory." Simple as that. Warming up for that game, I'd still never been flatter for a Test. Then the game starts: we suddenly started getting the ball and we're running all over the place like lunatics. The whole game just opened up.'

England won 25-14, scoring three tries to one. 'If you'd said to the coaches afterwards: "Did that go to plan?" They couldn't have honestly said yes because the plan was completely different. But we went with the game. We had a team that could do that.'

CHAPTER 7

HANDBRAKE OFF

At the end of the summer tour of South Africa in 2000, Clive
Woodward had a face like thunder. The team were staying at
the five-star Westcliff Hotel in Johannesburg, it was 8.30am
and there were three major incidents that required resolving.
One was a female guest, who was staying at the hotel with her
father, was missing. One was a crystal decanter, presented to
the hotel by Nelson Mandela, that had also gone missing. The
third was the fact that a golf buggy had gone through the front
window of reception.

The good news was that the hotel guest and the decanter
were both quickly returned, albeit that the decanter was now
empty. The mystery of the golf cart has never been resolved but
Lawrence, as someone who tends to know what is going on,
has an informed view. 'I'm not prepared to drop anybody in it,'
he says. He pauses, and then carries on: 'but to this day, I am
certain it was Austin Healey and Mike Tindall.'

There was a limit, however, to Woodward's ire. 'That's

because that tour was a real turning point for us,' Lawrence says. 'We weren't to know it, then, but we definitely felt it.'

England played two Test matches on that tour. The first, in Pretoria, they lost by five points, but they felt cheated out of a win, or at least a draw, when a late try was disallowed by a TMO decision – and the TMO, that day, was a South African. They bottled their frustration and unleashed it seven days later in the second Test in Bloemfontein. That was another five-point game but this time it went England's way. It was the first time that Woodward's England had ever won a game away in the southern hemisphere.

Lawrence: 'That result really did something for us. Clive would always say that the southern hemisphere were the enemy; these games told us that we were drawing level with them. That felt good and, regardless of who it was who happened to leave the handbrake off that golf buggy, we came back from that trip very united as a group.'

That wasn't the only lurch forward for the team that summer. The other was still in negotiation but would conclude with Clive Woodward persuading Jason Robinson that what his glittering career in rugby league required was a switch of codes to rugby union.

*　　*　　*

We are now sitting in the Landmark Hotel around the corner from Marylebone Station and Lawrence is telling Jason Robinson that his 'timing was incredible: June 2000 was our real coming together – and then you arrived.'

Yet it wasn't as if Robinson had timed his run at all. Robinson recalls the day he received that first phone call from Woodward: 'To be fair, I didn't know who he was when he called me.

That's rugby league for you, isn't it? Nobody knew who Clive Woodward was. Never watched rugby union.'

Robinson made his union debut for Sale Sharks in the November. It was only three months later that he was called up to England's Six Nations squad. 'I remember that,' he says. 'I was around all you guys and I didn't know who most of you were either.'

Lawrence finds this slightly bemusing. There wasn't a single player in that England squad who didn't know exactly who Robinson was. 'I remember you turned up with the number plate BLESSED on your Range Rover,' he says. 'I don't know whether we were blessed or you were. Either way it worked. We definitely felt blessed to have you.'

Robinson is now soon to hit his half-century; he looks well, better than he should do after nine years in rugby league and then another eight in union. He is absolutely delighted to be sitting back and pressing rewind on his World Cup story. And there is zero affectation, here, in his ignorance of the 15-man code that he was joining. Moving from Wigan to Pennyhill Park, it seems, was like moving to the other side of the world.

Robinson: 'Clive's approach was: "We're looking at building a team for this World Cup, three years down the line. We see you as potentially being a piece of that jigsaw." For me, it was just like being a new kid at school. I knew I had to get my head down. I had to learn and I had to prove myself and my mentality was: show some humility, ask the stupid questions, learn and just see what happens. One of the great things for me was Clive said, "Look, just play," and that took all the shackles off. But I look back at clips now and think: dearie me, I didn't have a clue. I was literally learning on the job. I'd love to see some of the games that I played in because I was raw and even when I scored, I knew I was still quite green because I didn't fully understand what was going on. I look back and there are some games where it was ridiculous – I was coming into the game from rugby league and I was just playing almost the same way.'

That's not exactly how the rest of the squad saw it. 'What surprised everyone,' Lawrence says, 'was how quickly you were able to do what you did.'

Robinson: 'It was a huge challenge because I knew it was high risk, high reward. But one of the great things for me was having you, Loll, and Backy and Hilda [Richard Hill] and just knowing that whatever happens, somebody's gonna bail me out. If you're surrounded by great people, it makes your job so much easier.'

Robinson did things differently around the camp too: 'When I came into the squad, I said to Clive: "If you want to get the best out of me, I need to bring my family." And that was accepted.' So he had his partner and their children all staying with him at Pennyhill. The children were home-schooled. 'It wouldn't work for anybody else. But at the time it worked for me, though when you have young kids and they're up all night and the following morning, you've got to go out and play an international for England, you do think: "What on earth am I doing?"'

Just occasionally, in between all these commitments, he would find some time to socialise and that normally meant a game of cribbage with Phil Vickery and Trevor Woodman, the two Cornish props. He loved their company, he says. 'They used to call me Stumpy.'

Yet somehow, this all worked. In fact, it worked brilliantly.

'When he joined the squad,' Lawrence says, 'we realised we'd got a one-off absolute gem of a player. For all of us, it was a pleasure to play with him really, because he was one of the greatest rugby players to have played the game. When you look at all the things that Clive did, getting Jason was as significant as anything. It was a gamble, bold, brave and it absolutely made an enormous difference. Clive takes a lot of credit for that. England were now getting ahead of the game.'

CHAPTER 8

A TEAM OF TEACHERS

Exactly a year ahead of the World Cup, Dave Alred was in Australia making a tour of the stadia where England were due to be playing. Specifically, he visited them at the same times that England's games would be kicking off a year later. Alred was England's kicking coach but for Clive Woodward, he was the best in his coaching team at detail. And that was what Woodward wanted. Most importantly: what are the chances of it being dewy? Is the ball likely to be greasy? What are the conditions? Alred, himself, wanted more detail specifically for Jonny Wilkinson and the other goal-kickers. What shape were the stadia? Ovals or rectangles? What was the background behind the posts that they would be kicking at? These are the things that matter to kickers and it is all detail you find easily online today; 20 years ago, there was no better supplier of detailed information than Dave Alred.

That demand for such specific detail is typical Woodward.

The fact that he saw the importance of the trip, rubber-stamped it and dispatched his man to the other side of the world is typical Woodward too.

In fact, the whole coaching group was very Woodward. Following his learning trip to Denver, it wasn't just Phil Larder, the new defence coach, or Alred, the kicking coach, that he hired. He hired different coaches for the forwards, for the scrum, for the lineout, for fitness. By the time they got to Australia, a year later, he had also hired a vision coach.

Lawrence: 'At the time, everyone liked to fire volleys at England: why do they need that many people? And they did that because no one else in world rugby was doing what Clive did. But Clive stuck to his guns. You can ask, 20 years on: was that innovative, was it visionary, was it ahead of its time? The answer is it was all of those things. It became the template for the future.'

Business studies students would have enjoyed Woodward here – because this gave him a big challenge: he was never going to be able to produce the best team of players in the world if he couldn't bring out the best in this new-fangled coaching team he had assembled to coach them. And the coaches were not exactly shy, retiring personalities. There was also an unspoken competition between them too because, naturally, they each wanted their area of specialism to thrive. This competition revealed itself most clearly on the training pitch, where they would wrestle with each other for training time. Larder, for instance, would remind the group that 'defence wins matches' – so therefore his defence sessions should have the most allocated time. So, while some might label Woodward the crazy professor, others would call this an essay in man management.

For Larder, Woodward was less a coach and more a CEO:

'He handled us as though he was the chief executive of a multinational company. He appointed the best people that he could to take charge of each specific area and he gave us complete control. But obviously, we had these "World Cup standards" and if we didn't live up to them, we'd be history. But I think he's still the only person that operated like that and it was so successful. It really was.'

For Phil Keith-Roach, the scrum coach, Woodward made you feel valued. Keith-Roach had also worked occasionally in the previous regime, for Woodward's predecessor, Jack Rowell, and not once, he says, did Rowell ever speak to him. 'I was honoured to do the job,' he says, 'and I loved doing it. But I also wanted to be acknowledged, but he didn't acknowledge those of us on the edge.' Woodward was the opposite; everyone was in the team.

For Andy Robinson, the forwards coach who was his number two, it was Woodward's skills as a salesman that stood out: 'He didn't doubt where we were going,' he says. 'His ability to carry it off – to say something and carry it through – was huge.'

Larder saw that too. He remembers one of the first occasions that Woodward ever spoke to the coaches as a group: 'He said to us: "Most England coaches in the past have had the ambition of winning the Grand Slam. Ours is to win the World Cup and be the best team in the world." Christ, that inspired us all.'

For Dave Reddin, the fitness coach, it was the mix of personalities he recruited and the way he allowed them to blend. 'Lots of leaders like to surround themselves with similar characters,' he says. Not Woodward. 'And we were a bit like an Italian family. Woody was very good at keeping the arguments going. He loved an argument amongst a management team, just stirring it up, playing the provocateur, asking people's opinions, never allowing people to get comfortable about the way we were doing things.'

For Alred, there were two elements that were very specific to the group that Woodward had recruited. One: with rugby on its fast track into the professional age, and with each nation competing in this race to professionalise as fast and as effectively as possible, Woodward only wanted personnel who were prepared to lead the way. As he says: 'The culture within the group was to be a pioneer.'

Two: Woodward had done a post-grad in education at Loughborough University and he understood the value of learning. Fancy ideas, modernisation, the transglobal search for minute detail – these were important and are maybe what he was best known for. However, his foundation philosophy was far more grounded. In answer to the question: how can we give the players a World Cup-winning education? His answer was: by employing teachers. It wasn't just Woodward who was a trained teacher; so were Larder, Robinson, Keith-Roach and Alred too. 'And teaching,' Alred says, 'is just another word for coaching. It's about developing the learner.'

What did the players make of it? They found the internal competition hilarious. At team meetings, before training sessions, each coach would make a brief presentation on what was about to come – and even this became a competition. Yet this was a very wizened, cynical playing group that, over the years, had learned to sniff bullshit a mile off and, on the whole, what they smelled here smelled good.

Lawrence: 'Clive's vision was fairly emphatic – that, to create the best playing group in the world, I want to create an environment that is so good that everyone wants to be a part of it and no one wants to leave, that everything about England had to be better than at your club. He wanted it to be aspirational and a destination that everyone wanted to be at. That is what he achieved and the coaching team were very much a part of that.'

CHAPTER 9

PRIDE OF CORNWALL

We are en route to Cheltenham, to a very decent dinner in the restaurant that Phil Vickery had recently opened there, when Lawrence has one of those moments that we are now getting used to, when he suddenly rewinds by two decades. He talks about Vickery and recounts the joys of their days in opposition, when Lawrence was Wasps captain and Vickery was captain of Gloucester.

Lawrence: 'So we were opposing captains and at the coin toss before the game, Phil would always have this game face on: so moody, so miserable, all pumped up like he wanted to murder me. And I'd just say stuff to try and put him off. I'd say to the ref: "Look at him, ref. Look at how on edge he is. There's only going to be one person you're going to have a problem with today. And that isn't going to be me." And Vicks was so wound up, he'd just stand there and say nothing back. Then, all those years later, Vicks joined Wasps so we were teammates at last and he said to me, about those old times: "Loll, you were a fucking nightmare."'

And here we are in Vickery's restaurant, No.3, and Lawrence recounts the story again to Vickery and Vickery laughs at the recollection and says exactly the same thing: 'Loll, you *were* a fucking nightmare.'

Vickery chooses dinner for us. (Highly recommended from the small plates menu: the arancini and the aubergine.) Lawrence, being half Italian, considers himself something of a foodie sophisticate and he is impressed. And then Vickery tells the story of him and Trevor Woodman, the two Cornish props who started in the World Cup final, one of the great double acts of English rugby, and how it all began.

Vickery: 'Trevor and I first played against each other when we were 11 or 12, Budehaven School versus Liskeard School and Community College. I can't remember if I was front row or second row but Trev was inside centre. They weren't even rugby schools; we're not talking Truro College or any posh schools, we're talking shit-kickers. I was a big fat kid who no one had much time for. Bude Rugby Club was the inspiration for me; it was their welcome: come in, good to see you, we'll help you. I made my debut for the Bude under-19s, aged 13. Technically, that probably shouldn't have been allowed but they looked after me. I remember seeing the boys – the first-teamers – wearing the Bude badge. I so wanted that. After GCSEs, Trev stayed at school and I went straight home to work on the family farm. I never had any thoughts of pursuing rugby as a professional; it wasn't a professional game, was it? Then Redruth came calling – would I play for Redruth? I remember two great men of the club coming up to the farm. I was actually late, milking. They were in the farmhouse; I apologised for being late. Neither one of them talked about playing for England or anything; all they talked about was wanting to get the best out of me. We think we can help you.'

So Vickery never did play for the Bude firsts because the next call, after Redruth, was the one from Gloucester.

Vickery: 'At that point, I didn't want to leave home. I wanted to do my milking, do my dairy, help my cows. But Gloucester said they'd get me a job on a local farm working with the cows. And Mum said: "Phil, home will always be here for you." So, I came to Gloucester and everyone hated me because, coming from Cornwall, I was a foreigner. You work your way.'

Vickery and Woodman worked their way into the England Colts system together. Woodman initially joined Bath partly because it was the closest Premiership club to Cornwall. But then Vickery started getting in his ear.

From the comfort of his Cotswolds living room, Woodman takes up the story: 'Vicks was on the edge of the first team up at Gloucester and was giving me grief because I seemed to be progressing more slowly at Bath. We were 19 at the time. He just got into me enough so that when Richard Hill, who took me to Bath, became director of rugby at Gloucester, it was just a simple fit then to come to Gloucester with him. And that's when Vicks and I started living together. The house we lived in was right next to Teague's Bar. Coming from a sleepy village in Cornwall to suddenly being in the high street of Gloucester; fuck, it's a bit different, isn't it? So we lived together for four years.'

It's not that they are short of housemate stories to tell, but they settle for just this one. Vickery asks Woodman to drive down to the garage to get some cigarettes. Woodman says: 'Go yourself.' Vickery replies: 'But you're dressed and I'm still in bed.' The house that they lived in overlooked a supermarket car park so Woodman, looking out of the window, says: 'OK. There's a trolley over there in the car park of the supermarket. You run over there naked, get the trolley and wheel it round the car park. And then I'll go and get the cigarettes for you.' Vickery accepted the challenge, 'and it was about a 40-metre run up the street to get there,' he says. So Woodman got the fags.

Eight years after moving in together at Gloucester, Vickery and Woodman were still co-habiting, but by this point it was in the room they were sharing at Pennyhill Park.

* * *

There is, as Lawrence says, another considerable influence in the development of the two Cornishmen: 'With any front-row story, there is another man involved. And that is Roachie.' He is referring to Phil Keith-Roach, the scrum coach, a man with an unusual passion for the scrum, a man who proudly admits: 'I never met anyone who loved it or was as interested in the detail of it as I was.'

'I remember Roachie scrumming with my dad's mate in the hotel,' says Vickery. Keith-Roach was in his fifties at the time.

Lawrence: 'Roachie had to have two hip operations. I told him: "If you stopped scrummaging with everyone in the hotels, it might help."'

Vickery: 'I remember Roachie scrummaging someone else in the wine bar here. Oh God, I miss that bloke.'

Keith-Roach himself, now in his late seventies, has brilliant memory recall; at least he does when it comes to scrummaging. All these England props – he can remember when he first clapped eyes on each of them. Vickery, for instance: 'We went down to a Bath game and that was where we found him.

Boy, he could scrummage! He'd only played about 19 full games for Gloucester. Did a great job, that day, on Dave Hilton (the Scotland loosehead). Then he plays for England, against Wales (his debut, 1998), and England score a pushover. The scrum changes direction with the arrival of Vickery. Thank God. Vicks could do a million things.'

Or this, for instance, is when he first saw Julian White: 'We didn't find White until I went down to Bridgend in 1999. I thought: "Fucking hell." He had everything. We took him to South Africa (for his debut in 2000). White was phenomenal.'

From that point, Keith-Roach had two tightheads whom he loved. 'The arrival of White and Vickery transformed the England rugby team,' he says. 'Rivals! Two rivals! Vicks would say to me: "You like him more than me." Then he invited me to his wedding. Then Julian invited me to his. I loved both of them. Fantastic beasts of men, very different players.'

Phil Larder, the defence coach, once told Keith-Roach that White couldn't defend. For Keith-Roach, this is like insulting one of his children, so he defended his man and happily accepted when Larder later reconsidered. When Keith-Roach recounts Larder's retraction, he does so doing an impression of Larder in his strong Yorkshire accent: 'I decided: Whitey's not very mobile sideways, but in a smaller channel, he's a fockin' nuclear bomb!'

On the loosehead side, Keith-Roach had even more to choose from. 'England used to have a lack of depth,' he says. 'Then more came in. Jason Leonard, Graham Rowntree, David Flatman and finally Trevor Woodman. Look at that, we're suddenly four deep. They are all different. And I love all of them.'

What is abundantly clear is that the love was reciprocal. There is also huge respect for Keith-Roach's knowledge.

Woodman, who is now a coach at Gloucester, still rings him to discuss scrummaging, so do other coaches, and so does Wayne Barnes, the referee.

Vickery: 'He cared about rugby, but also he cared about *you*. He'd come up to see you – yes, for some training, but it was also for going for a meal and having a chat as a human being. When you talk about going the extra yard, you'd do anything for that bloke because he cared about you.'

There was one other thing he did for his front rowers: wherever in the world they were playing, he would take them out for 'the front row dinner'.

Woodman: 'The front row dinner was unbelievable. Wherever we were, he'd do it. Whenever we arrived somewhere new, it was almost the first thing he did. He would go off, get a driver to take him around all the best restaurants and he'd find a restaurant that he thought would fit. And he had the luxury to take us out. We'd go to these amazing restaurants – six or seven courses, all the drink and everything.'

Lawrence, being Lawrence and a foodie and someone who won't miss a good opportunity, eventually managed to get himself on to the guest list: 'I said it's no good the front row doing all that hard work if they can't get rid of the ball at the base of the scrum. So Roachie said, "Loll, we need to bring you in."'

Woodman: 'I can't remember what trip it was, I think it was Argentina, when Clive said, "Obviously, the front row, you're going out tonight, just don't do anything stupid." And Roachie stood up at the back and said, "Clive, what do you classify as stupid?" And you could see Clive's face just drain. All the front rowers were chuckling.'

Yet always with an eye on the bigger picture, Woodward was

delighted with what Vickery and Woodman could bring to the team and with how that matched his vision for a World Cup-winning side: 'It was a very simple philosophy that I took to the team,' Woodward says. 'It wasn't rocket science, but the most important thing was: can we play quickly? From 1 to 15, can we play that way? The key was 1 to 8. I knew the backs would love this style, but could we get a forward pack, 1 to 8, playing with real pace, real passion, for 80 minutes? Can we still have the power, still have the scrums, still have the lineout but also run teams off the field of play?'

With Woodman and Vickery, he thought he had the answer.

CHAPTER 10

NO ONE CAN BEAT US

When they had both finally graduated up to the England training squad, Vickery and Woodman soon found themselves room-sharing. Of course they did. At Pennyhill Park, England's training base in Bagshot, Surrey, their room name was Ash. It had an angle out of the window where Vickery could have a cigarette without being exposed.

If he wanted a more relaxed spot for a smoke, they would pop round to Highgrove, the room shared by Lawrence and Jason Leonard. As long-term occupants, Lawrence and Leonard had managed to work the rooming system to their advantage, having identified Michael, the Pennyhill concierge, as a valuable friend.

Lawrence: 'I said to Michael: "We're going to be living here quite a lot of the time. So it would be great if we could have a fridge-freezer. And we need a microwave."'

Leonard: 'And a coffee machine.'

Lawrence: 'And we need a bar.'

Leonard: 'So we had it all there. All the sort of modern comforts, really. And the guys would come down. Because of the fridge we had, we had juices and all that. And we had beers in there. And the room was tucked away with this little terrace. There was a little nine-hole golf course behind our rooms but where we were, it was completely surrounded by trees, so we could see people coming down the golf course and that, but they couldn't really see us. So a couple of the guys would use it as their excuse for a sneaky cigarette.'

In particular, they recall the visits of Vickery and Woodman. 'They used to walk into our room,' says Lawrence, falling into a Cornish brogue, 'with Trev going: "Vicks, this is how the other half live. This is the West Wing."'

One of Lawrence's favourite Clive Woodward stories is the origins of their Pennyhill base camp: 'Early on, Clive asked: "Where do the All Blacks stay when they are here?" It was Pennyhill. So he went and had a look and declared, "Well, the All Blacks don't stay there any more."' England have been based there pretty much ever since.

Whether it was the 18th-century main house, the elegant chandeliers or floor-to-ceiling tapestries, the five-star Pennyhill certainly matched the environment that Woodward had in mind for his England squad.

Lawrence: 'Clive wanted to create an environment where there was elevation in everything. If you play for England, every aspect of it should be better than your clubs. In his words, what he wanted was for it to be so good that everyone wanted to be part of it and no one wanted to leave.'

Leonard: 'That's how it felt. It was something you had to earn. I was playing in a Quins side who were forever underachievers. After playing on the Saturday at Quins, I couldn't wait to jump in the car and just drive down the road to Pennyhill Park to catch up with all these guys and be part of that environment – because it was so much better than the club environment.'

His Quins teammate, Will Greenwood, felt very much the same: 'The weird thing is if you ask me what I remember, I remember the times together, the training at Pennyhill Park. I don't remember the games. I remember springing into the car off to train, ready for another week, ready for another campaign. I remember four or five years' driving through the gates of Pennyhill. My room was Sweetpea. I remember bumping into Wilko in the morning and he'd be coming out of his room and you'd walk down for breakfast and there'd be Johnno and Loll and Backy and Hilda and you'd think: "Fucking hell, no one can beat us." If you're a professional sportsman and you want to be in an elite surrounding where you're of total belief that no matter what comes out of the opposition changing room, you're going to win – it's pretty tough to beat that.'

CHAPTER 11

HOW RUGBY WAS

But it wasn't all breakfasts with Wilko and illicit fags on the terrace, was it, Lawrence?

'Well, no. Not when you talk to Stuart Abbott.'

Abbott was the last man in. He didn't get his first cap until seven weeks before the World Cup started; he had only arrived in England 18 months earlier. He was born and raised in Cape Town but had an English mother and had fancied trying his hand at the sporting experience overseas. When he moved to play for Wasps, international honours weren't remotely a consideration. Certainly not a World Cup. But then he found himself called up for the England tour of New Zealand and Australia, the summer before the World Cup. 'And at first,' he says, 'it was pretty tough, I'm not going to lie. It was: "Who's this guy from Cape Town?"'

What he specifically remembers from that tour was his 25th birthday. He remembers it because of what happened when the team manager presented him with a birthday cake. Did his new teammates sing him 'Happy Birthday'? Did they hell. 'Everyone just stared at me,' he says. He then pauses to accentuate the awkwardness of the reception. 'Obviously nobody knew me, so I had to earn my right to be there. It was: I've got to prove myself. I did feel like a bit of an outsider.'

It is amusing to observe Lawrence here. Instinctively, Lawrence doesn't like the idea of Abbott receiving this cold-shoulder experience, particularly because Abbott was his Wasps teammate. So he challenges this version of events. 'But you came on tour as a winning member of the champion side,' Lawrence says. (That's Wasps, 2003 English champions.) 'That gives you a chance, surely, to walk in and hope to have a little bit of credibility.'

'No, Lawrence,' Abbott replies. 'It didn't feel like that. That team had been together since '99. Everyone had 20, 30, 40, 50 caps. I was pretty much new. It was a bit of an intimidating experience.'

Lawrence doesn't attempt to disguise the essential hardness in the squad environment. 'We were pretty brutal,' he says. 'Spiky, competitive people – as you'd expect in an international team. We used to put pressure on each other. I'd look someone in the eye and say: "You need a fucking big game otherwise you won't be here next weekend." Or: "Last chance saloon for you this weekend, pal."'

'Very Darwinian,' are the words that Joe Worsley, another Wasps teammate, used to describe the environment. 'It built very mentally strong people. The way people were treated – these days, that just wouldn't fly. But we had so many mentally strong people at a time when it was quite normal to speak the way we spoke to each other and to put pressure on people in a certain way – which, today, would probably be seen as bullying. It certainly wouldn't be seen as proactive in building a comfortable team environment. But that's just the different generations.'

This is how Josh Lewsey recalls it: 'All high-performance environments are challenging; they make you pretty honest, so you can see through any bullshit. Like most of the '03 guys, I have never really suffered fools very well. Those guys were great because they could sniff you out if you weren't up to scratch or not adding sufficient value. We shared a lot together. And whilst that group was a challenging environment, I think there was also huge loyalty and deep care for each other too underneath. That was never actually shown or said but I think it was there.'

But this environment was, as Worsley says, very much of its time. Mike Catt agrees with that assessment, and he, like Worsley, is one of the few from the squad who are still in high-level coaching and therefore have that frame of comparison. 'This new generation that's coming through now,' he says, 'you can't scream and shout at them. This day and age, it is about putting an arm around them and getting them to believe in themselves. So, it's completely different.'

This is very much a theme in current conversations about modern coaching. You need to challenge your athletes but how far can you push them – and where do you draw the line? 'Championship-winning environments aren't easy environments to be part of,' says Dave Reddin – and he has worked with rugby players, footballers and Olympians. 'There's a certain level where you're going to need to have to cope.' Yet Reddin, too, reflects back 20 years and agrees that 'the old-school environments were not appropriate for everybody.'

Occasionally this went too far. One of the stories that has survived 20 years is the pen clicking – when, during a meeting,

Clive Woodward lost his patience at a squad of players who were clicking the tops of their biros. It is a revealing story purely because of the pettiness of the event.

'I remember that meeting,' says Lewis Moody. 'You could hear all these pens going in the background. No one's doing it intentionally, it's all unconscious. And Joe [Worsley] is the one person that gets picked on. It felt like Joe was always the person to get picked on.'

Lawrence: 'On a couple of occasions, Clive would use Joe as a bit of a punchbag. I mean, if everyone's clicking their pens, are you going to take on Martin Johnson? But there's no one that should be above any criticism and there's a certain way of speaking to people and Clive, most of the time, got it pretty right. There were just a few times where he got it pretty wrong and Joe tended to be on the receiving end.'

Worsley: 'I was 19 years old when I first had Clive as a coach and I don't think we ever got quite beyond the teacher-pupil relationship. And in those situations, in no way did I feel comfortable with replying to him because I felt any comeback would be met with issues about getting picked in the future. I'd say there were probably five or six guys who would be pretty safe with that. But, for the rest, you wouldn't be. Putting down the head coach in front of the whole group would be an interesting proposition. So, it was difficult to sit there and take some shit like I did. As a coach, now, I would never dream about doing that. Eventually I spoke to Johnno about it. I said, "Mate, this is ridiculous."'

Lawrence: 'Johnno and I actually had a word with Clive eventually about the way he spoke to Joe publicly. We just said, "You can't treat players like that. It's just not fair. You wouldn't do it to me. You wouldn't do it to Johnno so why are you doing it to Joe?" And that was the last we heard of it really. Everyone needs their wings clipped every now and again, including the coach, and including me. If you do something that you think is OK but actually isn't, it needs to be said. I think it's called self-policing. Look, from what I saw in my rugby career, all this would actually hardly touch the sides. A lot of coaches that we worked with, Joe and I, they will single out players who they know can take it. I could name six or seven England coaches who've done far worse. And actually, Clive genuinely cared about everyone in the squad. The point is that Joe Worsley wouldn't have been there if he wasn't one of the best players in the world and if Clive didn't 100 per cent trust him.'

Worsley: 'It is really hard to comment on some of the things that happened because you're talking about a different era. That Darwinian thing, it was a sink or swim attitude to things. But it was there in the Wasps environment too: when you first turn up at 18, you say the wrong thing at the wrong time and you take a load of shit. It had eased off a bit with England by 2003, there was a bit less of: you're a young guy, you come in and you shut up, you don't talk. But we come back to the fact that you can't compare it to what's happening now because of the way things have moved on. And it was the norm at that time. We're not talking about an England environment here, we're talking about how rugby was.

'And whichever way you look at it, you've still got to realise the reason we won the World Cup is in large part because some of the things that Clive did.'

CHAPTER 12

SURVIVAL OF THE FITTEST

It is when we are on a road climbing out of Bath, en route to visit Dave Reddin, that Lawrence brings up a game against the All Blacks at Twickenham in 1997. 'That game was a real moment for us all,' he says. 'I remember I came down the tunnel at half-time and I was throwing up; everyone was throwing up.' At that point in that game, the scoreboard suggested that England were in good shape; they were 23-9 up. 'But we were nowhere near fit enough,' Lawrence says, which largely explains the All Blacks' comeback and the epic 26-26 finish.

Why are you bringing it up now? 'Because we are going to see Dave.' And it was Dave who, as the team fitness guru, ensured that nothing like that would happen again. By the World Cup, Lawrence says, 'we genuinely felt we were, scientifically, in terms of measurement, the fittest team in the world.'

But everyone says that, don't they?

By now we are in Dave's kitchen overlooking a beautiful

Avon landscape. Isn't it the case that every major team rocks up at every World Cup claiming to have pushed to new limits, to have taken the human body to extremes of speed, power and endurance never previously known?

'Yes,' says Dave. 'I think all you can probably ever hope to do is believe it. I think that's the most important thing. But in terms of the test results and stuff, yes, we were better than we'd been at any time in the preceding six years. And you all believed it, Lawrence, because of those horrible, brutal, nasty sessions that we did that tied into the style of play we wanted to have. To me, that created some of the mentality to say: "You can throw anything at us." And that's also the mentality that says: "OK, extra time, no problem."'

Horrible, brutal, nasty sessions. 'The hardest thing I've ever done in my life,' is how Lawrence remembers it. When his teammates recall it, they use the language of survivors: 'they were killing us', 'we were dying every day out there'. This was England's training camp, at Pennyhill Park, leading up to the World Cup, all 11 relentless weeks of it.

Lawrence: 'The camp was like no other I'd ever been on. We had four training sessions a day, four days on, three off. Those days at Pennyhill, we were absolutely at breaking point on almost every one. We were all pushing boundaries further than we'd ever been before.'

It was competitive too, because 43 players were called up to the training camp and only 30 would go to Australia. 'What was on the line was being in that 30-man squad,' recalls Trevor Woodman. 'So everyone was pushing everyone. It didn't matter if you had 70 caps and you thought that you were on that plane, everyone was pushing the standards. It didn't matter how fit you were; everything was painful.'

Lawrence, like all his old teammates, recalls the one session that everyone feared the most: 'We did two morning sessions before lunch and then you were told to have a two-hour sleep. Because then, at 4.30pm, well, there is a session, we're not even going to tell you what it is, but it's going to hurt. That's great. You try and sleep and you're worried about what that fucking session might be. But you were so knackered that you did sleep and you got up and you just thought, I'm really not going to like this next hour, whatever it is, whether it's rowing, whether it's running, whatever it is, it's going to be horrific.'

The rowing is the one they still talk about. They were split into teams of three, one ergometer per group, one minute on, two minutes off, and round and round – for 90 minutes – and, obviously, with all the numbers being recorded because that is what makes for competition. 'Ninety minutes – that's a long time,' Lawrence says. 'And does that two-minute break go quickly!'

'That was when you'd see pure personality coming out,' Reddin says. 'You'd have someone like Hilly – he'd get through that session by moaning like hell all the way through. Greenwood would be the same. He'd be like, "How long left? How long? How many seconds?" He had to make a fuss of doing it but that was just his way of coping. But he'd do it. Whereas you, Lawrence, you'd be more, "I'm not going to admit it's hurting."'

Which brings us on to Julian White. Everyone remembers White and the rowing session but that's because they remember that he was in a team with Andy Titterrell, the Sale hooker, who wasn't rowing as fast as White would have liked. White was a personality whom Reddin describes as 'just sort of slightly under the radar, a bit quiet, gets the work done, but no big fuss'. Yet when under-the-radar, no-big-fuss White's patience could no longer endure Titterrell's laggard rowing pace, according to Woodman, 'Whitey just pulled him off the rowing machine.'

Woodman was the third member of the team. It didn't help, he said, that they had Simon Shaw (lock forward, long levers) on the adjacent ergo 'and he's going along next to you like Steve Redgrave.' So White 'just pulled him off and told him: "I'll do a minute 30. You just do 30 seconds." That's how competitive it was.'

How did it end up? Titterrell did not make the cut for Australia. White's flash of fury is still recalled with considerable joy.

There were a number of extraordinary feats of athleticism during that relentless training camp: Richard Hill's leg press, Mike Tindall's standing jump, the all-round decathlete Ben Cohen. Lawrence recalls the strength in the gym of Martin Johnson: 'He was phenomenal.'

'Johnno?' Reddin is slightly taken aback. 'He was a bit grumpy the whole time, wasn't he?'

Reddin nominates Neil Back for mention 'in terms of his ability to survive in areas that nobody else could' and Jason Robinson: 'for pure drive, physical resilience and ability to repeat high-intensity efforts – unparalleled.'

At the end of every week, there would be a bottle of Bollinger awarded to the player who had performed best in all the tests and it was rarely any of the above who claimed it. Pretty much every week it was Jonny Wilkinson. 'He was head and shoulders above,' says Lawrence. 'By the end of the camp, Mrs Wilkinson must have had a wonderful cellar.'

* * *

After leaving Reddin, we discuss Will Greenwood. Greenwood is fascinating because, outwardly, he always appeared bright and vivacious. But on the topic of training, Reddin has just called him 'the mental lettuce'. He has rolled his eyes and smiled as he has done so, as if he is teasing him.

Lawrence then explains that 'he was a terrible trainer. Maybe he didn't know it, but his body language was awful.' This is particularly peculiar if, today, you follow Greenwood online. 'It's just strange,' Lawrence says, 'that he is now the most enthusiastic trainer of all of us. Since he retired, he's trained like a beast. And he posts it all on Instagram.'

When we interview Greenwood a few weeks later, we make the mistake of thinking that he might laugh at his old self, the mental lettuce and all that, but he doesn't.

'Me and Dave used to fall out about this,' he says. 'It's assumed that, because I wanted to know exactly what the session was, how long it would be, how much rest there would be, I didn't want to do it. The flip side of it is, I can only train the way my brain works. I have a logical brain. I'm reading a book on fluke at the moment. I can tell you about Pascal's Triangle. Rugby is a game of chess. Always has been. So my brain is always wired, and it was always assumed that I was moaning about it because I was asking. Don't ask questions. Just get on with it and run. Now, how am I running? But if I'm doing 6 x 400 metres, it's a waste of time running the first one in 54 seconds? Because my next five, I won't break two minutes. So what level of intensity am I training at? Because I was always asking questions, I was perceived as miserable and not wanting to do it.'

'I don't care what he says,' Lawrence says, after some thought. 'He was still a terrible trainer.'

CHAPTER 13

JAYNE PICKS
THE TEAM

Lawrence was first picked to play for England against South Africa at Twickenham on 18 November 1995. He was named amongst the replacements on the bench. For the following England game, against Samoa, he was elevated to the starting XV and that is where he remained. He came off the bench once against Italy when he was making a comeback from injury, but otherwise he always started. It was a full seven years later before he was first dropped to the bench again, a decision upon which, to this day, you can still find him brooding. That's just a small window into what it's like to be Lawrence.

Lawrence: 'It was the autumn internationals in 2002, we'd just beaten New Zealand 31-28 and we were playing Australia the following Saturday. That week, Clive said to me, "Right. We've had a look at the tape and we're dropping you." And I said, "Really? No. You're resting me, aren't you?" He said, "No, no. We're dropping you." I said, "On what basis are you dropping me?" And he said, "Well, you weren't very prominent in attack." And I went, "OK. Well, I've had a look at the tape too and there was a reason why I wasn't very prominent in attack – because I was the top tackler in the game. So, clearly, I was so prominent in defence that I didn't have much time to be prominent in attack."

'The way I see it is this: delivering bad news is the hardest thing for anyone to do, so don't make it any more comfortable for them. Clearly Clive was uncomfortable about having this conversation with me, so you want to make it as uncomfortable as possible so he never does it ever again. That's my rationale anyway.

'But on this one, it was pretty clear that we were going to have this agree-to-disagree kind of argument and, ultimately, I was not going to win it. So, I then started to get a bit sulky and pissed off and I went, "So you're dropping me for my 50th cap?" And at that point, you could see the blood drain from his face because he had thought about everything apart from the fact that it was going to be my 50th cap. And then a little smile came, a little tweak of a nervous smile across his face. I said, "If you think this conversation is uncomfortable – which I think it is, don't you? – you wait till you have to tell my mother," at which point he just laughed and we shook hands.'

But Lawrence can't really complain about the hand that selection dealt him under Woodward. As the Pennyhill Park training camp wore on and the weekends of the warm-up internationals started to pass by, there were some far tougher selection decisions to be made. The initial training squad contained 43 players; the squad to go to the World Cup had to be whittled down to the 30 who would go to Australia.

There was one game from earlier in the summer that would

command a large portion of the selection debate. In June, England had toured New Zealand and Australia, one Test match against each nation. Many had thought that Woodward was mad to take the team there; as it was, they won both matches, Woodward was entirely vindicated and England were able to arrive at the World Cup ranked number one in the world, knowing that they had given two key opponents something to think about. In the process, they had also done something incredible against New Zealand. They beat them 13-15, a game that Lawrence calls 'one of our best collective defensive performances ever'. Yet Lawrence wasn't even on the pitch when that game finished.

Very specifically, England held out with only 13 men on the pitch. In the final minutes of the game, the All Blacks had a series of scrums within touching distance of the England try line. One pushover or one penalty try would have won them the game. The pressure on the England scrum was massive and in the midst of it all, England started haemorrhaging manpower. First up, Neil Back was yellow-carded.

'When I came off,' Back recalls, 'I thought I'd ruined it. I knew how important it was for us to win there. It was critical. I thought I'd let myself down, the whole team down. I was gutted. And then Loll was yellow-carded too and I thought: "OK, I'm not going to get all the blame now."'

There was no blame to be pointed anywhere, though, because the England scrum held out, a six-man unit defying the full Kiwi eight. The props that day were Graham Rowntree at loosehead and Jason Leonard at tighthead, very much the heroes of the hour. At that point, there and then, anyone would have been delighted to book the pair of them on to the flight to Australia.

*   *   *

The selection process under Woodward was certainly respected amongst the coaches. Some head coaches believe that because selection is a pressure that, ultimately, falls on their shoulders, they should treat it as their sole responsibility; Woodward was the opposite extreme. Selection under Woodward was a broad, sophisticated democracy. Everyone's opinion was valued, and everyone here means not just, say, the scrum coach, Phil Keith-Roach, or Phil Larder, the defence coach, but the video analyst, Tony Biscombe, and the head of conditioning, Dave Reddin.

This is Biscombe: 'Leading up to the World Cup, selection was second to none. The selection meetings would primarily be the coaches speaking but everybody in the backroom staff had a say. The only people really that were missing were the medical staff and they came in, too, if they needed to give a report on how certain injuries were going. So, I would be sitting there, listening to selection, there'd be a long discussion about two players or whatever and you're trying to keep your head down, and all of a sudden, Clive would turn around and say to me: "What do you think?" That's the way it was. Everybody's view was respected.'

Larder: 'Clive's number one statement to the rest of us coaches was that his most important job was selection. The process of elimination and the process of selection was very, very, very intricate. On the Sunday before every Saturday match, we would be sitting down and picking the team. We were not only looking at people who were great rugby players, but we were looking at strength of character, we were looking at players that could handle pressure, we were looking at players who could make the right decisions when things were getting tough. The process was: we'd pick a team and Clive would write it up and, quite rightly because his head was on the line, he would then go away and sleep on it. We would all be there in those meetings and there were some big arguments. If you can imagine: my best mate in the group of coaches was Roachie; he wanted the best scrummagers yet my priority was the best defenders.'

Keith-Roach: 'Clive would listen to me for hours in that selection committee. And I'd go on and on and on about how he had to play Leonard at loosehead and not tighthead.'

Reddin: 'I was in the selection meetings. Now I don't know what rugby's like today, but if you go into football, there's a coaches' room and that's where the coaches sit, and you'd better be knocking on the door if you want to enter because you're not allowed in unless you're invited. It's very hierarchical and I think that way you miss a huge amount of the insight that comes from somebody else's perspective, which Clive really helped to create. Clive would get all the opinions and he would listen and stir it up; he was actively looking for stuff. I thought it was a very enlightened way of doing it. It was upstairs in Pennyhill Park in what we called The War Room; that was where people worked. Everyone had a voice and Clive would listen to them all. Then he'd go to bed, Jayne would pick the team and he'd come and tell everybody in the morning.'

This is interesting and Lawrence laughs when Reddin says this because the idea that Mrs Woodward was actually the number one team selector was always a joke amongst the players. 'We used to laugh about it,' Lawrence says, 'just going: "It's not Clive you need to worry about. It's Jayne." I mean, really lovely lady, but you want to stay on the right side of her, that's for sure.'

But then, when we are back on another Zoom call and talking to Clive and Jayne on the subject of selection, Clive offers this from nowhere – 'Jayne picked the team, don't forget' – and he then leaves us with a slightly cryptic grin across his face, and Jayne looks at him and then at Lawrence and replies, 'You always say that, but it's true, Lawrence, I did, he's not joking.' She is deadpan when she says this. 'He always used to call me when he'd got the team in his head. He'd say: "Now I'm going to sleep on it." And I'd say, "OK then." Only once or twice, I then said, "Are you sure?" When you put Jason Robinson at full-back – that was one time when I said, "Are you sure?"'

Quick as a flash, Lawrence is back on to the subject of his 50th cap: 'For six years, apart from one week, I thought she was a brilliant selector, Clive. But we all have off days! It's fine.'

Later, after saying goodbye to the Woodwards, we discuss this. Clearly Clive would indeed talk to Jayne about his selection thoughts, probably as a way of processing it all through his head. What is not quite so entirely clear is whether she actually did have any influence. 'He was probably only after validation, wasn't he?' Lawrence says. 'Maybe he did just ask her some questions. Shame they got one of the answers so wrong.'

Let it go, Lawrence, let it go.

*   *   *

The World Cup squad was announced on Sunday 7 September, the day after the final warm-up inter-national against France, and, of course, after one final, mammoth exhausting selection meeting.

'It was a massive process,' says Larder. 'Massive. We finished up with a squad of players the likes of which I'd never coached before. What a superb group.'

For Lawrence, though, three names stick out, all three of them omissions: Austin Healey, Simon Shaw and Graham Rowntree. All of them had been England players for over six years. Shaw would eventually get out and join the World Cup squad as an injury replacement, but in Lawrence's mind, all three are part of the World Cup, even if they weren't physically there. He felt particularly for Shaw, at the time, because they were teammates at Wasps. 'The reason Wasps did so well against Leicester all those years,' he says, 'was because Simon Shaw did such a good job on Martin Johnson.'

This is how Clive Woodward recalls it: 'The only one that I genuinely lost sleep over was Graham Rowntree; he was the one who kept me awake at night. And I've met Graham a couple of times since, and though he's fine, he's never forgiven me. He just says it's still the biggest disappointment of his whole professional life, which I can understand.

'Everyone else, I was cool about. Austin had done a great job for us and I know Austin was a great player, but he was a very versatile player and I decided that we didn't need versatile players in the World Cup, plus he had been injured. And with Simon, I was happy to risk Martin Corry as a second-row option. But Graham Rowntree, even now, if I saw him, I'd still want to go up to him and talk about it. When I rang him to tell him, he was genuinely shocked and said, "You're joking." He didn't believe me. And that was not a nice conversation, but that's the job. But also, I'm pleased that he's a head coach now. Because he'll be going through this himself; he'll have to make similar selection decisions where he has to look players in the eye, like I did with Lawrence. There's just no cop out.'

Jayne: 'Can I just say this: I think something interesting has happened over the years. When you have your own kids, they don't understand all the dilemmas and problems and decisions you have to make as a parent until they then become parents themselves. We're talking now about what happened back then, but a number of the players, on getting older, are now in the media, like you, Lawrence, and a number of them are coaching. It's almost like the players becoming parents. Clive and I regularly bump into players, if we're travelling, or at a game or a dinner and we all have big hugs. It's a bit like now the players have all grown up and they're having these experiences of their own, they actually get it. I think they understand now better what it was like being us, or Clive. Because when you're a player, you are only concerned, really, about one person, and that's yourself. That's your responsibility. Whereas when you're a coach or a head coach, you're bothered about everybody, and you've got so much more on your plate and you have all these decisions, these selectorial decisions that you've got to make and whether they're right or wrong, they're your decisions. And you've got to stand by them. And I think that lots of the players now see that, and understand it much better. Does that make sense?'

Yes, it does. It's a nice metaphor: the team as a family and the players now turning into grown-ups.

Whether Rowntree made the World Cup or not, Lawrence still regards him as one of that family. 'I look at him,' he says, 'and think: "You were a part of our success." The way I see it, he helped us win that World Cup.'

CHAPTER 14

GRAYS AND CATTY

What were Clive Woodward's strengths as head coach?

Lawrence: 'Well, certainly one of them was selection. Clive always said that he never got everything right, as we know. But as a coach, selection is such an important part of the job. And he certainly got selection right. That call on Rowntree was harsh; really, really tough. But you can't say he wasn't vindicated. And there were other big calls that went his way.'

Lawrence is referring in particular, here, to two selections, two similar players, two old hands. A few months previously, no one would have guessed that both Mike Catt and Paul Grayson would make it on to the plane; maybe one, but never both. Catt was 31; Grayson was 32. Catt hadn't played for England for two years; Grayson was even further from the picture.

In the four years since the previous World Cup, Grayson had won just two caps, both off the bench. Between World Cups, the only time that he had toured with England was to Canada in 2001 and that was a real statement of where his career appeared to be moving because he didn't go as a player, he was invited on the coaching staff as an up-and-coming wannabe kicking coach. Around the same time, he was actually contemplating retirement – and that was a whole two years out from 2003.

Lawrence is impressed, if a little surprised, by Grayson's studied realism. 'We'd played in age-group games going back many years,' he says to Grayson. 'I had no idea you were thinking of stopping. You must be quite pleased you didn't.'

'Well, I was almost retiring,' Grayson says, explaining how his club, Northampton Saints, had nosedived before 2001 and taken some of his self-belief and aspirations with it – and then it all changed when Wayne Smith, the widely admired Kiwi coach, took the Saints head coach job. 'Wayne Smith came in and said to me, "Everyone tells me you're going to quit." I said, "I think I could still play." And he said, "Well, go on then. Prove it to me." And then there was a complete turnaround for me.'

Yet even by the summer of 2003, Grayson wasn't sure whether to bother with the pre-World Cup training camp. Back in July, when his name was announced in a list of 43 players – a group who would form the initial England training squad and would be playing in three warm-up international fixtures – he rang Woodward to ask if he'd be wasting his time.

Grayson: 'I'd always had quite a good relationship with Woody, and I'd always thought I could be quite open with him. And I said, "Listen, if you've got no intention of taking me to Australia, I'm not playing for the A-team." I said: "If it's just filling a shirt and you've already got who you want on the plane in your mind, don't bother. But if it's based on the form that I'm in and the form that I can show, if I play well enough, will you take me?" And fair play to Woody, he said, "Yeah, I wouldn't even be talking to you if I didn't think that you could be a valuable part of the team."'

And so, Grayson did pitch up for the training camp.

At that point, Catt wasn't even that close. He didn't go to the training camp. He didn't get invited. He wasn't even in the 43.

Catt: 'Prior to that World Cup, I'd had 18 months of injury. Every time I'd played for Bath, I snapped a hamstring, left and right. I just couldn't get it right, couldn't understand what was going on. But then that summer, when you were all in your Pennyhill training camp, Loll, I was in Spain in the sun and I don't know why I did this, but I trained the flipping house down. Every morning I was up, I just trained and trained. And, I don't know why, but I had this inkling. Honestly, I trained the hardest I'd ever trained, had a good few beers too, really loved it. It was brilliant. Time with the family too. Evie, my daughter, was still very young.

'But I couldn't get anything out of Clive. I was texting him all the way through the warm-up games, saying, "Clive, give me a chance. Let me just play one of the games." His classic text to me was, "There's no easy way into this team." And he also said, "I've got to see you play." But I couldn't play – there weren't any club games.

'But then Bath did have a midweek pre-season friendly against Celtic Warriors at Pontypridd. I texted Clive straight away, saying, "This is my only opportunity to show you. What do you think?" and he replied pretty quickly, saying he'd be there. And then, when we got to the game, it wasn't just him who was there, it was all the England coaches: Phil Larder, Andy Robinson and Dave Alred as well.'

Lawrence: 'Wow. No pressure there, then.'

Catt: 'I actually had a stormer in the game that night, but I remember looking to the stands at the end, hoping for a sign from him, a thumbs-up or something, but his seat was empty. I then texted him again: "Where did you go?" He replied saying they'd left ten minutes from the end, and I said: "That was when I was at my best!"'

England's series of warm-up games started with a whopping win over Wales; then they lost by a point away to France in Marseille, but even that was a victory of a kind because it was a largely second-string England against a first-choice France.

Catt: 'I got a text from Woody directly after that Marseille game. And he said to me, "It's not over until the fat lady sings." And I sat there thinking: *Well, what do I reply to that?* I've been begging this bloke to give me an opportunity. What is going on with this bloke?'

Lawrence: 'Well, how did you reply to him? Can you remember? Because Woody's funny. He sends all sorts of messages at three in the morning. You know that better than anyone. But did you reply or just let it go?'

Catt: 'I let it go. I think I let it go because I just didn't know how to reply to it. I just kept telling him, "Look, I'm fit." Then finally I got a call from Clive: "Could I come in for a fitness test?" "Of course I could," I said. But that was only on the Thursday before the Sunday when the World Cup squad was being announced.'

Lawrence: 'I remember you turning up at Pennyhill and I was like, "Oh, Catty, nice to see you. What are you doing here?" We had no idea. And then the next thing you're doing fitness tests on the pitch.'

Catt: 'What I remember is walking into the camp and you guys were dead. You had done such a hard pre-season, it was brutal. And there I was, I'd been on the piss in Spain, fit as anything, in the sunshine. And I just boomed this fitness test. Then, I still remember: I was on a train out of Waterloo on that Sunday, looking out of the window and I got a call from Clive. I thought to myself: "This is it. Another let-down." And he said, "I'm taking you to Australia."'

Lawrence: 'Part of why Clive was so smart was because he knew that you and Jonny [Wilkinson] could work well. Jonny obviously didn't feel threatened by you; if anything, it made him feel more comfortable and stronger.'

Catt: 'It was more taking the pressure off Jonny – so Jonny could be Jonny. Listen, I love Jonny and, really, Jonny and I, we got on really, really well. I think he just knew that when we played together there was a lot of help around him.'

In Lawrence's view, both Catt and Grayson were smart picks for Jonny Wilkinson reasons: 'Both of them worked well with Jonny. Both fitted into his orbit well. I'm not saying that Catty and Grays weren't also deserving selections in their own right, they completely were, and I remember the minute Catty was fit, everyone going, "Well, that's fantastic." But they also worked for squad reasons, and they could both help bring the best from Jonny.'

Grays says: 'The fact that I was the age that I was and the type of person that I am, I knew my role.'

Lawrence asks him what he means by that. Grayson says: 'I knew when Jonny was a kid that he could do some things that I couldn't do and I could see enough in him, when he was 18 and 19, that I thought, "Well, this lad will go past me at some point." And I was happy to look after him when he first got in the England team. I used to drive him to training and make sure he got a lift because it was a scary environment for a normal human, let alone an 18-year-old kid, because there was still half a toe in the past, where England training was an intimidating place to go. And I spent more time with him than any other player: the hours that we spent on the field, post-sessions, kicking together, and then we were always eating late together because everyone else has eaten and buggered off and we were having the last scrapings out of the tin in the meal room. So, we spent an inordinate amount of time together, and I watched him grow.

'And I understood it: I was either playing or I wasn't. There was no bench role or any of that. But in the back of your mind, you know that there are icons throughout that team: yourself, Loll, and Johnno and Jason Robinson and the names that trip off the tongue. But Wilko at that point – the public perception was that he was almost absolutely pivotal, and I was in the position of: well, if he snaps in half, that responsibility falls to me. And I was more than happy with that because it was such a good team, a good bus to drive.

'And I absolutely loved our practice together. Wilko would go for ages and ages. I'd get to a point where enough is enough, but I loved it. When I look back at myself and my career, I can say, "Well, I was a good player, I was an international player, but I was a world-class kicker of the ball." That's my bit where I'd happily go toe to toe with anybody. Kicking the ball off the floor, open play, that was my thing and I loved doing it. So being with Wilko – I loved it. And we had a good time. We laughed a lot, and we kicked a hell of a lot of balls.'

CHAPTER 15

I CAN'T GET ON THAT PLANE

On the eve of departure for Australia, Jonny Wilkinson was threatening not to travel. He wasn't happy with his game. Therefore, he said, how can I possibly go?

It all came down to the last training session that the squad would do at Pennyhill Park before boarding from Heathrow the next day. This was the schedule: they would complete this final training session, then they would all get suited up for a big eve-of-departure dinner hosted by O2, their main sponsors, and the next day would be doors to manual, wheels up and away we go. The dinner wasn't exactly high on anyone's list of priorities. Before leaving home, the only thing the players really wanted to do was to spend some time with their own families; a big corporate event could hardly have been less welcome. Of the lot of them, Wilkinson was the most disgruntled, but for other reasons altogether.

Clive Woodward had asked Phil Larder to take that last training session.

Larder: 'I'd developed a drill which was very competitive. It was a little corridor and each player had to tackle five runners coming at them, one after the other. I encouraged the forwards to try to run over the top of the defender and the backs to try and sidestep them.'

To this day, everyone remembers the alleyway drill. It was hard and unforgiving, there was nowhere to hide, and it doubled up as an exhibition man test. In fact, everyone remembers those entire defensive sessions. They were very much of their time. Modern professional rugby is now in a place where it is desperately trying to explore how it can be a safer sport and one area where it is making gains is in reining back on the amount of full-on tackling and bone-to-bone contact work done in training. The more advanced coaches, these days, keep contact down to a minimum, just a few minutes a week. Back then? No way. No one even thought to question it; the most advanced defensive coaching they had ever experienced, it seemed, was exactly what Larder was giving them.

Lawrence: 'Some of those defensive sessions were un-believable. I know that things have changed now regarding the amount of contact there is in the game, but back then, they were what they were, and, in many ways, they were great. When we used to run those little alleyways that Phil set up, usually at the end of the session, we'd all be there, the whole squad would all be watching each other. There was no hiding place. If you got stepped or you got beaten or you got run over, it was in front of the whole group. Puts a wee bit of pressure on you.'

Larder: 'That's how you inspire one another, isn't it?'

The experience is still scarred on full-back and wing Iain Balshaw's mind. 'Phil obviously would give you some shit if you missed a tackle,' he says, laughing at the recollection. 'I think I had the whole front row running straight at me. It's like: "If you want to be part of the World Cup squad, you've got to tackle properly."'

This last session in this Colosseum was watched by a very nervous Woodward. 'He had specifically requested that I take the very last training session before we flew out to Australia,' Larder recalls, 'But he asked me afterwards, "Why the hell did you put that drill in?" because, he said, "I was shitting myself that somebody was going to get injured." Anyway, we did it and I think there were only three missed tackles made during the entire session. It was really outstanding. But two of them were by Wilko.'

Here lay the problem.

Lawrence: 'Jonny was not only the best goal-kicking fly-half in the world at the time, but he was also probably the best defensive fly-half ever.'

Larder: 'That evening, at the O2 reception, I was sitting there, Backy was on my table, and this old woman starts coming towards me. It's always these old women that come and chat me up; I thought she was going to ask me for a date. Anyway, she poked me in the chest and she said, "Are you Mr Larder?" I said, "Yeah, I am." She says, "I'm sitting next to Mr Wilkinson and he's not eating any of his tea because of what you've done in training." So, Backy went over to speak to Wilko and then reported back. He said that Wilko had said it's just part of his preparation. He'd said, "I can't get on that flight and lie down in the bed when I've defended so badly." He'd said, "I couldn't do it if I kicked badly in training; I can't do it if I defend badly either. Everything's got to be perfect before I land in Australia."'

This called for drastic action. Wilkinson wouldn't travel until he had completed the alleyway defensive drill to his own satisfaction.

Larder: 'So Backy had to find five runners to run at Wilko and we all had to get up early the following morning before leaving for Heathrow to do it. We had to have the medical staff there too, just to make sure nobody was injured. Wilko then did his tackling perfectly. And off he went.'

Even Lawrence, who had worked with Wilkinson for five years, is astonished by this. He had not remembered the incident. He was clearly not one of the five that Neil Back approached for extra work that morning. (A wise recruitment strategy from Back.)

Lawrence: 'Jonny took it to the absolute extremes, didn't he? He was a perfectionist.'

Larder: 'He was. That's how he prepares. Dave [Alred, his kicking coach] always said he was murder if he missed a couple of kicks. He's got to get everything right in his head.'

Lawrence: 'I'm not sure it made him any calmer or any more chilled out in Australia. To be fair, I think it may have made him worse.'

CHAPTER 16

YOU MIGHT WANT TO DISABLE THE CCTV

The World Cup started for England in Perth, but the squad had been there before, only two and a bit months earlier at the end of their summer tour, on what a generous description might call a reconnaissance mission. Dorian West has a very specific recollection of those three days' 'reconnaissance'. As he puts it: 'I nearly died on that trip.'

They were staying in the Sheraton – because that is where they would stay for the first three weeks of the World Cup. West was room-sharing with Graham Rowntree who, of course, wouldn't make it back for the World Cup itself.

This is how West nearly died.

'We'd had a good drink,' West says in a very rugby understatement. 'I was in bed before Graham. The dickhead then came back and he'd lost his key so I let him in and he brought Johnson and Ben Kay and Martin Corry back, and they beat the shit out of me.' That's not a bullying kind of beating the shit out of someone, it's a rugby kind of pissed pile-on.

'They smacked me on the arse with a shoe, they were really belting me and then Cozza (Corry) tackled me into a window, and we are like 30 floors up, and well ... the window was rocking. How we didn't go through this window, I will never know. When I have nightmares, I still think about that now.'

When recalling this with Lawrence, they both find it hilarious. 'What a trip that was,' West says. Oh yes. 'And a good thing we didn't go through that window.'

If that sounds very old-school, that is the point about this squad: they were caught between the old school and the new. And when they returned to Perth, where they would spend the first three weeks of the World Cup, it was back to old-school again. There were two weeks before their first game and that was against Georgia, who were not regarded as a threat. They were also given 'jet lag protocols', which meant no big training sessions for four or five days.

What do you remember about it, Lawrence?

'I'm sitting there in the hotel room, it's midnight and you're wide awake, thinking: this jet lag protocol needs a little bit of readjusting – ten pints is surely the best jet lag protocol; that's how to get yourself to sleep when you're wide awake. Then a text goes and it's from Jason [Leonard]: "Beer. Reception, downstairs, five minutes, Jase." "OK, see you in reception."'

It helped, of course, that the squad had been to Perth so recently. They knew exactly where they could get those ten pints and Lawrence, as was his wont, had gone out of his way to befriend the concierge. 'You had to stay ahead of the game,' he says. 'So, I had a little word with the concierge and said, "Listen, you might just want to disable the CCTV for the next five hours as Mr Woodward might ask for footage."'

Thus did a group assemble and the first four nights were spent on the readjusted jet lag protocol. As Dawson recalls it: 'Jason and Loll were like: if we're going to feel hung-over, why don't we just be hung-over?'

Dawson was part of this group which, at different times, also included Vickery, Woodman, Catt, Balshaw and Tindall. Balshaw says that 'my biggest mistake of that entire World Cup was when I said to Leonard: "Jase, I will drink you under the fucking table." Well, youthful exuberance and all that. It did not end well for me. We'd all been given these Kodak cameras and Tinds had a picture of me where Jason's holding me up by the bar, literally just unconscious, and he's just pouring shots down my face.'

On the sixth day, proper squad training started.

Lawrence: 'It's the full thing. Breakfast meeting, red socks, blue shorts, red tops, the whole lot. This is it now. This is where the World Cup starts. And we look around the room and there's about ten minutes before the meeting starts and no sign of Leonard whatsoever. We had a buddy system, so you always checked your buddy's there – I was with Neil Back. Phil Vickery was Jason's buddy. I said, "Vicks, where's your mate?" He goes, "What, what?" I said, "You'd better go and find him because the meeting starts in ten minutes." He goes to Jason's room and he's face-planted, still fully clothed. This is the most experienced player that we've got on the trip. Anyway, we managed to get him dressed and into the team meeting and I'm thinking: "Clive, please just don't ask him anything. Just don't. If you ask him anything, he's got no chance."'

All this does seem somewhat surprising. This is the fittest England rugby team of all time. They have just put themselves through the hell of an 11-week training camp. Is the boozing not detrimental?

Lawrence: 'No, I wasn't worried about that at all because it didn't touch the sides. There was no concern that you were going to lose the conditioning.'

Balshaw's view is that 'these little outings' as he put it, peppered through the length of the tournament 'when we could let our hair down and enjoy ourselves', were some of their best moments and 'what made it very special'. In the modern professional age, little outings are almost extinct.

'We were seasoned campaigners,' West says and, because he is still coaching, he knows how times have changed: 'Lads these days, they go out for a drink and it's ten days before they feel right again.'

Ask Lawrence if he would repeat those Perth nights if he was in a World Cup squad today and he says 'Absolutely not!' and that is nothing to do with fitness and conditioning and whatever modern sports science might say. It's because in 2003, mobile phones didn't have cameras.

CHAPTER 17

THREE NINES

Which is the most important position on the field? Lawrence doesn't hang around with his answer and he doesn't say that it is his own.

'When you play in the back row,' he says, 'rarely do things actually cost your team the game. But when you play scrum-half...'

It was harder, still, for the England scrum-halves, Matt Dawson and Kyran Bracken.

'I made my debut off the bench against South Africa,' Lawrence says, 'and I played my last game off the bench against South Africa 12 years later. Almost all the 83 caps in between, I started. (Yes, apart from his 50th cap for which Woodward dropped him to the bench.) I can't imagine what it was like for those two.'

His point is that while he spent his career firmly established as first-choice No. 8, Dawson and Bracken spent almost all that same period scrapping to be first-choice No. 9. They were born

11 months apart, and they were first capped two years apart; they both won over 50 England caps and though Dawson won 16 more, that was in part due to Bracken's repeated back issues.

How was it between them? 'Cordial, that's all it was,' is how Bracken puts it. 'I don't mind saying it. I am just being honest. People say, "It's a team sport," but it's actually not, it's an individual sport. We all need each other. But it's a real individual journey as well. I don't imagine any player would sit on the bench and hope that the person in their position scores eight tries and is Man of the Match. Actually, it's a dog-eat-dog world. It's hard. It's not what people think. People think it's this harmonious environment and everyone loves each other. But it's hard.'

It got to the point between Dawson and Bracken where they called a kind of a truce. 'I remember having a conversation in Richmond,' Dawson says. 'I think it was in The Roebuck on Richmond Hill. When you're younger, you're looking at the papers: how did he do? Did he score? I was doing that, and I know he was. But now the press were battling us out and we were both thinking: "I know you're a decent player, you know I'm a decent player." So, we sort of had a bit of a chat to say: "Fuck it, I've had enough of this."'

Dawson poured his personality into every element of competition and his approach came at a cost. He laid that very bare in his autobiography, where he wrote that he had been 'revered and reviled' and that 'Through it all I have never given anything but my best, and yet it feels my motives and I have often been misunderstood. I have been called arrogant and worse.' He says he came close to chucking it in altogether. With the benefit of 20 years' hindsight, though, he says, 'I don't think I'd change too much.'

We meet in another pub in Richmond, where he is utterly self-effacing and takes complete ownership of his years as an elite athlete. 'I'm quite philosophical about the shit things as well as the great things,' he says. 'I think it makes you the person you are. It was a period of my life where, because of what I was doing on and off the field and the way I got the job done, it wasn't necessarily appealing to everybody. It was born out of wanting to be successful in rugby. I know that a lot of my teammates didn't particularly like me; that didn't really bother me because I wanted to win, and as long as we were winning, I was happy. I had a very hot-cold relationship with the media, which didn't bother me in the slightest. I handled all that in the way that someone in their early-to-mid-twenties would. In my late twenties, there were certain moments when you go: "OK, maybe I need to tweak myself accordingly. I know that I've done a lot of shit things and been a dickhead, but I am quite happy to forgive myself, learn from it and move on."'

Lawrence is impressed with his honesty. 'You're not teammates in order to be friends,' he says. 'You're teammates to respect each other and do a job. There's no one who didn't respect what you did, Daws. If you happen to get on with others as well, that's a bonus.'

Dawson says: 'I think it's gone the other way now. Today, everyone's high-fiving, patting each other on the bum and being great mates.'

Lawrence: 'They get on so well that what they don't say is: "You were shit today!" You've got to call each other out, but you're not allowed to do any of that.'

Dawson: 'In our era, if you made a mistake, you knew you'd have to answer to Loll and to Johnno.'

And when you look at it like that, it's hard not to conclude that a bit more of the inner Matt Dawson is what England in the early 2020s could do with right now. Plus, the Lawrence and Johnno police. Or maybe that's just not going to fly any more.

*   *   *

As it was, barely had England's World Cup campaign got going than they had neither Dawson nor Bracken available. Bracken was on the very steps up to the plane in Heathrow when he considered turning round and going home: his back had gone again.

Jason Leonard was right next to him. Bracken: 'Jase said: "Don't fucking say anything. Just get on the plane and once you are on the plane, there is nothing they can do." I was like: "I need to tell them." Jase was: "Don't tell them at all."'

Leonard had to be at his most persuasive. 'Kyran was going: "I'll have to come clean and pull out." I was like, "What are you talking about? Don't be so daft!"'

So, Bracken endured the journey. In Perth, when training started, he was still struggling. 'I was thinking, "Should I say something?" but by the time the Georgia game came, I was fine.' But backs are eternally unpredictable and in the warm-up for the game, it went again. 'I was suddenly in a really bad way. I took a suppository, just to get through. Honestly, it was horrific. I was thinking: "What do I do?" and it was only 30 minutes before kick-off that I just had to tell Clive: "I can't pass a ball." So I was out. That was so upsetting.'

As it was, the Georgia game came and went with a predictably lop-sided score – 84-6. The most significant news from the game was the injury list: two hamstrings, one belonging to Richard Hill, the other to Dawson. The knock-on effect of Dawson's injury was the opening of the door to the other scrum-half in the squad, Andy Gomarsall. Of the three nines, it was Gomarsall who had the best pass. He had gone to Australia clearly knowing that he was the third-choice No. 9, but with the ambition of clambering his way up the pecking order. Suddenly opportunity beckoned.

'At that World Cup,' Gomarsall says, 'there were moments that I loved.' Those would be the ones when he thought that he was taking that opportunity. 'And there were moments when I was fucking pissed off.' Those would be the ones when Dawson and Bracken were fit again and he realised that he hadn't changed the pecking order at all. 'But you can't show you're pissed off because that's just sapping the team. Then, once the quarter-final team was announced [Dawson starting, Bracken on the bench], there was a moment of acceptance for me. I remember going up to Daws and basically saying: "Well done, because you're going to play every single game." He probably didn't ever even see me as a threat or competition. He knew he was the man. Look, back then, he and I never got on or saw eye to eye and that was because we were so competitive, but I basically accepted where I was at and said to him, "Right, every training session now we're going to work on the passing. I think your passing is shit, so I'm going to try and make you better because we've got every chance to win the World Cup if I make your pass better. The rest of the game I probably can't help you with, you're an amazing player, but I can at least do something and help you." And that for me was acceptance and that's what I did.'

And how did that friendly offer of free coaching tutorials go down?

'It was a bit of the two Matt Dawsons. The arrogant one was going, "Fuck you, mate," and there's the other one going, "No, you're right."'

CHAPTER 18

MATE, YOU'RE MAD

The two injuries from the Georgia game would not recover as fast as had been hoped, as Lewis Moody would discover only two days before the next game – which was South Africa. 'I remember getting the call,' Moody says. 'It was a bit shocking. I was walking down the street and it was Clive saying, "Mate, you're going to have to play on Saturday."' Hill had not come through. 'I was like, "Fucking hell," because all our training had been building up to that one game, hadn't it? All pre-season, everything was about us beating South Africa. And I was like, "Fuck. OK." Because I was 25 at the time, a pretty nervous young lad in that side, and now getting to go and play in that massive game.'

Already this is interesting. Moody never played as though he was pretty nervous. If anything, completely the opposite. And he, famously, never displayed any concern for his own safety. Yet when we meet him over a long Zoom call, he happily exposes the obvious truth – that though this England team are preserved in our memories as sepia-tinted superheroes, they are all infinitely more complex than that.

Just because of the very way that he played, Moody had always seemed more comic-book warrior than most. Lawrence has a pretty good idea of what it was that set him apart. 'Most people,' he tells Moody pointedly, 'can flick that switch between being calm and not reckless to being in the head space that you need to be on a matchday. And that's the key, isn't it? As you get older, you realise that actually I'm quite good at flicking that switch now.'

'That off switch never happened for me, sadly,' Moody replies.

'No,' says Lawrence. This was his point. 'Yours was on all the time.'

This was the magic of being Moody or, if it was his own or other players' self-preservation that was of any priority, you could maybe call it his curse. But it is what made Moody the player he was: in love with the game, in love with being able to contribute in any way to helping his team, in love with the fearlessness that was his personal stamp on the game. 'Love' is his word, here, that he keeps on using to tell Lawrence about his appetite for the game.

'I genuinely loved it,' he says. 'I did, I genuinely loved it. For me it was a boyhood dream coming true, right?'

Lawrence: 'But you always had this mindset. You wouldn't rationalise and think like I did or anyone else did. You'd just throw yourself into it and think about the consequences later. Is that fair?'

Lewis: 'Yeah. People used to go, "Oh mate, you're fucking mad. Why do you do all that shit?" Well, my simple approach to rugby is that if I could benefit the team by using my body as a tool to get the ball back, or to get to someone, or take someone else out of the game, then fuck it, it didn't matter what happened to me. It was about the benefit of the team.

'And I absolutely loved it when I first played with England. I loved the fact that I got given the ball at the back of the lineout, got to smash it up into four Welshmen, or whoever, and maybe make half a yard so that the other players could run around the corner and score. Loved it.'

Moody pauses and then continues: 'In hindsight, there's one thing I would've changed which would be my approach to training in the latter stages of my career. Because people say, "Look, you don't have to go fucking flat out all the time now." But I just grew up in a mentality where if I came into the England side, let's say that World Cup team, I had to prove myself in every session if I had a hope of getting in past you, Lawrence, or Backy or Hilly. And that was the way it was. And it was the same at my club, Leicester. And it just stuck with me for the rest of my career. And it meant often getting injured in training, which is a stupid thing to do really, in hindsight. But hindsight's a great thing. People kept saying, "Oh, you shouldn't be so fucking reckless." I was like, "Mate, if I was less reckless, I wouldn't be a benefit to the team so I wouldn't be playing."'

Amongst Moody's many qualities was one which was absolutely true to the personality that he took to the pitch: his undying, completely dogged, relentless pursuit of the kick-chase. The role of supreme kick-chaser was one with which he had been anointed at Leicester a full five years before he even got to this World Cup.

Moody: 'It only came about because we played a game against Gloucester and the fly-half scuffed the kick. I happened to be chasing it, caught it and scored under the post. And I think from every kick-off after that, they thought that the same result was going to happen. So, I then ended up chasing every kick-off I think that was ever kicked in any game that I was involved in. I fucking loved putting myself in positions that were awkward and uncomfortable for the opposition. That was how I saw my role in the team and yes, I loved it. And yes, it meant that I had maybe more injuries than I should have done.'

By the time Moody got to the South Africa game – as a replacement for the injured Richard Hill – he was actually already injured himself too. 'A little foot strain', was how he described it after the Georgia match, but it got worse, he had a couple of scans, nothing showed and he just played through it, all the way through the tournament. That was how it was with Moody.

Two weeks after the final, though, back playing for Leicester Tigers away against Stade Français in the Heineken Cup, his foot was stamped on, right on the very same spot that had been causing him those problems, and that was it. This time the scan showed a stress fracture in the navicular bone.

Moody: 'Imagine if I had found that whilst I was in Australia; that would've been it. I would've been out. I look back now going: with that fractured foot I was just lucky to be there to the end.'

He then faced payback time. 'A stress fracture to me is a tiny little fracture that doesn't cause many issues and that you can recover from quickly,' he says. Quite the opposite with this one; it was another year and a half before he would play again.

And when you take rugby away from Moody, you are extracting an essential source of his joy. It was literally as though the sun had gone in. After around eight months, he toyed with a comeback, found that he was still not properly mended and went back into a boot. 'That,' he says, 'was when I hit a really dark point.'

When the tap of adrenaline is finally switched to off, it can be a huge personal challenge and, as one of the game's extreme adrenaline junkies, Moody experienced this as much as anyone.

'I think Annie [my wife] would tell you that I needed to be active and in a gym,' he says. 'If I don't do stuff, then I can be quite grumpy and miserable to be around and the whole mood changes, doesn't it?' He is now looking to Lawrence for encouragement. 'I don't know whether you experienced this, Loll?'

He continues: 'When you don't have a physical outlet, your mood or your ability to manage your mood swings diminishes, I found. And it would come out at different points that weren't acceptable – whether talking to Annie or friends or whoever. Often, it's at home, isn't it? So, one of the key parts of me being able to deal with life after rugby was still being physically active or having a physical outlet that allowed me to manage my emotions, which at times got away from me a bit.'

From one of the sunniest characters in the game, this is really striking. But Lawrence is nodding away empathetically.

Moody continues: 'I am a glass-half-full approach to life person but, like anyone, we all have shit and dark times. And if you don't have an outlet for that emotion, then it comes up in the wrong situations, right? And you'll have outbursts at people. I remember having a go at a waiter once just because they brought the wrong thing over. And that was nothing to do with him; it was because I was dealing with shit in my own head that I hadn't sorted through a physical outlet.'

But Lawrence gets all of this; it's not as if rugby hadn't become the definition of his life too. And as is his way, he heaps reassurance on his old teammate. 'I know what it's like,' he says, 'when you're used to living life fairly active and fairly fast, and then suddenly you don't get that outlet. Alice [my wife] used to say to me, "Please carry on exercising because you are a nightmare to be with anyway, let alone if you haven't had the exercise." So yeah, I'm with you. Completely.'

CHAPTER 19

MOST PRESSURISED GAME EVER

We ask Martin Johnson: What is the most pressurised game you ever played in your career? And he doesn't even pause for an answer. 'By a long, long, long way,' he says, 'it was the World Cup pool game against South Africa.'

South Africa were the big hurdle. They were the only genuine hurdle in the group stage and if you beat them, you got the better half of the draw. Lose to them and you were likely to get New Zealand in the quarters and Australia in the semis. 'People had no comprehension,' Johnson says about the pressure. 'If we went out early, we couldn't go home. We wouldn't be able to show our faces. Like if we'd lost to Wales in that quarter-final – how do we go home?' He talks about 'nerves' before the South Africa game being like no other and this is not a guy who talked about nerves. Not really ever.

For Lawrence, that game was steeped in narrative. It wasn't just that both teams knew that their success in this World

Cup hung on the result, it was that the previous autumn, at Twickenham, England had beaten the Springboks 53-3. That's more than a rugby score to the Springboks, it was an unprecedented humiliation for a proud rugby nation in the course of which they lost touch with their integrity as rugby players. 'Probably the dirtiest opposition I ever played against,' is how Lawrence remembers that day. South Africa had one man sent off for an illegal hit on Wilkinson and the others carried on in the same spirit until the death.

They were led from the front by Corné Krige, the Springbok captain. In the media following the game, Krige would be compared to Freddy Krueger and Osama bin Laden. He was certainly in the thick of it and Dawson was certainly on the receiving end of much of it. It was when Dawson started calling moves that were not England moves but moves for Northampton Saints, his club, that it became apparent he had sustained a concussion. Whether that came from Krige's flying head-butt in a ruck or poleaxing him later from the side, we will never know.

'I'll never forget,' Lawrence says, 'we scored a pushover try at the end which took us over 50 points and then, as we came off the pitch, they went: "See you in Perth." I said: "We'll fucking see you in Perth, don't worry."'

After that final try, Krige was 'almost in tears', according to Johnson. 'As we were walking back, I said to the referee: "Blow the whistle now. Nothing good's gonna happen now." And he did.'

Yet Krige was still not done. In the function after the game, he wouldn't let it drop. 'Martin,' he said, 'you twisted the knife today. This is not Perth; we'll see you in Perth.'

So there was a lot riding on Perth. There were a lot of

injuries in the England camp too. The result of one of those was that Lewis Moody, in for Richard Hill, went into the game with a very specific thought in his head, lodged by Phil Larder, the defence coach. In his analysis of the opposition, Larder had noted Louis Koen, the Springbok No. 10, and the fact that he would sit deep in the pocket when he wanted time to get a kick away. 'He doesn't like to be pressured,' Larder said. 'You may have an opportunity to get to him.'

Who would play scrum-half was the biggest issue. Dawson was still injured and Bracken was touch and go right up until the game. 'How he played that South Africa game was a miracle,' Dawson says of Bracken. 'He was having daily injections into his back, full on, like those horse tranquilisers. It was brutal.'

None of this helped Johnson much, who had in mind Joost van der Westhuizen, the Springbok No. 9, one of the all-time greats. 'I used to defend one out from the ruck,' he says. 'That was my job: they don't come through here. Someone like Joost, if you let him go through, that will kill your team. All my thinking was: don't let Joost go through a hole. Joost was so good at that, for a tall guy – he'd be lower than the sofa. My whole focus was: do not get done by Joost. So, I am basically going into my bag of experience and saying: don't worry about all the bigger picture things, just do your job right.'

On the eve of the game, Johnson went down to the stadium, something he never usually did – but that was a mark of the importance of the event. 'I never did that,' he says, 'but I just wanted to visualise everything. Just the thought of losing that game was beyond anything. It was horrendous.'

* * *

The game itself was a really edgy, early tournament encounter, though at least South Africa had left the extreme violence of the previous confrontation behind. What they were, though, was an even match for England; indeed for parts of the first hour, they were better. Two elements fell strongly in England's favour. One was that while Wilkinson could barely miss with his goal-kicking, Koen could barely hit; at half-time, when the score was 6-6, Wilkinson had converted two from two and Koen two from six. Also in England's favour was the fact that they had cracked the Springboks' lineout calls. In the week before the game, Ben Kay, England's lineout captain, had asked for the assistance of Dr Sherylle Calder, England's vision coach, who was South African. He wanted help with his video analysis because he was watching the Springbok lineouts and thinking: they're calling the lineouts in Afrikaans, aren't they? Yes, she said, they are. And so, she translated; it wasn't hard.

'They had literally done as their lineout calls the numbers 1, 2, 3, 4, 5,' Kay says. It wasn't hard for him to learn to count in Afrikaans. 'So we had a decent lineout day against them.'

'I actually played pretty shit in the game,' Moody says. 'But I had a couple of involvements and one major one.'

Indeed, 63 minutes in, the game played out just as Larder had envisaged: Koen, deep in the pocket, Moody chasing him down because, as he says, 'that was what I fucking loved doing'. 'I managed to exert enough pressure on him and, to be fair, he had an absolute shocker.' The charge-down then fell perfectly for Greenwood, who dribbled the ball over the line for the try. From that point, South Africa weren't coming back.

England finished 25-6 ahead, happy in the knowledge that this would not be a game to remember. Amongst their achievements was the job they did on Koen; he would never start a game for South Africa again. 'Yes, well done, Lewis,' says Lawrence, though the player that he recalls most from that day is Bracken. 'He was just so bloody tough that day. Be in no doubt, that was the day that Kyran helped us win the World Cup.'

Observing him closely from the stands, and knowing the state of his back, Dawson was similarly in awe. 'I was looking at Kyran, going: "How are you going to get through this?" He caught the ball from the kick-off, didn't give it to anyone, and just ran it back at them. I thought: "What are you doing?!"'

Bracken had high hopes for what he had achieved that night. 'I thought after the South Africa game I'd have a chance to keep the starting spot.' As it was, England had five more games and he didn't start one of them.

'It's funny,' he reflects two decades later. 'During the Covid lockdown, those games were all shown again on ITV. After that South Africa game had been shown, Clive texted me saying: "I just realised how well you played in that game." I was thinking: "Thanks, but you dropped me after that." But it was quite nice to get that text out of the blue.'

There was one other delayed follow-up to the whole Springbok saga. In 2018, out of the blue, Krige put out an apology on Twitter to Dawson for that 2002 Twickenham game. 'My sincere apologies,' he tweeted. 'I was and am ashamed of my behaviour that day. Hope my kids never see the video. DM me your number, would love to stay in touch?'

And no, they never did quite become buddies. The fact that it took 16 years did not make the apology OK for Dawson. 'I'd love to say I remember it well,' he replied on Twitter, 'but he knocked me into the next day... unfortunately, I do fear there'll be plenty of consequences in the long term for me.'

CHAPTER 20

IS THAT ALL YOU'VE GOT?

One of the more amusing reflections on the England team at the World Cup was this, in the Australian *Daily Telegraph*: 'The English have always been an arrogant race. Go back in history, look at the English army. Who goes to war dressed up in red coats?'

Take note that this was the *Australian Daily Telegraph*; nothing to do with the British version. Nevertheless, though its viewpoint was extreme, it was not uncommon.

'Everybody seemed to hate us,' wrote Will Greenwood in his autobiography. 'For as long as I had been playing with England, we had gone out of our way not to sound the least bit arrogant... but we still got abused wherever we went.'

Did any of these accusations of arrogance have foundations?

Lawrence: 'Before the World Cup, I phoned my mum and dad saying: "You've got to come out to the World Cup. Look, I can't say this publicly, but I genuinely believe we're going to win this tournament." Now if I was arrogant, I would've been saying that publicly, but I didn't. The perception is that maybe England were, but I don't think we were. Certainly, that group of players wasn't.'

At any rate, two games into the World Cup, the Pom-bashing was fully under way. Before they had even arrived in Perth, Corné Krige had gone public with his view that 'Martin Johnson is one of the dirtiest captains in world rugby' (pot, kettle and all that). Once in Australia, the *Mail & Guardian*, a South African newspaper, called Greenwood and Mike Tindall 'the Laurel and Hardy of the England backline'. The *Sydney Morning Herald* chimed in with the view that 'the lumbering English front rowers look like giant turnips'.

Lawrence: 'It's interesting, the minute you arrived in the southern hemisphere, the press and the rhetoric about England was pretty obvious. And we found it quite funny, I think, to start with. And then over a period of time it just became boring really and a bit tedious. But I don't know whether they were writing it and just having a bit of fun in their own offices or whether they were writing it because they believed it or whether it was because they were insecure. I mean the biggest threat to Australia's national security in a rugby sense was England, really. Because we were the number one side. We'd beaten them six times previously. And it's a home World Cup. So, the papers are probably thinking, let's just try and unsettle them. The same thing happens when you go on tour in New Zealand. They've got such amazing things to talk about but instead of celebrating all these wonderful players that play for countries other than New Zealand, they just seem to find a way of attacking every other player that doesn't wear an All Blacks shirt. And you know, that's fine.

But there was definitely a determination for us to go and prove people wrong.'

Three themes would develop in the Aussie media around this England World Cup team. The first – their supposed arrogance – really dates this England team. Consider the two decades of underperformance that followed 2003, the idea that the current England team would be arrogant or even have anything to be arrogant about is just silly.

It seems a joke, too, that it was a barb ever thrown at Lawrence and his England team. Certainly, he and the players now look back and laugh but at the time, they didn't always find it quite so amusing. 'There is arrogance in rugby,' wrote Dawson in his autobiography, 'but it doesn't wear a white shirt.'

The second theme was the team's age. It was Toutai Kefu, the Wallaby No. 8, who first called England 'Dad's Army'; it was a nickname that would stick. At the start of the tournament, John Muggleton, one of the Wallaby coaches, asked publicly of England: 'I question how much you can teach a 34-year-old.'

'Oh, I thought it was quite amusing,' is the reflection of Dorian West, who was the oldest in the squad, turning 36 just before the Georgia game, 'because we were the fittest we'd ever been.'

Again, 20 years' hindsight makes a mockery of the whole Dad's Army storyline, but it would be wrong to suggest that it didn't get under the skin at the time. 'It was the one slur that really hit home,' wrote Dawson. 'There was a lot of disrespect there. Backy, aged 34 and about to become England's most-capped flanker, was livid.'

The day after the South Africa game, a third theme re-emerged. It was directly linked to Jonny Wilkinson – the fact that he had successfully converted seven kicks from seven against the Springboks, two of them drop goals, and the perception that, apart from his boot, England couldn't do much and certainly couldn't play entertaining try-scoring rugby. It was the *Australian* whose headline that day would stalk England all the way through to the final. Over a picture of Wilkinson kicking, in bold letters, the headline demanded to know: 'Is that all you've got?'

Lawrence's view is that 'You take it as a compliment, in the end, because you realise that whenever their press are on the front foot and having a go, it's because they see you as a threat.'

Yet there was also something ingrained in all this, about rugby and about who really understood how to play the game and that, for some reason, this was to do with which end of the earth you happened to be born in. This, at least, is how it struck Greenwood: 'In those days, I don't think the southern hemisphere believed anyone else could do it [win a World Cup]. And the reality is no one's done it since. I do genuinely believe, if you've ever spoken to a Kiwi, an All Black or whatever, lovely blokes, but their mindset is: "Why are you even on our pitch? What are you doing here? Are you still here?" And I'm not trying to call them out, it's just that they're born with it. They feel the only people who can win the World Cup are the southern hemisphere.'

CHAPTER 21

THE WEIGHT ON JONNY'S SHOULDERS

The weekend after South Africa, England played Samoa, a game which threw a new light upon Jonny Wilkinson and suggested, for the first time in the World Cup, that perfectionism, the ideal that he had set himself, was not only one that he would struggle to live up to but was becoming a burden too.

England made a slow start against Samoa; they went 3-0 behind, conceded a try and were suddenly 10-0 down. And this was not a match that was expected to overly stretch them. They then won a penalty, 40 yards out, which Wilkinson missed though that is only a minor footnote; 40 yards out is not a sure-shot, it was just a point of interest because up until that point in the World Cup, he'd had a 100 per cent kicking success record.

Just before half-time, though, there was a major footnote. England had a penalty directly in front of the uprights, Wilkinson blasted the ball and it bounced back off the post. No one could really believe what had happened. From his seat in the stand, Paul Grayson remembers the moment acutely. 'That's what happens when you're nervous,' he says. 'I was like: "Oh, maybe he is human after all. He is feeling it."'

It wasn't as if it was a disaster game for Wilkinson. England were still 13-16 behind at half-time, but when they were finally pulling ahead in the second half, there was a gorgeous Wilkinson highlight when he hoisted an inch-perfect cross-kick which Iain Balshaw caught without breaking stride to score England's third try.

Yet Matt Dawson, who was his scrum-half that day, could also sense that maybe something was up. 'At one point, I've flung out a pass to where he should have been,' he recalls. The pass went to ground. 'But it wasn't a shit pass,' Dawson insists. 'I remember he was so deep. It was more: "What the F are you doing there?"'

That was out of character for Wilkinson but Dawson had taken note of Wilkinson's introverted behaviour off the pitch too. 'I was on to him with: "Come on, come out, come and have a beer, come and play cards, come and do something!"' The more the World Cup progressed, however, the more Wilkinson became a hermit. Dawson acknowledges that he wasn't equipped at the time to understand why Wilkinson might be behaving this way: 'There was no consideration from me to say: "Why is he in this state of mind?" I was all about the rugby: I want to win the World Cup, let's get on with it. The one person who absolutely got it from the start was Grays.'

As the second fly-half in the squad, Grayson was obliged to spend a fair few man-hours with Wilkinson anyway, because of the kicking practice that they would do together. No one actually suggested that Grayson should then broaden his role as Wilkinson's support man, but he sensed that it was required and graduated into it naturally. It started in Perth when they went out together to the music shop and bought a guitar.

Grayson: 'We'd mess about with it in his room. I was more Jimi Hendrix and he was more Jack Johnson. It was a bit of a fun way to pass an hour or two. I remember walking to the guitar shop because nobody batted an eyelid as Perth's not necessarily a rugby city. If you're an AFL player, they know who you are, but rugby union just doesn't exist there. So we were not quite anonymous but not far off. And that would be the last time in his life he would walk anywhere without being instantly recognisable because of what that tournament did and his role in it.

'He was hardly somebody who was searching to be out and about anyway. He wasn't a guy who wanted to go out for coffee. Some guys go stir-crazy in their rooms and in the hotel; they just want to be out and he wasn't like that. He trained his balls off, would get back, sleep, play guitar, eat some food, chill out, watch a film, rinse and repeat. He always seemed to me happiest in his room. And at that point it was by his choice. Then, ultimately, it became not his choice because by the end of that tournament, you just couldn't move, could you? He certainly couldn't.'

Wilkinson hadn't always been so remote. Mike Tindall remembers their days playing England under-18s together and their (unbeaten) tour of Australia. 'I have so many good stories from that trip,' he says. 'Jonny: happy, having a drink, and everything else. It was fine. But he was fine all the way up until 2001 – when he just became massive, he became a pin-up boy and then he just made the decision never to go out again.'

In Australia, at the World Cup, Grayson could sense the impact that the tournament and Wilkinson's central role within it was having upon him: 'Think about the weight of expectation that was not only on England but also on him and then couple that with the way he thought about it and the amount of pressure he put on himself. He had this desire to tick every single box, to think: I've done absolutely everything possible to prepare for a game and therefore I can't fail. But we all know that's impossible. Think about the weight of expectation for somebody who's wired that way mentally.'

The best thing Grayson thought he could do was just to keep Wilkinson in a happy place: 'I used to make him laugh. The actual training, the physical aspect of kicking the ball backwards and forwards to each other for hours on end, we kept that competitive but there was still room for having a bit of fun. It's not head down slog all the time. We got into a good routine and he likes his routine. So yeah, there was quite a lot of peace in those moments.'

The other member of this team was Dave Alred, the kicking coach, who had worked with Wilkinson since his teens and knew him as well as anyone, and Alred could also recognise the struggles Wilkinson was going through. 'It was a cross between managing it on a daily basis,' he says, 'and, to some extent, fire-fighting.'

He remembers trying to manage Wilkinson's demand for perfection: 'You'd kind of shake him with a bit of reality. He'd become so good and had such expectation that every now and again, you'd need to say: "Stop! Fuck! This is really good!"'

Was Wilkinson coping with the pressure? Alred pauses before he answers. 'I felt he was.' And then he adds: 'That doesn't mean to say it was comfortable.'

What is strikingly clear, when you talk about Wilkinson to any of his old teammates, is the depth of their regard for him. It is a genuine affection for him as a friend crossed with a soaring admiration for him as a teammate, for the tireless professionalism that he took to his role, for his reliability, for the fact that they knew that if they put him in a position to win a match, then he would pull the trigger and never miss. He was both their trump card and the most modest of peers. He could bring them glory yet resist even the thought of basking in it.

It is not that the other players couldn't see the weight that Wilkinson was taking upon himself in Australia, their responses were confused in part because they didn't know what to do about it or really whether there was anything that they should do about it, plus this was Jonny – wasn't it? – and Jonny always took on the pressure and Jonny always came through. And that was part of the deal for all of them too. You are each there, in Australia, because you are one of an elite group who have each proved you have the mental strength to deal with the challenge ahead. Wasn't this just what Wilkinson was doing – just in a very extreme way? Yet Lawrence calls it a form of 'self-harm'. 'Torturing himself' are the words Dave Reddin uses to describe it.

Lawrence: 'I had concerns for Jonny all the way through the tournament because we were under pressure, and he was the main man, wasn't he? He's the No. 10; he was in the eye of the storm. And the longer the tournament went on, the more pressure he came under. And I felt sorry for him. I felt for him because he'd created this way of working, a way of being that didn't allow him to have the same release valves or the same outlets to relieve the pressure. I don't think he understood how to do that. And as a result, you could see that it was building and building for him. And that must have been really intense.

'I loved Jonny. We all did. And we admired his pursuit of

excellence, which was incredible. I don't think there's another rugby player in the history of the game who's done that much training. But we were all doing what we felt was the right way to get the best out of ourselves. And if he felt that that was the right way to get the best out of himself, then that's fine. We all had concerns about ourselves, about each other. It's called pressure. It's called nerves. It's called being the number one side in the world.'

Even from the outside, the pressure that he was under was all too apparent too. Three days before the Samoa match, Wilkinson was put up for media interviews and one of the questions asked of him was: 'Are you worried you're turning into a basket case?' Yes, that beggars belief. Twenty years ago, though, it was met by a ripple of sniggers.

Yet that pressure showed itself in that Samoa match and it would dog Wilkinson further into the tournament.

Dawson: 'It is a difficult pressure that the coaches are under, too, when all the players know that your star player is nowhere near performing well enough. It's proper senior players going: "What are you going to do?"'

Lawrence: 'No one really wanted to tell him. That was the problem. I felt so sorry for him.'

Richard Hill was one of Wilkinson's best mates in the group. He could see what he described as Wilkinson 'taking the weight of the world on his shoulders', but like everyone, he had his own job to get on with and that job was recovering from a hamstring injury. 'Part of me was having to be selfish with having to sort myself out,' he says. But he also found it well-nigh impossible to dig Wilkinson out of his slavish routine. In the last week of the World Cup, he finally persuaded him to walk a couple of hundred yards round the corner from the hotel to enjoy a change of scenery. Their destination was only a bookshop, but he describes that as 'a triumph'.

Long before the World Cup, Reddin had identified Wilkinson as a special project. What he saw in him was what he calls 'a self-discipline and an ability to beat himself up, or almost a necessity to do so, that was unheard of. His volume of kicking practice particularly was a problem.'

Reddin could see that by over-practising, Wilkinson was in danger of damaging himself. 'But you've got to be respectful,' he says. 'He's a senior international, he's been successful because of the way he's done things.'

In their years before the World Cup, Reddin would try to put a limit on the number of kicking hours that Wilkinson could do in training – not that Wilkinson would necessarily follow the guidance. Reddin would also factor into his calculation his assumption that however much Wilkinson was allowed to do in the England camp, he would almost certainly go home and do a whole lot more.

Reddin: 'I think one of the biggest things you have to be able to do as a coach or a parent is say "No" sometimes. Just because Jonny wants to do it, doesn't mean that's the right thing for Jonny to do. Now, psychologically, a player might not feel he's done enough, but if all you do as a coach is nod your head at the player, particularly a senior player, then I don't think you're doing your job. You've got to disentangle the player's massive motivation to get better from what you know as an expert to be the right thing to do at that time. And that's tricky.'

Reddin had already made it his job to earn Wilkinson's trust and confidence. 'Having a bit of a window into Jonny's personality was important,' he says. He knew that, because Wilkinson lived in Newcastle, he would sometimes not go all the way back home on a Sunday after a game. Reddin therefore made it his own routine to return to Pennyhill on Sunday afternoons, where he knew he would often get Wilkinson to himself.

Reddin: 'We'd often go for a kickabout with a football just out on the pitch at Pennyhill Park. Or we'd do keepie-uppies in the dining room and just mess about. It was just a way of developing a bit of a relationship. The more you can get inside somebody's head a little bit and find out what is bugging them, the easier it is.'

At the World Cup, Reddin, therefore, could see that there was plenty on Wilkinson's mind. 'I could tell he was really struggling with the pressure,' he says. 'I realised how much he was torturing himself at the time just with the ability to cope with what was going on.'

In the week after the Samoa game, then, when England had moved up to Queensland and were staying outside Surfers Paradise, Reddin hired a Jeep one day in order to get Wilkinson out of the bubble and away from the hotel. He took one of the physios, too, Richard Wegrzyk. That meant that they could also bring Hill. That then meant that it was an easy sell for Wilkinson.

Hill: 'We went to this amazing beach, middle of nowhere. It was 1) to get Wilko out. He could then do keepie-uppies on the beach with no one bothering him. It was 2) for Richard to do my treatment on the beach – and then join Jonny with the keepie-uppies too.'

The idea that Wilkinson's therapy was keepie-uppies on the beach is a statement in itself about the world in 2003 and how far it has moved on in 20 years. In today's world, where mental health is so minutely monitored, if a player is struggling with pressure, this would be quickly identified, addressed and a plan put in place to deliver the required support.

Dawson: 'If we knew what we know now about mental health, we'd be having a very different conversation than we did at the time about Wilko. We'd have handled it very differently. I genuinely had no idea about mental health or what he was going through.'

Lewis Moody: 'Wilko – he's a great example of someone that needed a bit more support, but you always thought he was so mentally strong that actually you don't need to go and chat to him, he's clearly got all his shit sorted, look how great he is. But I look back now, I think: actually, there were plenty of things that I could have done better. But you're just blissfully unaware, aren't you? You're cracking on in that rugby bubble, just trying to win everything.'

Yet here, finally, is one last reflection on Wilkinson, another reminder of how he was regarded, and that a Wilkinson off day would have been regarded as an on day for most of his peers. It comes from Will Greenwood who, as an inside centre, spent most of his international career playing outside him. In this conversation with Greenwood, he is talking about his own emotional mindset and the mental process that he required to build himself up for a game.

'I needed prodding or poking,' Greenwood explains. 'I needed a cause. I needed to be pushed into a corner. I needed to feel a siege mentality. I needed to feel like someone had slighted me on the telly. I needed to feel like someone had doubted us. That was my emotional fuel.'

Question: 'So yours is a kind of Michael Jordan mindset approach then?'

Greenwood's answer, quick as a flash: 'There was only one Michael fucking Jordan on our team. And that wasn't me. I was the one standing next to him.'

CHAPTER 22

JONNY ON JONNY

What did it actually feel like to be Jonny Wilkinson?

That requires a long answer, but the word that strikes you, above all, is fatigued. Fatigued in Australia; fatigued, in fact, throughout his entire career. 'I'm not sure,' he says, 'that I can remember a game I didn't play fatigued. This idea of "going out there and feeling fresh" – I never felt fresh. I just never felt fresh. How can you feel fresh from being on your feet that long during the week?'

This is what he means: 'For every single game, I went out, and my kicking session before kick-off was somewhere between 40 minutes and an hour. That's pre-game. That's over a half of the time of a game I spend practising one thing. And then I run into the changing room and have five minutes before we all go out as a team to do the normal warm-up. So my entire warm-up would be longer than the actual game itself. And that's just game day. And bear in mind that I kicked every morning of the game as well. So you have to put in another half an hour to an hour in the morning, sometimes over an hour if it wasn't going well. Even in my last year in the game, I was the same: I would do probably about 20, 30 reverse passes off each hand at the end of my pre-game warm-up. Now, that's like 60 passes of something that you're just not going to do in the game. But I'm literally just thinking, "What else can I do?"'

So, yes, fatigued. Which makes you wonder: what kind of a rugby player might he have been if he was fresh?

Ask Lawrence that question, though, and for pretty much the only time in this entire tour around the team of 2003, he is lost for words. You can almost see his brain computing the information that Wilkinson has just shared with him, checking it because it doesn't sound right, and then rechecking it. Eventually, he summons a natural challenge: 'How can you possibly? You can't play fatigued! At the time you thought it was a really good idea, but fuck, it's not a good idea! You can't be like that! There's no human being that can be like that!'

But Wilkinson has thought all this through. There may be no rugby player who has put in as many practice hours as Wilkinson, but you are unlikely to find another who has thought it all through to his depth either.

'I know how I did everything,' he says. 'I worked out everything I was going to do. My kicking stance, my style, the ball I hit, everything was scripted by me. I didn't have the capacity to just say: "It'll be all right, don't worry about it, trust it and just see how it goes." I'm like: "No, that is the epitome of the darkness for me."'

These are conclusions that he has come to after 20 years of working it out. It is not as if Wilkinson is asking himself 'What if?' or 'Could I have done it differently back then?' He is, it seems, pretty much at peace with his rugby life and that young man who was the focus of 2003.

We meet him at Pennyhill, which is entirely appropriate. This is where one of the great England careers was developed, where he invested so many preposterous hours honing his kicking craft. It is like a second home. He keeps himself to himself as much as possible these days and he certainly doesn't seek out social contact with his old teammates. Yet he is delighted to see Lawrence. They exchange family news. Wilkinson is trying to decide on schooling for his young daughter; that is a stressful parental responsibility for anyone, but it seems that, Wilkinson being Wilkinson, he is pushing the anxiety to the extreme.

Lawrence exhibits the same clear affection for Wilkinson that is expressed by so many of his teammates. He is the man they adored, yet also the one they struggled to understand.

This is what Lawrence says of Wilkinson, before he arrives at Pennyhill: 'Jonny's relentless drive and desire to become the best and improve himself was just so admirable and you have to respect people's ways of working. But I think he made enormous sacrifices, like enjoying his childhood, really. I mean enjoying his life. In Australia, I felt for him because he'd created his way of working, a way of being that didn't allow him to have the same release valves or the same outlets to relieve the pressure. And as a result, you could see that it was building and building for him. And that must have been really intense.'

Then, when Wilkinson arrives, Lawrence doesn't take long to get to the point and share the thoughts that he and so many of the squad have expressed: 'We all kind of saw what was going on in your head, but no one came and put an arm round and said, "Jonny, are you okay?" No one said, "Can we do anything about it? Can we help you?"'

Yet Wilkinson rejects any such suggestion: 'People have different memories. A lot of people did – well, maybe not put an arm around. Maybe that's what you're thinking: "I didn't put an arm around." But the way that people interacted was the same as putting an arm around physically. The way they spoke, the things they said.'

Lawrence asks: 'Do you regret being the way you were then? Or do you just think you just couldn't have achieved that if you hadn't been like that?'

'No, no,' says Wilkinson, 'it's not that I regret that or I couldn't achieve that. It was inevitable. I look back and I just think: it is what it is. There was no other way. The alternative wouldn't have worked. I had this sense that there wasn't another option. Me being happy, joyfully, explicitly happy whilst trying to play rugby just wasn't going to happen at all.

'In the middle of a game, that was where I was completely at one. That was my happy place. In between those moments was suffering. And as I understood it, that's how it had to be. I had this understanding that in order that I can have my happy place, my preparation needs to be a form of suffering. I had to earn my happy place on the field. I wanted to suffer because, in a way, that was my dynamic that worked. I had to feel like I was suffering. I had to feel like I had to be the saviour. I had to feel like I had to be the warrior. And I had to suffer because I was so massively driven by the fear of letting people down.

'Even the idea of having a good time on a Friday before a Saturday game, I felt desperately rocky on that. Or before a game, if someone said something funny to me, I'd laugh and then go stop myself: don't do that, you're inviting the gods. I was surrounded by this fear, constantly worrying about letting my guard down.

'So when people say, "Oh, you're out in the field again doing your two hours' kicking; I don't know how you do it," I'm like, "I don't know how you *don't*. I don't know how you can sit there in your room and chill out and watch a damn film on a Friday before a Saturday game. I don't know how *you* do it. It makes no sense. Why aren't you out there turning over every stone, covering every base, writing pages of notes, walking around your hotel room doing press-ups and air kicks?" You know how people swing golf clubs without a golf club? I'm like looking at people thinking, "How can you not?" Because I have this presence around me saying: "What if you don't?" The only thing that gave me solace was thinking I've done all I can and therefore if I fail, there's a thread I can hang on.

'I would feel guilty about going out and exploring. People going out into Sydney or going out in the cafes and stuff – I just didn't do it. Because I felt like: "Shit, you're out of your jurisdiction here. Something's going to go wrong." But also, I didn't like other people seeing me doing it because I was hugely driven around how I was seen, image and recognition. That was also part of my perfectionism – that I couldn't let people down. So I needed them to see me on the field. That helped as well. I needed that narrative of like, "He's always trying, he's so dedicated."'

Lawrence knows he can't, but is nevertheless trying to make sense of it all. He says to Wilkinson: 'Most people work on the law of diminishing returns. I mean, I love training, but it gets to a point in training where if you carry on training, it's not good for anyone.'

'Yeah, I didn't have that,' Wilkinson replies.

Lawrence carries on: 'I've said to coaches: "Are you getting something out of this session? Because none of the rest of us are; we've reached our peak."'

'You wouldn't have heard me say that to a coach once,' Wilkinson replies. 'Not because I wouldn't agree, but because I didn't have that kind of awareness. I didn't have it. I was a blunt object. While you were saying that, if I had spoken, I'd have been saying: "We need to be out there more."'

Lawrence is entirely perplexed. It is in his nature to wish the same joy and fulfilment for his teammates that he himself experienced. Wilkinson – or, at least, the Wilkinson of 20 years ago – could not be further apart.

'How much was there of "I love being here" – I'm not sure if we ever had that,' Wilkinson says. 'I don't know if other people had that, but I didn't have it once.'

At least, as he says, he has moved on so far since. 'I'm largely unfamiliar with who I was back then,' he says.

And where would we have been, wonders Lawrence to himself, if he hadn't played fatigued?

CHAPTER 23

BRISBANE

'Quarter-final week is a kind of a crossroads,' Lawrence says, and then he explains: up until the quarter-finals, there is enough incentive and opportunity for every player in the squad to convince themselves that they might just make the cut for the team for the knockout stages, yet once the squad for the quarter-finals is announced, big dreams are dashed. No one wants to say as much or express those feelings, but the numbers are simple: 15 players are in the starting team, seven are named on the bench and then the other eight wonder what the next three weeks holds for them beyond holding tackle bags in training and waiting for an injury.

'That's when you know what your fate is,' Lawrence explains. 'It's the acceptance moment. There's still another three weeks to go and that is a hell of a long time.'

Touring rugby squads tend to have a name for those who don't make the cut. On British and Irish Lions tours they are the mid-weekers or the 'dirt trackers'. More brutally, some non-first-teamers are referred to as 'drift' as in the driftwood. In Australia, once the England team for the quarter-final against Wales had been picked, Mark 'Ronnie' Regan, the Leeds hooker and a man widely acknowledged to be a 'good tourist', produced terms for the different groups of players: the bench players, he declared, were 'drift', the other eight were 'double-drift'. Regan was double-drift.

At least England's last group game, in Brisbane, was against Uruguay, who were World Cup minnows and therefore provided an ideal opportunity for drift and double-drift to be given a game. They won 111-13; Josh Lewsey, who was neither drift nor double-drift, scored five tries. England would then stay in Brisbane for the quarter-final and that is where Regan and others came to terms with their double-drift status.

'So we'd go out and enjoy ourselves,' he recalls happily. 'Back then there was no social media, no Facebook. What goes on tour goes on Facebook nowadays. But there was none of that then.'

A new member of the driftwood that week was Simon Shaw, who had been called up as an injury replacement. He wasn't sure if he'd be drift or double-drift but he feared the worst: 'You get voices going on in the back of your head saying, "Am I even going to get a touch?"' He didn't. 'I literally thought I was getting flown out there to sit around the hotel for two or three weeks until the end of the World Cup.' That's kind of how it panned out. 'And I'm thinking: "What's the purpose of that?" The other part of me is going: "There's always a chance. And never give up." Well, luckily, I had my sidekick Ronnie, who was always entertaining enough to distract me.'

Shaw was the new man to replace Danny Grewcock, who'd had a really unfortunate World Cup. Grewcock was named on the bench for the first game, against Georgia, but broke a toe in the warm-up. The medics then reckoned that he would be fit in time for the Uruguay game three weeks later, which he was, but he finished that game with a broken bone in his hand and that was it. His World Cup was finished.

He never discovered how he broke it. 'Collision,' he says. 'Hand hit something hard and then that was it.'

'So it wasn't striking an opponent?' says Lawrence, feigning surprise. 'That makes a change.'

One of the complications here was, with the business end of the World Cup now beginning, some wives and girlfriends were starting to arrive from England. 'Yup, that was when my missus had just turned up,' says Grewcock. 'So essentially, we just got shit-faced that night in Brisbane. I may have been sick in the morning. I know that I couldn't unblock the sink, there was so much food in there.'

And then you went home? 'No. we booked a camper van, went to Fraser Island, went to Noosa. It was brilliant.'

One other uncertain arrival in Brisbane that week was Richard Hill's partner, Claire. 'That week became a little bit make or break for me,' recalls Hill. 'There was a point when she was going to be on a plane on the way over to Brisbane and potentially I was gonna be diagnosed as not fit and on a plane going back the other way. And she wouldn't have known until she arrived.'

The hamstring that Hill had torn three and a bit weeks earlier in the Georgia game had been refusing to mend.

Hill: 'Clive was very supportive, saying: "Take as long as you need. We don't want to risk this." But that still doesn't stop your own head saying: "I'm a burden on the squad. How is it being viewed? How do other players see it? I'm not enjoying it. I'm doing everything I can and yet I can't get out on the pitch."'

Lawrence: 'Yes, we'd be saying to you: "Are you still here?"' The banter was quite brutal.'

Hill: 'In Brisbane, I basically made the decision: I am either tearing this properly or I am back in the game. I remember turning up for training one day just as you guys were leaving. It was a really hot day. I had to do a whole load of shuttles, repetitive actions. I didn't have a clue if I'd survive it. But I pretty much finished the session, lying on the floor thinking: I got through it. That's when I think I started to piss the medics off because I've got through this session and I'm like: "I'm fine, I'm ready." They said: "You're not." "But I'm fit." "No, Hilly, you're not."'

One of the other arrivals from the UK into Brisbane that week was Jayne Woodward. She has a very specific recollection of her arrival: 'I didn't expect Clive to be at the airport. I thought he was too busy, but he came to the airport to meet me himself. In the car on the way back he was telling me that he'd been worried all week because he didn't think the players were quite right. He could feel it in his bones, this uncertainty of whether they were ready for the match or not. He said to me in the car: "I can't put my finger on it, but we're just not there. We're not on the money. This is going to be a much harder game than everybody thinks it's going to be." He just knew.'

CHAPTER 24

LUGER'S LAST STAND

Clive Woodward's premonitions about the Wales quarter-final turned out to be right. Wales shocked England, their fly-half Stephen Jones scored arguably the try of the tournament and at half-time they had a 10-3 lead. And, not that anyone knew it, Wales had brought Dan Luger's England career to an end. That is the same Dan Luger who had scored 24 tries in 38 caps; he was still only 28 years old but he was already England's fifth all-time highest try-scorer. To this day, amongst England's multiple try-scorers, no one has a better tries-per-game ratio than him. But at half-time that day, his time in an England jersey was finished.

Luger's career end tells us a lot about the game and how different attitudes were to it at the time. It also says a lot about the intense competition in this squad and quite a bit, too, about sliding doors moments and how opportunity can be presented and then snatched away.

At the beginning of the year, there had been three leading contenders for the starting trio of back-three places in the team: Luger, Jason Robinson and Ben Cohen. There were a number of other peripheral contenders but, significantly also, Iain Balshaw was fighting to establish himself again back from injury as was Austin Healey, a uniquely versatile player who was also a potential World Cup scrum-half. Josh Lewsey, the Wasps full-back, never even seemed in the picture. The last of Lewsey's six caps had come two years previously, but then midway through the Six Nations, after injuries to Robinson and Cohen, he got a call.

Lewsey: 'Clive didn't speak to me for a number of years. I called and messaged him and I wrote to him repeatedly, trying to explore "What do I need to do or improve?" I never got a response. In international rugby, your entire career is effectively dependent on one person, whether they like you or not. And this may sometimes be more about personality than logic. As such, I was told by others that that was the case and that I just wasn't liked. As a young person, I think that can be quite hurtful and damaging when you care so deeply about one person's approval and you can't even find out what you've done wrong to create that impression or what you should do to change it. So yeah, I don't think my face fitted for a while. And then after relentlessly knocking on the door, through repeat games and playing well for the club, I eventually got a chance. Out of nowhere, and for the first time in a number of years, I got a call and Clive said: "You're in. This is your one chance, don't fuck it up."'

That one conversation was so crucial to Lewsey's career that he would name the title of his own autobiography exactly that: *One Chance*.

What did Lawrence make of this scrap amongst the back-three players? 'Wingers are sort of strange individuals,' he says affectionately. He laughs as he tells the story of Paul Sackey, another Wasps and England winger, who once handed back a feedback form to his coaches, where he listed 'chilling' under his 'likes' and under 'dislikes' wrote 'rugby training'.

Lawrence: 'Wingers are clearly very talented people and they can do things that no one else can. I've played with and against some of the best wingers in the world. But you've got keen people that sit in the front of the class and go, "Yes, sir. Yes, sir. Right, I'll answer that question and I'll do that training session," no questions asked. You know what I mean? And then you've got the No. 9s who know how to align themselves to the coach who's going to pick them. And then you've got other people who are individuals, who'll challenge and question and that's what you want. Wingers are like that. They're quite selfish people. They're only interested in scoring themselves.'

Lewsey happily admits that he 'ruffled feathers' and 'had never played or been good at politics'. Luger was not much interested in playing that game either. Yet when that 'one chance' came around for Lewsey in the Six Nations, against Italy, he took it with aplomb, scored two tries, one of which was a 65-metre sprint in which he corkscrewed the Italy full-back into the Twickenham mud in the process. From that point on, Lewsey was a fixture in the starting XV.

Simultaneously, that Six Nations was both traumatic and defining for Luger. On the eve of the opening round of games, when England were due to play France, the news broke that Nick Duncombe, the Harlequins and England scrum-half, had died suddenly at a Lanzarote training camp, having been rushed into hospital with what turned out to be meningitis. Duncombe was 21 years old, he already had two England caps and his star was expected to continue to rise. He was also one of Luger's closest friends.

Luger somehow managed to get through the France game and next up was Wales, where he won plaudits for his contribution in attack and then Italy, where he scored one try to Lewsey's two. At that point, though, he came clean with himself; he acknowledged that he couldn't quite battle on through it any more.

'Things did change for me after Nick died,' he says. 'It changed me mentally. I think I was never quite the same after that in terms of my love of everything. I was thinking, "Shit, there's a bit more to life than the sport." After that [Italy game], I spoke to Clive and I asked to be on the bench. Because my good mate had died, I said, "Look, I want to stay involved but I just want to be on the bench."'

Woodward listened and did exactly as Luger asked. For the next two games, against Scotland and then the Grand Slam decider against Ireland, Luger was out of the front line, on the bench. At the same time, though, Robinson and Cohen had returned from injury. The starting back three in those two games, from which Luger had asked to be vacated, then became Lewsey, Robinson and Cohen. That was how it would remain all the way to the World Cup final.

Luger's one last opportunity was in this quarter-final against Wales. Lewsey had been injured so Luger started. Yet it was the wrong game to re-establish yourself because Wales surprised everyone with two early tries and no one betrayed the sense of unease more than Luger. 'I had a chance to show myself,' he says. 'No one played well but I didn't play well particularly. I missed tackles, I smacked a kick into touch. I kind of got half knocked out.'

This is really interesting. Half knocked out? 'At half-time,' he recalls, 'they go, "How are you feeling?" I said, "I'm not feeling great." At the time, I didn't really question it. I mean, I was in the changing room. I was like, "Yeah, I'm not feeling great." When Clive had said, "How are you feeling?" I should've said, "I'm fine. I'll stay on," but I said, "I'm not feeling fantastic."'

So, Woodward replaced him – which was the correct decision. In the modern game, though, the chances are that Luger might have been identified as a possible concussion victim at the time he sustained it, that he might well have been brought off immediately for a head injury assessment and may not have lasted until half-time. He may not then, for instance, have sliced that kick into touch; he may not, then, have been perceived to have responded poorly to the intense pressure situation in the game. Twenty years ago, though, Luger was left wondering the opposite. Should he have subscribed to the sentiment of the time? Should he have been tough, shown no weakness? When asked by Woodward how he was feeling, should he have said, 'I'm fine, thanks, and I can't wait to get back out there'? 'I probably should have stayed on and carried on,' he says, 'but I didn't, and *c'est la vie*. That's how it goes. Yeah, there were opportunities there. There's no one else to blame but myself.'

Blame is the wrong word here. Essentially Luger was ahead of his time. Worried about his mental health during the Six Nations earlier in the year, he had taken a step back. Then, in the Wales quarter-final, one of the biggest games of his life, he was honest about a brain injury. Twenty years on, both decisions would be applauded; back then, mental health wasn't a term you ever heard around any sports field and concussion was something players believed they should battle through.

Both decisions leave you wondering – what if and what might have been? – because in the immediate case of the World Cup and the England back-three selection battle for the semi-final and final, Lewsey would be fit again and back in the side and Luger didn't just drop out of the starting XV, he tumbled further down the pecking order and wasn't even retained on the bench.

This is what Lawrence says to him: 'It was such a competitive squad. You give someone else an opportunity in that squad and you never know when you're going to get the opportunity back again. I mean, look, you did the right thing by saying, "My best mate's just died. I don't feel right to play this game."'

This is Luger's perspective: 'Hindsight's a fantastic thing, but how I look at it is: would I change where I am now in life? Would I change being a World Cup winner, having played 38 times for England, living in Monaco? No. But would I have fought harder for my place? Yes, but I don't know if other things would've changed because of that. I do sometimes dream in the middle of the night. You get upset why you didn't, why you weren't playing in the World Cup final. But on the flip side, I felt very thankful to be part of that amazing squad, amazing people I love. I feel very lucky and blessed to have been part of it all.'

And forever, tattooed on his right arm, remains the initials of his great friend Nick Duncombe.

CHAPTER 25

CATT RESCUE JOB

The Wales quarter-final has been recorded as a massive malfunction for England and one that nearly sent them tumbling out of the tournament. Lawrence doesn't quite remember it that way.

Lawrence: 'Everyone just expected us to beat sides: roll them over and smash them to pieces. But Test rugby's not like that. We never imagined that the World Cup would be like that. But that fact remains: we hadn't been playing great up until the quarter-final and we definitely weren't playing great in it. We all knew that; we'd been grinding our way through the tournament. Against Wales, we started poorly. We looked leggy. We kicked quite badly. By his standards, Jonny was not having his best game. We played to Wales's strengths and they got their tails up. But at no stage did I think: we're going to lose this game. We were 10-3 down at half-time. We still had 40 minutes to sort it out and I knew that we couldn't play that badly again. We got together in the changing room and said: "We need to sort our shit out." But there was no sense of deep panic.'

Different people have different perspectives here. Andy Robinson didn't exactly share Lawrence's confidence. 'If it had been a boxing fight,' he says, 'it would have been stopped at half-time and we'd have lost. We were hanging.' He also questions the players' mindset at the time. 'Ben Cohen does a cross-field kick from a quick tap penalty to Neil Back. Where does it come into our mindset to kick cross-field to our smallest player when we are five metres from the line? That wasn't us.'

Dave Alred felt that Wilkinson was being forced to do too much: 'The issue was that we didn't have a second kicker in the backs. We were only kicking from one pivot. I was screaming that we must kick from 13. My annoyance was that Will Greenwood wouldn't kick.'

At half-time, Clive Woodward made the substitution that seemed to resolve everything. Until that point, Mike Catt had been a player on the outer edges of the squad; he had only started one game, which was the Uruguay match for which most of the big guns had been rested. That was about to change in a big way. Woodward hooked Dan Luger, he moved Mike Tindall out on to the wing in Luger's place and brought Catt in to inside centre to try and take some of the pressure off Wilkinson.

Having watched the first half, Catt felt, like Woodward, that he knew what was required. On so many occasions, he had played No. 10 for his club side, Bath, and enjoyed the support given to him by the No. 12 outside him, the former England captain, Phil de Glanville. He knew how a No. 12 could work as extra eyes and ears, how he could share the kicking responsibilities and step in as playmaker if required. In Catt's words, de Glanville made him feel 'comfortable' and that's what he intended to do for Wilkinson.

Catt was another who had been watching Wilkinson closely

during the preceding weeks. 'It was really bizarre to watch him,' he says. 'There was so much pressure and he, as we know, put so much pressure on himself. Yet I was in such a good mental state. I was just like, "Right, come on, Jonny, you've got to enjoy this." I sort of took that upon myself. I love Jonny, we'd always got on really well. At the 1999 World Cup four years earlier, we'd been on the bench together when we lost to South Africa. Then, when I joined up with the squad in '03, I hadn't played with him or seen him really for a good 18 months and I sort of felt that Jonny just wasn't Jonny; he wasn't the Jonny that I knew. And I really hated the fact that this guy was living the dream with the best team in the world and not enjoying the moment.'

By playing the de Glanville role, Catt thought he could lighten the load: 'I think Jonny just knew that when we played together, there was a lot of help around him. It was taking the pressure off Jonny, so Jonny could be Jonny. It was just a classic case of me just giving Jonny a breather.'

Lawrence likes the idea of Catt arriving on his white charger. 'Did you actually feel like, "This is my moment"?' he asks him. 'Because, up until then in the World Cup, you were sort of on the fringes. But then, against Wales, you'd had the perspective of watching what was going on in a pretty poor first half; Jonny was struggling, the team was struggling and suddenly you were given your chance.'

Contrary to general opinion, Catt didn't actually think that Wilkinson was having such a bad game at all. 'I actually thought that Jonny was phenomenal in that first half,' he says. 'If you watch that game again, he was everywhere. He was unbelievable. He made a try-saving tackle in the far left-end corner.'

This is also true. Wilkinson was everywhere, getting involved in so many parts of the game that weren't really in his job description. That was both a strength and a problem, and that was where Catt came in.

Catt: 'When I came on, I sort of said, "Just give me the ball. I'll beat this thing 60 metres down there." We then won our lineout, we finally got on the front foot, Jonny kicked his goals, and it was as simple as that. We just got everything right again.'

Indeed, the second half seemed hardly connected to the first. It was ignited by Jason Robinson who seemed to be saying: enough is enough when he tore through the Wales defence. Robinson beat five men, made the offload to Will Greenwood and with a Wilkinson conversion, England were level. From that point, they pulled away, winning 28-17. 'By the end of the game,' says Lawrence, 'we won comfortably really.' Comfortable maybe. Happy? Definitely not.

*　*　*

Here, though, is a different perspective, from Greenwood. 'In the World Cup, we would have to come back from behind in four out of the seven games. The greatest macro view I can give you of that is if you're losing four games in a World Cup – and you've got to win seven to win the World Cup – to come back and win all four, that does make you a great team. It takes a good team to dig themselves out of three of those at best – to find a way to change, to change on the hoof, not to panic, just to stay and trust. A lot of players say this now: trust the process. But it wasn't the process, it was trusting the individuals in the right place at the right time to see something and do it. And, by the way, Wales should have beaten us in the quarter-final. They bottled it; they properly, properly had us.'

CHAPTER 26

DEATH BY OVER-TRAINING

After the Wales game, a few of the players went out for a wind-down beer in Brisbane. The victory had taken them to the semi-finals, but no one was pretending that they felt in any way satisfied. 'We ended up in a bar,' Lawrence says. 'Nothing out of the ordinary,' he insists. 'I think we were playing pool.'

'We were playing pool,' says Mike Catt.

'It was you, me, Jase and I'm pretty sure Grays,' Lawrence says.

'And Cozza,' Catt adds, filling in the missing facts on a nothing-out-of-the-ordinary night out.

What followed shows that England had a coaching team who listened. It also demonstrates that though they would listen, the coaches nevertheless commanded considerable respect.

Lawrence, you weren't able to bite your tongue, were you?

Lawrence: 'No, I wasn't. In the bar that night, we were all talking about what we thought wasn't going right and what we were going to say about it. The coaches – they were over-training us, we'd been on a ridiculous training schedule. We all agreed that the next day we would say something. And then of course I remember the next day, in the team room, when we did this review session of the game, which was also a sort of honesty video session. And those of us who had been out the previous night were probably feeling a bit dusty because we'd had one or two beers. And at the end, Clive did his usual thing: "Does anyone want to say anything?" And no one said anything and I felt you, Catty, looking at me thinking: "Well, I've only played half a game of rugby so I'm not going to say too much."'

Catt: 'Yes, it was: you'd better stand up, Loll.'

Lawrence: 'So I put my hand up and I remember saying something along the lines of, "Can I just ask a question? We're supposed to be the best prepared team that's ever gone to a World Cup, right? We all agree on that. So why are we training at 98 degrees Fahrenheit at three o'clock in the afternoon when the games are all at seven o'clock in the evening?"

'There was then this tumbleweed moment, this hushed silence. And I think the coaches sort of looked at Clive and Clive looked back at them and then went, "Yeah, that's probably quite a good point." And that was it. After that, we did almost no training at all. We did walk-throughs at seven o'clock every night, didn't we? That was the end of it.'

Pretty much everyone was immediately happy and on board with the new arrangement. 'Clive trusted us,' says Leonard. 'When you've got Loll and Martin Johnson coming to you going, "I'm tired, the players are tired," he's going to listen.'

Probably the only dissenting voice was Wilkinson's, though he kept that to himself. 'On the physical side,' he says, 'I would be like, "I don't give a shit." Genuinely, if you want to do another

20 minutes of full-on defence, yeah, whatever, I'll do it. I mean it was child's play for me. Because I didn't stop, even when I went back to the room, I didn't stop.'

*   *   *

The Dallaglio-Leonard brigade were not the only ones out for a beer that night. There was a double-drift night out too. 'City Rowers,' says Mark Regan, dredging up the name of the venue, plus the fact that there was also double-drift there from Wales and Scotland, who had been beaten the day before by Australia.

Regan: 'We all decided that we made a very good Lions team and that we would be ready to take to the park to play for the Lions the following day.'

Amongst the faded details, we know that Stuart Abbott and Simon Shaw were in the English double-drift, that Tom Shanklin and Rhys Williams were there representing Wales and that, at some point late into proceedings, Williams, a utility back, would scrum down against Regan and Regan would make him squeal.

Regan: 'We had a drinking competition, a boat race. The English won the drinking competition. We had Shawsie there, right at the end. He drank everyone under the table. There were 50-odd vodka Red Bulls on the bar. And it wasn't any of the Scots who paid for it, put it that way. They were doing their laces up by the door.'

At least that's the way Regan tells it – and most of these facts have been verified. Twenty years on, though we know that much of it is true, we cannot be absolutely sure where Regan's recollection ends and his storytelling begins. He isn't completely sure either.

Shaw disputes part of Regan's story anyway. 'I do remember that night,' he says, 'but I'm not very good at downing pints.'

143

CHAPTER 27

DROPPING TINDALL – CLIVE'S BEST EVER DECISION

When the World Cup squad had been announced eight weeks earlier, Austin Healey was one of the players most hard done by, but he got extremely close again when, late into the tournament, he was flown out to Australia as injury cover. Before the quarter-final, England had two wingers, Iain Balshaw and Josh Lewsey, who were carrying injuries, the result being that Healey was put on a flight on a just-in-case mission. If one of Balshaw or Lewsey didn't mend quickly enough, Healey would take their place and Clive Woodward wanted him in Australia and recovering from the jet lag so that, if necessary, he could step in immediately. It was a mission which many of the squad remember well, largely because of the way that Woodward broke the news to them: 'Josh, Balsh, please do everything you can to get yourselves fit so when Austin gets here, I can send him straight home again.'

Lawrence: 'He obviously didn't mean it, but everyone pissed themselves laughing.'

The World Cup's rules around squad sizes were peculiarly strict. Squads were limited to 30 players. A substitute player could only join when another player was officially declared injured and no longer part of the tournament. So while Woodward waited for Balshaw and Lewsey to recover, Healey wasn't allowed to train with the squad; he wasn't actually allowed to see or socialise with the squad – he was supposed to be kept in a kind of quarantine.

'I do remember that,' Lawrence says, 'because Jase and I went and played golf with him.'

Which was therefore an illegal game of golf?

'Yes, I mean, what a stupid rule.'

It wasn't just Lawrence who paid Healey a visit. In Sydney, four days before the semi-final against France, Mike Tindall went out to see him too. Tindall had just been informed by Woodward that he was being dropped from the starting XV and, needing to manage the fact that he was feeling so angry and frustrated, his response was that he needed a beer and a break from the camp. Healey would be his outlet – and camera phones would have loved it.

*　　*　　*

To recall all this, Lawrence and I meet Mike Tindall on a warm, clear-blue June afternoon in his beautiful Gloucestershire house. It is not like a royal palace; there are no portraits of dead monarchs, no tapestries of the Crusades, no suit-of-armour statues. We sit in the airy kitchen/dining room, the glass doors out on to the garden are pulled back. Tindall is suffering terribly, having been at the races at Royal Ascot with his wife Zara the day before. He is consuming coffee copiously and worrying that he's expected back at Ascot later in the week and will have to inflict the same damage upon himself all over again. Zara is somewhere else in the house, he says. He thinks she might be asleep on the sofa. Twenty years on, this is one player who seems extremely content with the direction that life has taken him.

Then he tells the story of how he got dropped. He had been a fixture in England's midfield pretty much ever since his debut in the Six Nations three and a half years earlier. On the Wednesday before the France game, though, Clive Woodward spoke to him in the reception of the Manly Pacific, the hotel that England had as their base for the last fortnight of the tournament. Woodward explained that Mike Catt had done so well coming on in the second half against Wales, particularly in the way that he had taken the pressure off Jonny Wilkinson, that he was going to start with him against France.

Tindall: 'He also said that he knew it was going to be raining against France and that it was therefore going to be more of a kicking game.'

This decision to go for Catt ahead of Tindall played to the differing skills of the two players. Tindall was the more physical, ball-carrying centre and a better defender; Catt had played a lot of his rugby at fly-half and full-back, so he was more of a play-making centre and was recognised more as a kicker. Tindall, however, felt that his own game was more nuanced than his reputation suggested and that he could have done any job required.

Tindall: 'I wasn't happy about it. I was kicking more than I'd ever done and I could've played that role in the semi-final. I think, against France, Clive wanted an older head. But I thought I was probably playing better than Will [Greenwood].

So, I said to Clive, "Well, I think it could be beneficial not having Will involved."'

But Woodward's mind was made up. Catt and Greenwood would be his centre pairing; Tindall was on the bench. 'Anyway,' says Tindall, smiling, 'it turned out that dropping me was the greatest decision he ever made.'

Thus Tindall headed out from the Manly Pacific. He went with a frustrated Martin Corry, who was coming to terms with the fact that Richard Hill was now finally fit to return to the fray – so he was therefore one spot further from a place on the pitch too.

They went to the Manly Wharf Bar, which looks right over the harbour, where they had agreed to meet Austin Healey. 'I was a bit pissed off, obviously,' Tindall says. But not only did he meet Healey there, he says, 'I met Zara for the first time.'

He points out of the kitchen into the house. 'We've got a picture of the Manly Wharf Bar just out there,' he says. That's their memento, that's where it happened.

Lawrence: 'Austin tells the story that he was the one that brokered the deal. He had nothing to do with it, actually.' Well, he did have a small hand in it. 'Anyway, 20 years on, Tinds is now one big plane crash from being king of England.' Actually, as things stand, his wife is 20th in line to the throne.

Tindall: 'Because all the stories are so twisted up now, you're not even sure what's true any more. The way I tell it is that I was the one who was responsible for rewarding Clive with his knighthood.'

* * *

That was the last impact that Austin Healey had on the 2003 World Cup. Lewsey and Balshaw were both passed fit for the semi-final, so he was never actually needed as an injury replacement and instead he was flown back to London. The following Saturday, when England were playing in the World Cup final in Sydney, Healey was back home, playing for Leicester Tigers away at Rotherham in front of 2,900 people. They won 27-17 and Healey scored a try.

CHAPTER 28

THE HOLY TRINITY

Seventy-five minutes before the semi-final kicked off, England fans who had arrived early were treated to a famous old ritual that hadn't been seen for five weeks: Lawrence, Neil Back and Richard Hill trotting out on to the pitch together. They went out at a slow jog, straight up along the halfway line and then didn't turn towards where England were warming up, they went the other way. Two laps of the French half of the pitch.

That was quite a statement, wasn't it? 'We weren't doing it to wind anyone up,' Lawrence says. He is smirking as he does so. But they always did this, always a slow jog to get the heart rate up, always two laps circling the opposition half. 'Sport is often quite ritualistic, isn't it?' Lawrence says. 'It's about doing the same things over and over again.'

The point here was that they had Richard Hill back in their number. The third musketeer had finally been passed fit. This reunited a back row who had played a record 39 times as a trio. They were known to fans and media as 'the Holy Trinity', not that they would ever refer to themselves as that. 'Though,' says Lawrence, 'it's not as if we ever minded it!'

To play with this unit of three, says Phil Vickery, was a privilege. 'You tell me: when has there ever been a better England back row than Hill, Back, Dallaglio? Still, to this day, there hasn't been. Without a doubt.'

There is a fair bit of history here. 'The thing is,' says Lawrence, 'we spent some of the early years as rivals.'

That's certainly how Hill remembers it: 'I'm not sure how much Backy and I spoke to each other in that first year because we always thought we were in direct competition.'

Lawrence too: 'Backy probably had a voodoo doll of me and a number of other players who should never have played seven, but got picked there ahead of him.' Lawrence certainly didn't think of himself as a No. 7. He remembers getting the phone call from Jack Rowell, the England coach before Clive Woodward, giving him his first start. That was autumn 1995. 'I was in Sainsbury's, and I've got my daughter, Ella, on my front. Jack says to me: "I'm picking you at seven." Now, I'm not going to argue with the England coach but I've never played seven in my entire career. So, I'm thinking: what do I do? Do I phone back and say I don't fancy playing seven? Obviously, I just kept my mouth shut.'

Back is the oldest of the three and was the first of them to be picked for England, playing at No. 7. He was an out-and-out No. 7; there was no other position for him. But then Lawrence and Hill came along and they were both picked at No. 7 too. What Back had to overcome was that at 5ft 10in, he was considered by some coaches to be too small.

Lawrence: 'He was always up against it, because of his size, and was always going to have to overachieve in certain areas, and fitness was one of those. His attitude was: "I'm going to make sure I am the fittest person ever, so therefore you've got to pick me."'

Between the summer of 1995 and the autumn of 1997, it was mostly Lawrence or Hill being picked at No. 7 for England. In that time, Back got two caps for the British and Irish Lions but not one for England. Then Woodward took over; in his first two games, he selected Back on the bench and in the second of those, for the whole of the second half, he staged the premiere of the Holy Trinity.

In a rare one-off, England were playing New Zealand at Old Trafford, Manchester. The starting back row was Lawrence at six, Hill at seven and Tony Diprose at No. 8. At half-time, Diprose was subbed off and the back row shifted so Hill was at six, Back at seven and Lawrence at No. 8.

Hill: 'We'd never trained together in those positions. At one point, Zinzan Brooke picked off the base of a scrum and walked in to score and we all looked at each other and went: "What were you doing?" We also said, "That's never happening again," and I swear that before every scrum in every international after that, we spoke about our roles before the scrum went down.'

Lawrence: 'From that moment, we recognised that the more time you spend together, the better you become as a group. That was where the warming up together came from. We said: "Let's warm up together, all the time, because then we can continue to talk about what we're going to do in the game." So we'd be reminding each other of the things that we would have to do collectively and the individual responsibilities: "You've got him. I've got that. I'm going to do this, this and this." So we became very close. We spent a lot of time together on the field and a lot of time getting inside each other's heads. And we got on very, very well. We still do now.'

Back: 'I think the strength that Loll, Hilly and I had is we understood each other's strengths and we played to those strengths.'

Lawrence: 'Hilly was the one player who never got dropped. His consistency of performance was unbelievable. Everyone used to say that he was "England's most underrated player"; Backy and I always told him: "You're England's most overrated underrated player." And Backy: well, all sevens are a bit quirky, aren't they? They're wired slightly differently. I mean, think about it: for a start, it's an odd number. Plus, they have a unique set of skills. Maybe it's an incredible coincidence, maybe it's chromosomes, but they are lone wolves, killers, assassins. The rest of us are able to integrate better into the pack. They are a bit weird, wonderfully weird. And thank God we have them; I couldn't think of anything better than having Neil Back. He's the bravest and one of the most incredible blokes I've ever met. Luckily, rugby celebrates difference, because sevens – they just don't conform. And Backy didn't conform either in his approach to fitness because he was so far ahead of all of us in his approach. He was the catalyst for driving the standards of the whole group.'

Collectively, they made a huge impact and not just in their areas of responsibility or the all-court game that they allowed England to play or in the outcomes of games, but on their teammates too. This is Will Greenwood: 'The matchday, for me, was all gallows humour. I was laughing but I wasn't laughing; I was actually just shitting myself. I was trying to laugh to make myself relaxed about it. There were all these different things that you have to go through, particularly in a violent game, to get yourself up to the mark. So, before the warm-up started, I used to go and sit down on the post pad and watch because these three dressage ponies – Back, Dallaglio and Hill – would come out in full tracksuit, get to the halfway line and if we were warming up on the left, they'd turn right and they'd just trot around the opposition half, like stalking horses. I often thought, "They should pee on the corner flag," because it was like they were marking their territory. And despite any of my own fear, I'd be thinking: "Well, at least those fucking idiots are on my team. That other lot have got no chance.'"

CHAPTER 29

LET'S JUST GO OUT AND PLAY

Lawrence describes the last two weeks of the World Cup as 'our happy place': 'We got to the semi-final stage and all of a sudden, there was a calmness that descended on the group. We had two weeks to win the World Cup. That was a happy place to be. Plus, the heat was turned on France more than us. They'd been playing some spectacular rugby and the world's rugby press was talking about how wonderful their front row was and about how they had the best back row in the world – as if we needed any more motivation, and against France, you never did anyway. Given all that and our performance against Wales, that was a spicy little cocktail for a pretty spiky performance. Plus, Jonny had not fired in the Wales game; he was no doubt personally motivated. We all were. It was an intense build-up; everyone was very motivated.'

There were a few scraps of evidence to suggest that England were indeed in a happy place.

One: in the warm-up games before the World Cup, a France first-string team had beaten an England second string in Marseille with a 17-16 win which England had nearly stolen when Paul Grayson missed a drop goal at the death (England didn't always get their last-minute drop goals). It was the aftermath of that game that was so revealing.

Grayson: 'They celebrated it like they'd won the World Cup. But we were only a mixed team, nowhere near full strength. It was like: if you get to the semi-final, you're going to play the real England, so you're screwed now psychologically.'

Two: Despite all the admiration being lavished on the France front row, England were quite happy with where their scrum was too.

Phil Keith-Roach: 'That week in training, we never did any scrummaging work because Johnno came up to me and he said, "Roachie, we know how to scrum." And then he walked off. We'd bussed this bloody scrummaging machine all the way across Australia, but here was Johnno saying that our job was done already. That meant more to me than almost my whole rugby career put together – that he felt satisfied and I hadn't been a complete waste of time.'

Three: It seemed that England were at last starting to find the right emotional wavelength.

Martin Johnson: 'Lawrence felt we'd been a bit dry and a bit robotic and he felt that needed to be said. Before the France game – I think it was the team meeting the day before – he just said to us: "Hey, let's just go out and play rugby. Let's go out and play like we do and get stuck into people, smash people about and just do what we do." And it was a great call. It was a really good call because it just boiled it all down. Lawrence was always Lawrence. That's what he is: fantastic player, a great leader. He's always got a bit of chat. He always comes out with something that will make you smile or whatever. When he finished on that, it was like: that's it, let's go, bang.'

Four: England fans had been arriving in colossal numbers.

Lawrence: 'The night before the France game, we watched the other semi-final. What struck me in that game was that all you could hear in that stadium was "Swing Low" being sung. And this was a semi-final between Australia and New Zealand. The stadium was full of England fans. I thought: if it's full of England fans for that, what's tomorrow going to be like?'

Five: Actually, England were definitely on the right emotional wavelength.

Lawrence: 'Our semi-final was the best atmosphere of them all. You came out and there were white shirts everywhere. We were pumped. And that's the game where I famously started crying in the national anthem. I mean, obviously I was very proud every time I sang the anthem; I always thought about my immediate family and particularly my sister who passed and that always inspires you. Sometimes those feelings get the better of you.'

It wasn't until after the game that Johnson told him: 'When I saw what state you were in, I knew we'd be all right.'

*   *   *

The game itself didn't go remotely to plan – but that only reflected well on the England team. It was another example of a group of players who could adapt and change their game plan according to the circumstances in front of them.

'Obviously,' says Lawrence, 'there was the usual "let them go ahead early" thing.' Indeed, this was the third time in six games: this time, 11 minutes in, it was an England mess-up at the back of a lineout with Serge Betsen gratefully darting in for the try. Yet that didn't rattle England. What was more important was working out where to attack the French back.'

Johnson: 'Our coaches had said to us, "They're very strong up front, let's play to the 13 channel." We'd brought Catty in at 13 for his kicking game. So we were going to go to the 13 channel a bit, but it was not a lot in the end because we got on top of them up front.'

Johnson rejects any credit for this tactical switch. He says that there was no specific moment when they agreed to make a change of direction. The fact that they did it, he suggests, just tells you how mature and intelligent that team had become: 'No one actually said anything. I don't think anyone made a call on it. I wouldn't have said to the players: "There's a huge change of plan." It was just that Daws was smart and we could feel it, we were picking and going and it was working and we just went with it.'

Thus, as the first half progressed, England starting winning the small contests and gradually the scoreboard reflected that. France, meanwhile, struggled for a foothold and their frustration began to show: two yellow cards, one in each half, only helped England further. Most importantly for England, though, it was also a performance brimming with the kind of passion they had been desperate to get out on to the field.

Lawrence: 'Our front row were the key to that victory. They stepped up and delivered a world-class performance. Everything else came from that. Plus, Matt Dawson was an absolute menace and Jonny produced his best performance of the World Cup. Look at the score – 24-7 – it was a pretty comfortable win in the end.'

It was also a very wet night, which was largely why all

England's points came off Wilkinson's boot – five penalties, three drop goals. The absence of a single try would, of course, provide plenty of fuel for the week to come.

CHAPTER 30

IT'S A HEMISPHERICAL THING

When you say that only two players in the squad had ever been in a World Cup final before, Lawrence will remind you gently that 'that's not strictly true, is it?' because both he and Matt Dawson were already World Cup winners. They were both in the England team that won the Sevens World Cup in 1993, and in the final, the team that they had beaten was Australia. But distinctions aside, the two others were Jason Robinson, who was in the England team in the 1995 Rugby League World Cup final, who lost 16-8 to Australia, and Jason Leonard, who was a young man in the 1991 World Cup final which England had lost, again, to Australia, 12-6.

Leonard is not the sort of person to wear his disappointments publicly but, 12 years later, the wounds of that 1991 final defeat had certainly not healed. They still haven't really completely healed now.

'That regret, that pain that you have,' he says, 'it's still there. It's not like I think about it every day now. But is it there? It's there. So, the opportunity 12 years later to play against Australia in another final, and also this time, in Australia – what that meant to me was huge.'

For his 1991 teammates, that opportunity never came around again. Most famously, Brian Moore, the hooker in the 1991 England team, so struggled with the defeat that 18 months after the final, he couldn't bear to live with his World Cup 'runners-up' medal and threw it into the Thames. Thus it was, in that final week in Sydney, in the lead-up to the final, Leonard started receiving messages from those old 1991 teammates. 'I got them from a lot of the guys: Wints (Peter Winterbottom), Teaguey (Mike Teague), all those sorts of guys, obviously Paul Rendall and Jeff Probyn, Mooro.' Rendall, Probyn and Moore were the other members of the 1991 front row union. They felt that Leonard was carrying a part of them with him, still carrying the flag for the 1991 team, that he could maybe deliver a semblance of redemption.

In this vein, Andy Robinson, the forwards coach, saw that Leonard and the 1991 final was something that the 2003 team could tap into. So, in that final week, he asked Leonard to address the squad in one of their meetings. 'It was just to talk to the players about what it means,' Leonard recalls, 'about the pain and regret. About how we couldn't go through that again.'

Meanwhile, in the Australian media that week, the idea that an England team should finally get their hands on the Webb Ellis Cup was not playing well at all. Certain papers were merrily indulging themselves with anti-England sentiment and the fact that all of England's 24 points in the semi-final against France had come off the boot of Jonny Wilkinson only invited them to wallow further in their latest point of attack. England, according to the host media, were still arrogant and were still Dad's Army has-beens – that much hadn't changed; what they were accused of now, in particular, was being a dull team incapable of playing entertaining rugby.

'They're killing the game,' the (Australian) *Daily Telegraph* declared. 'They are so bloody boring.'

The next day, the *Daily Telegraph* continued the campaign: 'So, England play boring rugby. You're kidding. What else is new? The Pope is Catholic? Hitler was a bad guy? Kylie has a cute rear end? News Flash. England has ALWAYS been boring. Down through the years, English sporting teams have turned boring into a fine art.'

At a stretch, some of this could be described as wit. Over the road from the Manly Pacific Hotel, where England were staying, was Manly Beach, where there were danger signs hammered into the ground: pictures of a swimmer with a danger sign superimposed with the words: 'Danger, strong current'. Next to these, one morning that week, appeared some new signs: an image of Jonny Wilkinson with the same danger motif superimposed with the words: 'Danger, boring rugby teams train here'.

The *Daily Telegraph* wouldn't let it drop. Another article headlined 'Ancient Art of the Bore: it's the national English pastime' featured a list of English bores: Nick Faldo, Steve Davis, Geoff Boycott, Tim Henman and Hugh 'Tedious Twit' Grant. On another page, under 'Very important correction', it gave the following clarification: 'The *Daily Telegraph* reported yesterday that the English rugby team was boring. This was incorrect. The entire country of England is boring. The *Daily Telegraph* wishes to apologise for this error.'

Did it go too far? On the day Jonny Wilkinson was up for media duties, the *Daily Telegraph* sent a reporter wearing a 'Stop Jonny' T-shirt. On the Friday, the eve of the final, it published the address of the England hotel (hardly a secret) and tried to deprive England players of a good night's sleep by encouraging cars to hoot their horns outside and for local fire alarms to be set off at night.

Were England ever bothered? 'Not ever, I don't think,' says Lawrence. 'I certainly wasn't. We took it as a sign that they were so worried about us.'

But it was one of those arguments that you cannot win. Before the France semi-final, Clive Woodward had been pushed into addressing the 'boring England' debate and said, 'It doesn't matter how we win. We're not Torvill and Dean; we're not here to get marks out of ten.' This was followed by a *Courier-Mail* article in which the description of him as 'adolescent, surly, complaining and resentful' was accompanied by some analysis explaining that these character traits were not 'his fault': 'It is just the sort of bloke he is. The type whose natural arrogance cries out to the typical Australian: "Come on, knock me down a peg or two."'

England were certainly accustomed to being the enemy wherever they went. That was and always has been part of the deal with being in the England rugby team. In that last week in Sydney, though, they were surprised to find that, just very briefly, they had actually won some friends.

Leonard recalls meeting up with Keith Wood, who was his old Harlequins teammate and had been Ireland's captain at that World Cup until their quarter-final defeat by France: 'It was the Thursday or the Friday before the final and Keith came and saw me for a coffee. All you wanted to do at that point was get out of the hotel but by then, if you stepped outside, you felt like the Fab Four walking down the street, like The Beatles, it was like you couldn't go anywhere. Anyway, we found a quiet coffee shop and we're sitting down talking about players, about family, whatever, and at the end of the conversation, Keith's just gone, "Look, I've got to say this now, Jase, for the first time ever in my life, I want England to win. I really do want England to win." I said, "Cheers, mate, thanks." And he's looked at me and he's gone, "I don't think you realise what I've just said. I've put 800 years of history to one side to say that." He genuinely meant it. He'd never supported England before. Not that he was overly against England, but he just wouldn't ever be supporting England. But he said, "I don't want Australia to win. I want England to win." And it wasn't just Keith, it was more a hemisphere thing at the time and it was a big thing. I had some French boys saying the same to me. Philippe Sella was one. And I had some other Irish boys, Scots, Welsh. Remember, at the 1991 final, there were some Scots boys there, wearing kilts with Aussie shirts. Not this time. This time, I think it was the weight of history – New Zealand won in '87, Australia in '91 and '99, South Africa in '95. It was just all southern hemisphere.'

CHAPTER 31

THE NIGHT BEFORE

Everybody has their own story of that final week, about the way the tension built as the World Cup final approached and the manner in which they dealt with it. Here are a few, starting with how Mike Catt fretted about his fitness and about whether he could do himself and the team justice in the World Cup final.

Catt: 'What happened is Clive sat me down on the day after the semi-final and he said to me, "Look, I haven't made my decision on 12 and 13 for the final yet." He said, "Greenwood's definitely going to play, but I'm not sure who I'm going to pick between you and Mike." And I said, "Clive, stop right there. Listen, I've done really well coming off the bench. You've got Stirling Mortlock in the midfield for Australia. A big lump. I'm battered, emotionally and physically. Look, go with Tinds. I've done really well, coming off the bench. I'm quite happy to play that part and do it that way." And he went, "Phew, good. Thank you." And that was it. And off he walked.'

Yes, Catt genuinely talked himself out of the World Cup final starting XV. (Twenty years later, this leaves Lawrence astonished. 'I didn't know that,' he says. 'Didn't have a clue. I don't think I could've done that. Incredibly mature, incredibly sensible.')

*　　*　　*

Lewis Moody: 'I'd spent a lot of the downtime during the World Cup wandering around the different coffee shops and milkshake parlours of Australia with Thommo [hooker Steve Thompson], Ben [Cohen] and Joe [Worsley]. I'd made it my mission to try and find the best vanilla milkshake in Australia. That last week, I managed to get it down to an old surf shack on Manly Beach. They did a vanilla pod milkshake which was incredible, so we'd sit at this little table with the doors pulled back, looking over the beach, drinking vanilla pod milkshakes. I know, that sounds particularly manly, doesn't it? But it was one of the highlights of my tour. I loved it: just the peace and the time to step away from the playing and the pressures of the games.'

*　　*　　*

Without any of the management knowing, Josh Lewsey found his release in a regular early-morning surf: 'There was a lot of boredom in the hotel, so I'd end up sneaking out to go and try and do a surf on the beach at Manly. I'd go by myself, 5am when no one's around. And I was rubbish, and it wasn't even proper surfing but was just something different to do, a bit of a cerebral break, something that's a bit of a switch-off and a getaway from just the mundane sitting in the hotel room, waiting.'

*　　*　　*

For those who knew that they wouldn't be in the matchday squad, the last week was long and slow and a test of patience and endurance. To fill the time with something worthwhile, Andy Gomarsall decided to do some of the extra work that was set for the squad by Dr Sherylle Calder, who was with England in a novel role entitled 'vision coach'. Calder's expertise was to improve the players' peripheral vision and spatial awareness. She has now worked with two World Cup-winning teams and another team of World Cup finalists, but in 2003 there was some scepticism about her contribution. Clive Woodward, though, was so convinced by her that he would badger the players to do the extra exercises that she set and he had a board up next to where her 'eye gym' was set up, where players would fill in how much time they had done.

Gomarsall: 'It was a bit like being back at school. You'd have to fill in how much homework you'd done. So, I'm there and I'm bored out of my skull and I'm like, "I'm going to do Sherylle's eye coaching. It's good and I've got time on my hands." Did the eye coaching make a difference? Yes, I think it did. Did anyone do 100 per cent of what they were told to do? Did they hell. But I did a lot. I'd do an hour where some boys were doing ten minutes. I saw two players hadn't filled anything in and one was Johnno. He didn't put the numbers in because he didn't do it. He couldn't be arsed, right? The last thing he wants to do is any eye coaching. So, I was filling it in after my session; you had to put up on the board how many minutes you'd done. And I started to fill it in for Johnno instead; I was like, "I'm going to put him down for my 60 minutes today." I remember later: Clive was giving everyone a telling-off for not doing the eye coaching and he refers to Johnno and goes, "Look, Captain Fantastic, look at him, he's done more minutes than anyone." I'm like, "This is brilliant," and Johnno's looking around, thinking, "What the hell is he on about?" He had no idea, no idea. He knew somebody was taking the piss but still today he wouldn't know it was me.'

*   *   *

Richard Hill: 'I struggled with sleep in the final week; it was just the getting to sleep because it was on my mind: don't fuck up. Don't be the bloke who drops the ball over the line, misses a tackle, nothing that can ever put you in a pizza advert. I didn't want anything like that. I've always been driven by fear of failure. I know that's not a psychologist's best practice for elite sports people, but it worked for me. So, it could take me a couple of hours to get off to sleep that week, but you'd be aware that other people were struggling too. There were also rituals that you experienced at every Test match to know that people were catching up on sleep left, right and centre. If you went into the physio room at 4.30 on a Friday afternoon, Matt Dawson was asleep either with acupuncture needles still in him, or they've taken them out and he's still asleep and they've put a rug over him. That medical room was always popular anyway. Every week, they had a movie afternoon, and the players would order food to the medics' room that they couldn't order to their own.'

*   *   *

Martin Johnson: 'I remember going to the aquarium with my daughter, Molly, the Thursday before the final. I got back and Will Greenwood's saying: "My mates have been phoning me urgently. They've seen Johnno in the aquarium. What's he doing? What's he doing, pushing a pushchair on a Thursday before the World Cup final? What's going on!?"'

* * *

Trevor Woodman: 'In the build-up to the final, I'd be hanging out with Vicks and we'd be sitting there going, "How do we approach this then?" It's like, "Not so sure." Vicks is sitting there, having a smoke on the veranda, and he's like, "Suppose we just treat it as any other normal game, shall we?" I was like, "Yeah, probably."'

* * *

On the Friday evening, the night before the game, at 7pm, the squad convened for the usual eve-of-match team meeting, which would start with a video that had been compiled by Tony Biscombe, the team's video analyst.

Biscombe: 'The video was always the last reminder of what we were trying to achieve in the game and how we trained during the week. So sometimes there was quite a lot of training footage. For instance, if we were going to really attack the opposition in the scrum, then we'd show some scrum training sessions when we were knocking seven bells out of the scrummaging machine, just to remind them of what we were trying to achieve.'

The video for the final was entitled 'Saturday Night's Alright for Fighting' and came with the Elton John soundtrack.

Biscombe: 'Basically what we did was we didn't show the Wallabies in any good light at all. All we showed was England players battering the hell out of Australia, particularly the Josh Lewsey tackle from the game in Melbourne the previous summer, the one that bust Mat Rogers' ribs. We used that video not only as a congratulations for getting to the final but to stress the point: there's still one more game. But we also used the middle part of the video as a way of saying to the players who weren't playing the next day that they were still part of the team. We showed every player that wasn't in the matchday squad. I think that was a great move by us to do that.'

*   *   *

Lewis Moody: 'The first time I actually seriously felt the pressure of the tournament and the expectation, that I'd maybe never thought about as a young kid, was the eve of the World Cup final itself. I just remember looking in the mirror for the first time and going, "Fucking hell, we're playing in a World Cup final." It was really a feeling that only manifested itself as reality at that moment when I looked in the mirror. Until that point it had never dawned on me because it always felt like we were going to do that anyway. It was the most nervous I ever was and probably ever will be.'

*   *   *

Jason Robinson: 'The night before I remember well. Talk about shit preparation. I was just about to go to sleep when my phone started to go. Messages from family members in northern Scotland. It was a couple of newspapers trying to dig some dirt on me. They'd been up to Scotland, taking pictures of my kids. I was absolutely livid. So, I went from being really relaxed that night, thinking about tomorrow, biggest game of my life, to absolutely furious. I don't know what time I got to bed, crappy sleep and everything else. After the game I never did any media. You can't stitch me up the night before and then expect me to sing like a canary afterwards. I was a stubborn thing.'

*   *   *

On the morning of the final, Paul Grayson slipped under Matt Dawson's door a note he had written the night before. The note started off with some *Blackadder* jokes they had always enjoyed together, it then reflected on the long history of their friendship and then got on to what was to come later that day. 'Today is your day,' he wrote. 'All your growing has been done. You're in control of the World Cup final. This is where you belong. Enjoy it. The rest of the world can rejoice in Matt Dawson the finished article... Win the World Cup. It will happen... You'll make the difference.'

Grayson: 'We'd had a rugby lifetime of friendship and I was one of the few that would tell him when I thought he was being a dickhead, probably more often than you might expect. And he'd listen. The night before the World Cup final, I wouldn't have been able to say to him what I wrote down, even though it was really simple. Emotionally, I don't think I'd have been able to say it. And I don't think it would've carried the same weight as opposed to just putting a few thoughts down on paper and just giving him a pat on the back and saying: "You're a world-class player in a world-class team, this is where you belong. Enjoy the experience. Don't be frightened of it."'

*　　*　　*

Ben Kay: 'The day of the final was a beautiful sunny day. You have to try and occupy yourself. There were some humpback whales off the coast. We went up on to the roof of the hotel to see those – anything to occupy yourself. And then by the time we got down to go out, it was pissing down with rain.'

*　　*　　*

Lawrence: 'By the day of the final, you would look outside the hotel and it was a sea of England jerseys. You couldn't go out there.'

* * *

Robinson: 'It was like being in a zoo. Everybody's looking in and you're looking out, thinking, I'd love to be out there too.'

* * *

Lawrence: 'You were almost trapped. It was idyllic. It was almost the best place to be but the worst place to be – oh, just to walk down the beach. I packed and unpacked about six times that day, just to kill time. I'm thinking: "If we win, it's probably likely I won't be around for a few days. And if we lose, you just want to get out and exile yourself to some island for the next six months."'

CHAPTER 32

THE FINAL

The final would kick off at 8pm; that's a long time to wait. The coach journey to Stadium Australia was a good 90 minutes – and that's a long time to wait too. And there are only so many times on a coach journey that you can play 'Lose Yourself' by Eminem, the song that had become the squad's World Cup anthem. Could Eminem have been any more to the point with his opening refrain? 'If you had one shot, one opportunity to seize everything you ever wanted – one moment – would you capture it or just let it slip?' Yes, this was the thought that minds had been festering on all day.

Yet even on arrival, there was a genuine inner belief too. Lawrence: 'We drew confidence from the way we played against France. We felt we were coming to the boil. Plus, the last six times that we'd played Australia, we'd beaten them. We knew we were a better side than them; they knew we were too. We just had to go out and prove it.' Easier said than done.

* * *

The start of the World Cup final does not go to plan. It is wet, the ball is slippery, England kick off 'and the first thing I do,' Lawrence says, 'is to throw a pass that doesn't go to anyone.' Yet there is soon worse than that to come.

Lawrence: 'The player that we had discussed more than anyone was Stephen Larkham, the Australia No. 10. I know that's not rocket science; everyone targets the No. 10. But he was a player who was hardly ever in the breakdown – whereas Jonny couldn't stay out of them. So our approach was therefore to tie Larkham into every breakdown we possibly could.'

At set piece, however, they cannot get to him. In the sixth minute, second phase from a scrum inside England's 22 finds the ball in Larkham's hands and Larkham launching a high cross-kick to the opposite corner, where Lote Tuqiri has a seven-inch height advantage over Jason Robinson, the England full-back. Robinson has to back-pedal and has further to go than Tuqiri, who takes the catch well and only has to fall to the ground to score the try. Australia are 5-0 ahead already.

Robinson: 'As a full-back, I have to stand almost opposite the 10, just a bit to the right of him because I'm waiting for the chip over. So the fact that I got out to the ball that was in the corner was a miracle in itself. I've gone directly backwards to a ball that's coming over my head, but I hardly jumped off the floor to compete because I'm running diagonally back and the conditions were crap. But don't get me wrong, the kick was bang on the money. And Tuqiri had the ball in front of him, he had the momentum and everything. But I wonder: should Josh have been at that ball in front of me? I don't know.'

Josh Lewsey has done enough wondering about that too.

He was on the right wing, marking Tuqiri, and before Larkham delivered the bomb, he was doing his job: pushing up with the rest of England's blitz defence.

Lewsey: 'My personal memories of the final are more to do with the moments I might have been able to do better. When Tuqiri scored, again I think now actually, we were blitzing but should I have put the brakes on a little bit more and got back to help Jason? We're flying up and as Larkham was shaping to kick, do I put the brakes on a bit earlier to get back to block Tuqiri, so Jason had a cleaner chance of a catch?'

For Robinson, the challenge he faced was not just Larkham's up-and-under but how he would respond afterwards. 'That really was one of my tests there,' he says, 'because mentally, normally, if something like that happens to you, then that can plant the seed. So many players I know, wing or full-back, if something like that happens to them, they're gone. They're gone because now their mindset is: right, don't kick the ball to me. So, there was a massive thing in my mind. It was like: just get your hands on the ball, make a tackle, make a run, catch a ball. Because that could have just eaten away at me.'

*　　*　　*

It is another 32 minutes before Robinson exacts his revenge. By then, three penalties from Wilkinson have nudged England into a 9-5 lead, but this is increased with Lawrence on a curving run left from a ruck in the Wallaby half. Lawrence passes inside to Wilkinson and Australia have now been opened up and, at this point, it is just about whether Wilkinson feeds Robinson to his left outside him to complete the score or Ben Cohen on his right on the inside.

Robinson: 'I was so lucky because when you made that half

break, Lawrence, and got the ball to Jonny, you passed it to your right and Jonny, obviously receiving it from that side, can see me. He can't see Ben. That is the reason why I got the pass. The easier pass was back on the inside and Ben would have been in under the sticks. I say: "Well, Jonny wanted to make sure, so he passed it to me."'

Lawrence: 'I think Ben is probably still wishing Jonny had been a bit nicer and passed inside as opposed to outside. But also, the best way to unlock a defence is an inside outside pass. It's like a one-two in football.'

The inside ball would certainly have given Wilkinson an easier conversion. He missed it but, nevertheless, England were 14-5 ahead and very much in control.

CHAPTER 33

THE TWAT WHO DROPPED THE BALL

England's early dominance was eventually rewarded with that Robinson try in the 38th minute, but it should have come 13 minutes earlier. It is when we are in the car, en route to Leicester, that Lawrence brings this up.

'When we are talking to Ben Kay,' he says, 'he'll know that that is exactly what we are going to want to ask him about.' Indeed he does.

We meet Kay in that hotel outside Leicester, with Martin Johnson and Julian White, and when he arrives, he is completely prepared for it. Of course he is. He has been living with it for 20 years.

Yet it is not just Kay involved here. It is Josh Lewsey and Matt Dawson who are also wondering what might have been.

The chance goes by in a flash. This is the 25th minute. England have kicked through and recycled. They are about seven metres out, to the right of the posts, and Australia are scrambling to

Lawrence: 'It's the full thing... Red socks, blue shorts, red tops, the whole lot. This is it now. This is where the World Cup starts.'

© David Rogers/Getty Images

West: 'Johnno used to amaze me because [he would] be able to analyse the game and give an appraisal of what we've done and what we need to do – from that position where you can't see half of it because you've got your head in a scrum or a ruck.' © Don Morley/Getty Images

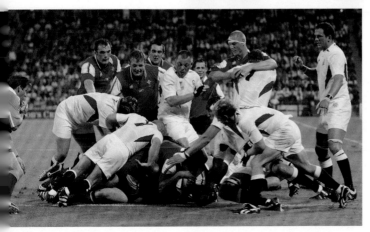

Johnson: 'If we went out early, we couldn't go home. We wouldn't be able to show our faces. Like if we'd lost to Wales in that quarter-final – how do we go home?'

© David Rogers/Getty Images

Lawrence: 'Our semi-final [versus France] was the best atmosphere of them all. You came out and there were white shirts everywhere. We were pumped.'

© Christophe Simon/Getty Images

Worsley: 'Whichever way you look at it, you've still got to realise the reason we won the World Cup is in large part because some of the things that Clive did.'

© David Rogers/Getty Images

Larder: 'We finished up with a squad of players the likes I'd never coached before. What a superb group of men.' © David Rogers/Getty Images

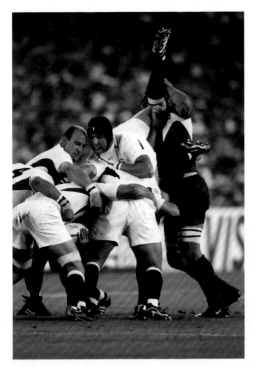

Left: *Lawrence on France semi-final*: 'Our front row were the key to that victory. They stepped up and delivered a world-class performance. Everything else came from that.' © *Stuart Hannagan/Getty Images*

Below: *Lawrence*: 'When you see and live and breathe each other's experiences off the field, when you go through things together and you share each other's pain, it makes you very united and that makes you very strong.' © *Ross Land/Getty Images*

Below: *Lawrence*: 'We genuinely felt that, scientifically, we were the fittest team in the world.' © *David Rogers/Getty Images*

Above: *Wilkinson*: 'In the middle of a game, that was where I was completely at one. That was my happy place. In between those moments was suffering. And as I understood it, that's how it had to be.'

© *Jon Buckle/Getty Images*

Lawrence: 'We recognised that the more time you spend together, the better you become as a group. That was where the warming up together came from.'

© David Rogers/Getty Images

Vickery: 'Our mindset was: you go at it, you finish people off. Did I need to depower the scrum and stop pushing? I'd sooner lose the Rugby World Cup than stop pushing.'

© Christophe Simon/Getty Images

Lawrence: 'When you look at all the things that Clive did, getting Jason was as significant as anything. It was a gamble, bold, brave and it absolutely made an enormous difference.'

© Nick Laham/Getty Images

Lawrence: 'We drew confidence from the way we played against France. We felt we were coming to the boil. We knew we were a better side than Australia; they knew we were too. We just had to go out and prove it.' © *Phil Walter/Getty Images*

Larder: 'You guys were all standing round Johnno and you were talking about what to do next: "This is what we're going to do." Clive and I saw this and said, "We're not going to say anything. Let them get on with it."' © *Bob Thomas/Getty Images*

Wilkinson: 'It happened almost out-of-body. I don't remember any effort, any of me trying to do it. It just took care of itself.' © *Stuart Hannagan/Getty Images*

Lewsey: 'To be amongst that group of people, to be part of that team was the greatest of honours, and for the first time I also felt I was someone.' © *Mike Hewitt/Getty Images*

Slot: 'Despite the Australian runners hurtling down on him, Woodman does catch it. The ball is then recycled to Mike Catt, who boots it out into the crowd. And, at last, the game is done.'

© Jon Buckle/Getty Images

Reddin: 'England were different. We were a different England. We were a different type of rugby team for that period of time. That's always been the stuff that's excited me.'

© Greg Wood/Getty Images

Catt on Wilkinson: 'The guy they dared to call a basket case, the guy whose frame of mind had been questioned, the guy who it was said would buckle under the pressure. Good on you, mate. You've been a genius in this tournament.'

© Tom Jenkins/Getty Images

Lawrence: 'I remember looking round and seeing all the people and all the emotions. For me, that was the ultimate moment of joy. You've got to treasure this because this is the absolute end of a very long journey.' © *Manuel Blondeau/Getty Images*

Lawrence: 'I want other England players to know what it feels like to win the World Cup. I want other supporters to be able to say: "I was there," or "I was watching you, pissed in the pub at eight o'clock in the morning."' © *Matt Cardy/Getty Images*

get back. Neil Back feeds Lewsey and there is immediately a three on two. Lewsey has Dawson and Ben Kay outside him and George Gregan and Phil Waugh in front of him. So he draws and passes to Dawson, Dawson likewise draws and passes to Kay. It should be simple, but Kay drops it.

'It goes so quickly,' Lawrence says, 'but in that very moment, Ben became forever the guy who should have scored in a World Cup final and didn't.'

Kay: 'People say that it was down to nerves. It wasn't nerves at all. People drop balls in rugby matches all the time; it just so happened that my drop was in a World Cup final. I know what happened: we made that break and if you look at the replay, Daws tries to hold the last defender, Phil Waugh, to buy me a little time, to make it easier for me. He throws a little tiny pump (dummy) pass. I've seen him start to throw it and I've started looking at Waugh, thinking how I am going to set myself for the contact. My thinking was: I don't want him to hit me and dislodge the ball. You tell every kid: never take your eye off the ball. I just chose the worst moment to take my eyes off it. So, when I saw Daws start to throw it, I thought it was coming. I effectively caught the first one, when he didn't give it, and dropped the second, when he did.'

So, if it wasn't Kay to score, could it have been someone else? Lewsey, perhaps? That is certainly what Lewsey has wondered, his mind playing a game of what he calls theory versus reality. 'The reality,' he says, 'was Daws was also coming around the corner with me, for a three on two overlap. So, I drew the pass, give, give, and you put Ben in at the corner. So technically we absolutely did the right thing, 100 per cent, but once he dropped it, part of me did think: should I have dummied and gone myself instead? Could I have made it? I look at it now: I'm two yards out, coming on to the ball at speed, dummy that pass, there's Gregan there and perhaps I can carry him over the line with me. That's the theory.'

And was it really Kay's fault? Did Dawson actually need to sell that mini-dummy which his own teammate ended up buying? Many months later, that is exactly what Phil Larder said to Kay: 'He said: "It should have been Daws getting the bollocking for that. Why is he making it difficult for you by throwing the dummy? Why make it extra complicated?"'

Dawson's not having this. 'It was a delayed pass to draw the man,' he says. 'He's slightly gone for it.'

Lawrence: 'This is a guy who catches the ball for a living. He's the lineout king. He catches it one-handed most of the time.'

Dawson: 'He can use as many excuses as he likes but he coughed that right up.'

'But I am not making excuses,' Kay says. Indeed, he isn't. He completely owns the error. 'I shouldn't have taken my eye off it. I was trying to be too clever.'

The interesting thing is what happened next. In the biggest game of his life, Kay has just committed a whopping blunder. 'The thing it does do to you,' he says, 'is it makes you start thinking: "Don't make any more mistakes." Which is the worst thing you can think. If you play trying not to make mistakes, it inhibits you. It would have been there in the back of my mind, but I focused instead on running round, trying to hit things.'

And then there is what happened in the immediate aftermath. In the changing room after the game, Will Greenwood was winding him up, saying to him, 'That's going to haunt you for the rest of your life.'

Greenwood didn't know how right he would be. 'It's not like I think about it all the time,' Kay says, 'but a week won't go by without at least one person mentioning it. Often more. At a dinner, you know someone will say something.'

So, he quickly learned to dine out on it too. 'I've had to use it to make jokes about it,' he says. 'When I'm doing an after-dinner, I start in the intro with the Will Greenwood story. Then I go through all my achievements and then say: 'But even my mum introduces me as that twat who dropped the ball in the World Cup final.' Then I go on to meeting the Queen at Buckingham Palace and at the end she is on the way over and she says: "Keep walking, Philip, there's that dickhead that dropped the ball."'

There is, though, a part in all this that does actually nark Kay and this is the bit that he realises he just can't affect and that he will have to grin and bear for evermore. 'The thing that actually annoys me,' he says, 'is that among those people who never really watched me play, at least not closely, I've now got a reputation that my hands were bad. And that was one of the best parts of my game. My hands were very good. But I've got a reputation for being the guy that can't catch.'

CHAPTER 34

ENGLAND VERSUS THE REFEREE

In the 27th minute, two minutes after Ben Kay's drop, England execute a scrum so comprehensively that you think: no worries, Ben, you don't need to hold the passes because England will just do them in the scrum instead.

The scrum in question is eight yards out from the Aussie try line, to the left of the posts. It requires one reset but, second time round, the Wallaby pack go into reverse at a pace that is rare for a scrum. It's not like they are being edged backwards through repeated efforts, it is a case of the England scrum getting the immediate upper hand, not letting the momentum go and taking them for a walk. England have already had the upper hand in the scrum, but this is the ultimate statement of their dominance. As Martin Johnson says: 'We could push those guys as far as we wanted to, down Sydney high street and back again.' Watching it back again, the only question is: how do Australia get out of this before they are pushed back over their try line?

The answer is this: with all the pressure coming through the Australian unit, the flankers break off. So, the referee, Andre Watson, blows for an England penalty. 'Nowadays,' Lawrence says, 'that would be a penalty try.' Instead, Jonny Wilkinson kicks the penalty, England extend their lead to 9-5 and, penalty try or not, it all seems to be heading in the right direction.

For a few years up to the World Cup, the England scrum had measured itself against what it called 'world-class standards'. They had a yardstick by which they would measure these world-class standards which was: winning 100 per cent of their own scrum ball and disrupting 25 per cent of the opposition. Usually, they would meet those targets. Phil Keith-Roach, the England scrum coach, says that, in 41 games out of the 45 leading up to this World Cup final, they hit them. They were so on their game at this World Cup that they hit them in all six games before the final. The irony is that the final, above all others, was the game where they thought they would ram the point home.

Lawrence: 'Australia had always struggled in the scrum and that was no secret. Meanwhile, the French had gone really well in the competition and were probably deemed to be the best scrummaging front row at the tournament – until we went into our semi-final against them, and our three front-row forwards demolished them. So, going into the final, we had the best scrum in the world, which we'd just evidenced by destroying the French, and, of the teams that were thought likely to win the World Cup, Australia had the worst scrum – by quite some way. So, it was best versus the worst. Yet somehow it didn't quite work out like that.'

Quite why it didn't work out remains, to this day, completely baffling. It is a subject still heaving with acute outrage and dark conspiracy theories. Bring up the subject with Keith-Roach and he says it is 'like itching a sore'. Johnson calls some of the decisions 'unfathomable'. Lawrence calls it 'close to daylight robbery'.

It started pre-game. England had concocted a plan for referee Andre Watson, a South African. That was standard practice; they always had a plan for referee management. England had brought their own professional referee, Steve Lander, as part of their touring party so that he could referee at training sessions and advise on how to best manage the different referees during the tournament. Different referees have different personalities, different communication methods and different ways of seeing the game and it was beneficial, therefore, to understand each one of them. Lander's advice with Watson was clear: he likes to be seen to be in charge, he requires utmost respect, he cares about how the exchanges look and he probably won't appreciate a towering Martin Johnson looking down and glowering at him when they have to communicate.

As Jason Leonard says: 'He's one of these referees who's a bit "Yes, sir, no, sir, three bags full, sir." So even if he makes the biggest mistake of his life right in front of you, you've got to look at him and go, "Good call, sir." Because if you say, "For God's sake, what was that?" then he's on you as a team and things swing the other way. So, you've got to bite your lip.'

The Johnson size disparity issue was easily resolved. To avoid Johnson having to look down on Watson when they spoke, it was agreed that Johnson simply wouldn't speak to him. At all. All communication would be left to Matt Dawson, who was a scrum-half and therefore wouldn't be looking down on anyone.

The communication with Watson starts in the changing room before the game.

Leonard: 'As all referees do, he comes in and he talks to the front-rowers in particular, but the back row as well because they're bolted on. And he tells you what he expects. I'm not matey with Andre at all but I sort of said, "Look, sir, we are a dominant pack. Just looking at it on paper, their front row is very weak. Are we going to be allowed to actually scrummage against them? It's a World Cup final." And he basically said to all the front rowers, "I'm South African, I love the scrum, of course you can." So, we were very confident. He'd said exactly what we wanted to hear. You're thinking: "This is meat and drink, this is lovely, we're just going to eat them alive."'

'What I thought he said to us,' recalls Phil Vickery, 'was: "I wouldn't give a scrum penalty unless I could put my mortgage on it." After the match, I'm thinking: well, you've obviously got no mortgage.'

The reserves of respect that the England front row had for the Australians were already pretty limited. England had played Australia twice in the previous 12 months and out-scrummaged them on both occasions. It didn't help Australia's cause that their first-choice tighthead, Ben Darwin, was injured from the semi-final and so they were forced to go with Al Baxter who, in his whole career, had only ever started two Test matches. On the loosehead side was Bill Young, known to Leonard as 'Bendy Bill'.

The way that that Aussie scrum had gone backwards in the 27th minute suggested that all these premonitions were right. Two minutes later, though, something strange happened: another scrum, another collapse and Watson awards the penalty to Australia. It looks like he is directing the blame at Trevor Woodman. Why? Why indeed? We are rewatching the game in Lawrence's kitchen and he thumps the kitchen table in frustration. Yes, 20 years on; he's still thumpingly frustrated.

Lawrence: 'You can understand our frustration – we'd just destroyed them, so why would we go down? We wouldn't. We want to scrummage against them. And the referee hasn't even given a reset; he's so sure that he gives a penalty against us! But the Aussies are just very clever. Look at their props, they'd rather collapse a scrum than have it go backwards at a hundred miles an hour because then they've got a 50/50 chance that the decision could go their way. It could go our way, it could go theirs. And we'd just comfortably won the scrummaging contest in the semi-final, so we've therefore taken this kind of alpha attitude into the next game when actually really, we should have realised we were playing against some really canny opposition who were going to cheat. Gamesmanship, sportsmanship, whatever, call it whatever you want.'

Leonard: 'For them, I'm guessing it would be a no-brainer to go: "We'll just collapse the scrum. If we try to scrummage against England, they're going to win the ball anyway because they're pushing us off the ball. But if we collapse it, the referee's got to go their way or our way. So why not drop the scrum, give it a go?" I think that's their mentality.'

Leonard was in the perfect position to take it all in. Woodman and Vickery were the starting props; Leonard was on the bench, and he had the feed of the ref-mic in his ear so he could hear all the exchanges.

'Even from the start of the game,' he says, 'the scrum was going up, it was going down, it was wheeling early and stuff like that. And there's a lot of resets. And as the game wore on into the latter part of the first half, the ref's language started to change.'

Maybe it was the fact that the match as a spectacle was being blemished by the mess at the scrum. Maybe Watson felt, as referee, that he had to deliver a better show. But by half-time, Woodman and Vickery are already baffled. As Watson walks off for half-time, he has Woodman and Vickery on either side of him, one in each ear. For a team whose strategy was to leave all the talking to Dawson, this wasn't quite the plan.

In the second half, it then just unravels. There is a scrum in the 51st minute in which England march Australia backwards again, just like that scrum near the try line in the first half. It is so comprehensive that on the home TV commentary, the Australian TV commentator says of the Wallabies, 'It's like they're on roller skates.' How, then, only six minutes later, does Watson give a scrum penalty against England when England, again, have the nudge? They have proven indisputably, again, that they have the stronger scrum, but Watson penalises Vickery. (Lawrence thumps the kitchen table again.) Soon after, Watson penalises Vickery again. And Vickery then tries to talk to him to dispute the decision. Again, this is unlikely to win Watson back onside; if anything, the opposite.

Vickery: 'I was trying not to get myself upset or frustrated. You've got to stay focused on what it is you are doing because before you know it, you could do something stupid.'

Leonard: 'My alarm bells were really going by about 60 minutes. That was when he pulled both sets of front rows over and said: "Look, guys, there's millions watching and you're stuffing it up. Listen to me!" So, he's saying that we haven't come here to watch a scrummage, which was a complete 180 from what he said in the changing room. We're shoving them left, right and centre and I've got to say, personally, I thought Woodman and Vickery were having great games against their opposite numbers and of course I'm going to say, "Yeah, we were obviously in the driving seat," but we really were. But what the ref wanted was a couple of very nice, neat and tidy scrums, a clean hook and he'd actually go, "Thank you very much." I remember, with 15 minutes to go, getting a message up to Clive. I said: "Listen to the ref, you've got to get me on." But Clive sort of didn't answer.'

Keith-Roach: 'The second half, for me, was excruciating. I couldn't understand why it was so different for our ball and theirs. When you look back, though, you see that Baxter [who was against Woodman] would scrum fair on England ball and, on their ball, would scrum in and down. Maybe that was the plan. But it meant that Trevor had nothing to bind on to.'

The second half saw four scrum penalties go Australia's way, the last being the most influential decision of them all. The penalty count against England allows Elton Flatley to whittle away at England's lead, kicking the three-pointers and bringing Australia back from 14-5 down at half-time until, with two minutes to go, they are 14-11 behind and have a scrum just inside the England 22. Maybe the Australian commentator has a sense of what's coming because he decides that now is the moment to list the history of England's failures as a sporting nation: 'England last won a World Cup in football in 1966. They've lost three Cricket World Cup finals. Australia has held the Ashes in cricket since 1987 and England last won the Davis Cup in 1936.' And now, here, in the second Rugby World Cup final England have ever played in, they are hanging on for dear life.

The scrum is Australia's put-in and notable for two reasons. One: England shove Australia backwards and eventually Baxter, the Australia No. 3, goes down. Two: Johnson lets his guard drop. For just that one fleeting moment in the whole game, he forgets Lander's advice. He says to Watson, 'You've got to ping three.' Watson spins round to him and snaps back, irritated: 'I'll ping what I see.'

Johnson: 'It's the only thing I say to the ref in the whole game: "You've got to penalise them." And what does he do?'

The answer is he doesn't reward England for the dominance of their scrum, he calls for a reset. The reset scrum then goes down right on the point of engagement – the ball hasn't even been put in – but Watson blasts on the whistle and his right arm goes up: he has given a penalty to Australia.

When you watch that scrum from the reverse angle, you can see Woodman pulling out of the engagement. Maybe that's because Baxter was giving him nothing to bind on to. 'Nine times out of ten, a referee calls that for a reset,' Lawrence says. Not here, not with a minute left of the World Cup final.

Johnson: 'That last penalty is a potentially World Cup-deciding decision. It's the last kick of the game. It's a huge call to make as a ref. Too big a call. And I am thinking to myself: what have you done? What have you done?'

Flatley then kicks the penalty. The score is 14-14. The game goes into extra time.

Leonard: 'When it got to 80 minutes, Clive said, "Jase, you're on." And I remember taking off my tracksuit top and bottom, I threw them at him and said, "It's about fucking time."'

Vickery: 'It didn't bother me at all that Jason came on for me. I wasn't upset. Couldn't be happier for Jason. But that was how our squad was.'

Johnson: 'The ref's decisions are unfathomable. We had a dominant scrummage, but we weren't allowed to show the dominance. Without being arrogant, we should have won that game by 9 to 12 points. We made mistakes. We probably lost our way a little bit tactically. But we couldn't dominate the game. I felt for guys like Vicks; they've practised all their lives to dominate in the scrum and they weren't allowed to do it. The frustration levels were immense. The Aussies are smart. They nearly won a Rugby World Cup without being able to scrummage – which is amazing. Our biggest enemy in the final was frustration – that we'd get frustrated with the situation.'

Leonard: 'So I went running on. I spoke to Johnno and then the rest of the pack and just said, "Look, all we want to do is stay straight and square on but don't push. Let them win their ball." For the previous 30 minutes, the ref had been getting nothing but abuse. So, for me it was a case of going to the ref and saying: "Excuse me, sir, I'm on the pitch now. You know me, I'll go forwards, I'll go backwards, but I don't go up and I won't go down. You'll get no penalties out of me." And he actually said, "Thank you, Jason." He really said thank you. It was the most civil word anyone had had with him for the last 20 or 30 minutes. So that's what we did: we kept it neat and tidy. We held the Australian front row; they win their ball, we win ours. And I remember running past him at some point in extra time and I said, "Excuse me, is everything all right? Are you happy with the scrums? Is there anything I need to change?" and he just looked at me and said, "Jason, they're absolutely fine. Thank you so much." That was it.'

Lawrence: 'That was what we needed: someone to come in and just explain that, that we needed to change the picture, to go: "Guys, trust me; the only way to resolve it is just to stop scrummaging."'

Keith-Roach: 'Jason is a very unemotional, hard-nosed guy and his experience, there, was priceless. He saw with great clarity what was needed.'

Leonard: 'The problem was that we'd been shoving the

Aussie scrum all over the place and the boys were thinking: "Hold on a second, so I've just pushed his head up his arse 10 yards that way; how are you penalising me?" The whole thing about a game of rugby is you can only play to that bloke in the middle and I think that we missed that a little. We were normally very good at changing stuff on the hoof, in real time. We'd normally be: "This is not working; what are we going to do? We're going to do this." But here, all we wanted to do was bludgeon them at the scrums and in my opinion, we were doing it perfectly legally but that doesn't matter. It's the referee's opinion that matters, isn't it?'

Twenty years on, this retelling of the World Cup scrum story seems as extraordinary now as it was back then. In short, in order to win the game, England had to stop trying. They had to play passively; in a phase of the game in which they were miles ahead, they had to neuter their advantage. You ask Lawrence how that sounds and he's still pounding his kitchen table. 'We'd never done anything like that before,' he says. 'And never did since.'

Keith-Roach spent years trying to answer the question in his head – could I have done something differently in the build-up? – but never really found an answer: 'I had never told them to hold off. Our aim always was to attack. Our tactics were never to scrum soft.'

And, as Vickery says, attacking was a game that the front-rowers enjoyed playing: 'Our mindset was: you go at it, you finish people off. Did I need to depower the scrum and stop pushing? I'd sooner lose the Rugby World Cup than stop pushing.'

* * *

There is one other story that Lawrence and Woodward tell: the conspiracy theory story. And Lawrence knows that we won't get through a retelling of the final without Woodward going there.

This is Woodward's clear recollection of returning back to the team hotel after training one day in that World Cup final week: 'When we got off the coach, this strange guy is trying to give me this bag of coins. But all my media training stepped in and I just ignored him. And then, Lawrence, you came up to me about a minute later and you had the bag and gave it to me, going, "This guy wanted me to give you this bag of coins." So, I open this bag of coins and there's this letter in there, saying that the World Cup final's been fixed and all these coins will prove it.'

And what came of it? Nothing apart from that it all sat for a long time in Woodward's head. You ask Woodward how long it took him to let it go and he replies with another question: 'What's the date today?' The answer to his question was 17 July. And he then answers: 'On 17 July, I still haven't let it go. I'll go to my grave thinking there was something wrong with that game.'

CHAPTER 35

JUST DON'T BE THE GUY WHO MAKES THE MISTAKE

In many ways, the 2003 World Cup final was a final of its time – albeit that every World Cup final is.

Right at the start, Trevor Woodman throws a punch. 'That's a definite yellow in today's game,' says Lawrence. 'If not a red.' But no one seems to even notice – apart from Matt Dawson. 'He just came over to me,' Woodman recalls, 'and said, "Get yourself under control. Calm down."'

Then Phil Vickery appears to take a blow to the head. 'Today,' says Lawrence, 'he'd be off for an HIA.' But no one bats an eyelid.

It is also a game where drop goals are very much on the mind. In today's game, drop goals are a rarity but in that final, Jonny Wilkinson attempts four and gets one (more on that later) and, in extra time, after coming on for Mike Tindall, Mike Catt tries one which is charged down.

'Yes,' Lawrence says to Catt, laughing, 'you hit that drop goal and then they nearly scored.'

Catt pays him an ironic 'thanks' for the memory. His drop goal attempt didn't exactly threaten the posts; instead, it ended up bobbling along the turf in front of Phil Waugh, the Aussie No. 7, who knocked it on. As Catt recalls: 'If he had picked that ball up and moved it, two passes and they would have been in under our sticks. Still to this day, I remember thinking, "God, Jeez, I've just lost the World Cup final."'

This is a game that is remembered for its drama, but certainly not particularly for the quality of the England performance.

Lawrence: 'We defended well but there was no other aspect that was great. Our lineout wasn't great. Our scrum was a problem. Our conversion of opportunities was not what it should have been. We were certainly nowhere near the level we had been when we beat Australia in Melbourne five months earlier. You don't want to be critical, but it wasn't a great performance. We lost the second half 9-0, which was a complete disaster. We went in at half-time leading 14-5, but we'd been so dominant, it could have been more. Yet even then, by our standards, we were pretty sloppy in that first half and then, in the second, they just carried on pegging us back.'

Certainly, there is an unusual element of nervousness creeping in.

Mike Tindall: 'My hamstring started to cramp in the last five minutes of normal time. And my immediate thought was, "I do not want to be the one that misses a tackle. The only way they're going to score is if someone misses a tackle. And, if I'm going to do a full stretch sprint, and my hamstring goes, I'll never forgive myself." So, it was two minutes to go, we're three points up and I'm like, "Just get me off." And then, as I've gone off, that was when they formed that scrum, the penalty was given and then, Elton levels the scores. So I always like to tell people: "When I went off, we were still winning."'

This is Lewis Moody, who was on the bench and came on in extra time: 'I was desperate to go on and make a difference. I felt I was a person that could do that. From the word go, I was thinking, "Get me on, get me on, get me on." But man! As it went on and Australia kicked the points and it started see-sawing between a point this way, a point that way, genuinely in my head, all I was thinking in those last 20, 30 minutes was, "Do I actually want to be the bloke that goes on and gives away the penalty?"'

Iain Balshaw's head was in exactly the same place. He came on, off the bench, in extra time too: 'It was quite nerve-wracking. You just come on, fresh off the bench. You don't want to be the one guy who makes the mistake. I got the ball quite early. I think it was Catty who gave me the ball quite early and Lote Tuqiri snotted me. After that, I was like, "Just keep it in the forwards!"'

The substitution of Tindall was certainly influential. It meant that Catt came on at inside centre with Will Greenwood shifting out one spot to outside centre, which left him marginally more exposed. Phil Larder, England's defence coach, recalls this specifically because Australia then targeted him.

Larder: 'For about ten minutes, they were absolutely running down his channel and he didn't miss a tackle. It wasn't just up to him, it was people on his inside and outside that were helping him. But it was a great defensive performance in that area. If I look back at the World Cup, our best defensive performance as a team was in the World Cup final because Australia played out of their skin that day. They played far better than I'd seen them before.'

They played well enough to equal the scores at 14-14 and push the game into extra time. This is where, over the last 20 years, legend and reality have taken certain different directions.

It has become part of the story that, in that period on the pitch between the end of normal time and the start of the first period of extra time, a nervous Woodward joined the players on the pitch, apparently desperate to unload on them excessive instructions. It has also become part of the story that Johnson used some particularly blunt language to instruct Woodward to leave them alone. In fact, says Larder, 'You guys were all standing round Johnno and you were talking about what to do next: "This is what we're going to do." Clive and I saw this and said, "We're not going to say anything. Let them get on with it."'

It is also part of the story that, driven by his eternal dedication, Wilkinson went off to practise his kicking. Yes, he did indeed go to the posts and hit some kicks but Wilkinson laughs at the interpretation of it. 'Yeah, it's a great story, isn't it? He's so dedicated, he's gone to hone his skills.' I'm afraid it's bollocks. What's happened is I've stood in that huddle with Johnno and everyone and I'm like, "I can't stand still and listen to talking." My mind's going, my mind's going. And suddenly I'm starting to feel like, I can't do this, I can't do this – so let's go do some kicks and show yourself you can. It was what I needed to do to get through that period. It was: I need to be doing something to cope. I'm going to kick some balls. It was pure coping. Nothing else.'

There was something else that Larder had noticed, in that period, when he got down to pitchside. 'I remember running down with Clive from up where we were positioned. We didn't know what would be happening. What we found was that the Australian team were on their bloody backs and all the substitutes and doctors and everything were massaging them. Meanwhile, our players were standing all round Johnno, talking about what to do next.' It was the comparison that struck him. 'Of all of the coaches sitting in the stand that day, it was Dave Reddin, the fitness coach, who was the most instrumental. I am convinced that it was our fitness that took us on from there.'

Johnson agrees with his assessment: 'So we come into the huddle and no one was chatting straight away and I just looked around everyone. I remember looking around and I thought: "We're going to win. I don't know what's going to happen, but we're gonna win." We were fitter than them. George [Gregan, the Australia captain] said it in a documentary a few years ago. He said: "Our idea was to run them about because they're old." But mate, our team was far fitter than yours. Honestly, that game doesn't rank anywhere in my list of hardest physical games. Australia were not that sort of team, not a grinding team. Physically, the game was comfortable.'

*　　*　　*

One of the more amusing ways of re-watching this 2003 World Cup final is watching Johnson and Lawrence watching themselves. There is still a film of this online, from 2019, when a sponsor booked a small viewing cinema in Charlotte Street in London and invited the pair of them to sit through the game together.

They are an entertaining double act. Johnson is very dry. He purrs sarcastically every time he is involved in the action: 'Hang on, I've done something good.' 'Great offload.' 'Why wasn't I Man of the Match?' Etcetera.

Early in the first half, when Lawrence makes a break, Johnson is on his shoulder.

Johnson: 'I thought at that point, when you make the break, you could have passed to me.'

Lawrence: 'I could have done. But then I looked up and saw it was you.'

It is not remotely Johnson's intention, but when you watch the game this way, you cannot miss the extent of his involvement and influence. This only increases through the second half and then into extra time. But point that out to Lawrence and he responds as if this is just a statement of the obvious. 'It's not a surprise,' he says. 'He was one of the best players in the world.'

Even when Lawrence and Johnson are watching it back 16 years later, as the game goes into extra time, the tension still grows.

In the second minute of extra time, Wilkinson kicks a 45-metre penalty. 'That was the best penalty I ever saw him kick,' says Lawrence.

Then, with three minutes left of extra time and England still three points ahead, a messy England lineout leads to a player handling the ball on the ground and Watson blowing up for another penalty to Australia. Lawrence watches this bit intently: 'I thought that player on the ground was me... Ah, hmm. Yes, it was.'

Flatley then kicks the penalty. The scores are level and the game moves to its conclusion.

CHAPTER 36

DROP GOAL

This is a moment in history. The ball is at the feet of Matt Dawson. He knows what's coming. The fly-half outside him knows. The whole heaving stadium knows; it can see the England players moving into position and as it recognises the unfolding gameplay, it seems to draw in a collective breath in anticipation. The match clock tells everyone that this is the last chance. This is the game.

The opposition know it too. They are like sprinters in the starting blocks, waiting for the gun. One flick of Dawson's wrists and they will be bolting forward. They have one job left in the game: to stop the England fly-half.

Dawson allows himself one fleeting glance over his shoulder. Just to check exactly where he needs to deliver the pass. If you didn't already know what England were attempting, if the opposition chasers were by any chance in two minds, here was confirmation. And then he reaches for the ball.

If you are a drop goal purist, though, you press pause

here and look at the set-up and your conclusion can only be: yes, one chance, but long odds. You see that the fly-half is around 34 metres out. That's pretty long range for a drop goal. Worse, though, the forward pack are too far left of the posts. That means that Dawson's pass has to be lateral – an infield pass to open up the posts as wide as possible for the No. 10's drop-goal attempt. And the fact that the pass is lateral means that the chasers have less distance to chase to put the kicker under pressure. So the kicker gets little protection. It's all a bit of a roll of the dice.

And so Dawson fizzes out the pass. Mike Catt catches it. Catt takes two steps and his right foot goes into its backswing. Yet the chasers, led by Rob Howley, are already close enough to be in his field of vision. As Catt hits the drop-kick, Howley leaps, his arms high and outstretched. Catt needs distance, accuracy and really quick execution, but the result is that his right boot gets under the ball and sends it slicing into the sky, midway between the right upright and the corner flag.

And that is it. 'That,' says Lawrence, 'is when our world caved in. I think that's the most I've ever hurt after losing an international game of rugby.'

*　　*　　*

If this is a book about the most famous drop goal in England rugby history, then we need to go back to 1999 and the one that missed. England versus Wales, the last game of the last Five Nations Championship. Thanks to a late converted try by Wales's Scott Gibbs, and then the wayward failure of this last-minute England drop goal attempt, Wales won 32-31 and England blew a Grand Slam and the rock 'n' roll celebrations ignited around Wembley were all red because Wales had just come back from behind to pull off the unlikeliest of underdog victories.

'I remember what it was like under the posts, after Scott Gibbs had scored,' says Lawrence. 'I remember getting everyone round. There were still a few minutes left. Plenty of time to win the game. Plenty of time for that drop goal. And yet everyone was completely panicked. It was like talking to a brick wall. I couldn't speak to anyone, let alone get their attention. We were all punch-drunk. It was as if a bomb had just gone off.'

Who was captain that day, Lawrence?

'Yeah, well, fair enough.' Lawrence knows that we can't rewind to that day without talking about his captaincy. 'Before that try,' he says, 'I'd had an opportunity to kick for goal. We were six points up and another penalty would've taken us more than a score ahead. I should have done that.'

Yet the error of Lawrence's captaincy that day is but a footnote in this story. There are two elements from Wales's victory that are not: first that extreme sense of panic under the England posts and, second, the long-odds hapless execution of the drop goal.

'Afterwards,' Lawrence says, 'when the smell of death finally left the changing room, when we eventually had the courage to even speak to each other again, I think we got to the point where the feeling was: "Yeah, Lawrence, you might have made a bad decision at the end of the game, but if we ever again get to the situation where we need to drop a goal to win a game, we probably need a call for it." Because we didn't have a call. We had an opportunity to win that game and we didn't know what to do with it.'

* * *

Four and a half years later, England now find themselves in a similar situation. They are standing under their own posts with time fast vanishing in another game that seems to be turning against them. This is the World Cup final and Elton Flatley is just levelling the scores.

There are now significant differences.

In the team room, back at the England hotel, there are a number of posters on the wall. These are the key messages for the team and because the players see them every day, they are ingrained. There is one which has a section entitled 'Build the Score' which stressed that you should always be accumulating points and that the easiest way to do that is with a drop goal. The call for the drop goal is 'Zigzag'.

Clive Woodward, who designed all this, explains Zigzag: 'What Zigzag means is: you win the ball, you go left, right, left, right. What we are trying to do with Zigzag is get closer to the posts so we are in position for the drop goal; we don't want to go wide, we want to keep the ball in the middle of the field. We punch left, recycle, punch right, recycle. It's a zigzag.'

Standing under those posts, with the minutes of the World Cup final vanishing and Flatley's kick successfully tying the scores, the England team now knew the call. For Lawrence, those two moments under different sets of posts on opposite sides of the world, four-plus years apart, are inextricably linked. 'And,' he says, 'at that same point, in the World Cup final, there was a complete serenity. We weren't exactly delighted with the situation but we were very clued in. Everyone was. There was no panic, it was just: right, this is what we are doing next.'

Zigzag.

CHAPTER 37

ZIGZAG

So there they are, with less than two minutes of extra time remaining, watching Elton Flatley nervelessly draw the game level again. But no one actually called 'Zigzag'.

'That was the joy of it,' says Martin Johnson. 'It was so much in our heads that no one had to. No one actually called it because we didn't need to. We just knew that that was what we were doing.'

And thus did the 2003 World Cup final move towards its denouement.

Even before Flatley has started lining up the penalty, Johnson is standing with Wilkinson and Kay, planning what is coming next.

'One of the challenges I have now,' Moody says, 'is trying to distil what's actually fact and what has kind of passed into legend. In my head, I remember standing under those posts and the message being passed.' Well, Moody wasn't actually under the posts at all, but he nevertheless knew exactly what was required. This was the most important kick-chase of his life.

Lawrence: 'Everything we did was the opposite of what Australia thought we were going to do. People probably think that, to get the ball back, you've got to kick short. So we kicked long.'

The intention instead was to force an attacking lineout. That was where Moody came in: Wilkinson kicks long, the ball is taken by George Smith, who is tackled by Moody. Moody is then straight back up on his feet because when the pass goes back out of the ruck to Mat Rogers, it is Moody again, fast up, diving at his kicking leg, pressurising him out of a long clearance.

The lineout is 10 yards beyond the Australian 22. The question now is: where to throw it? And bear in mind, here, the fact that England's lineout had been appalling. All Steve Thompson wanted was a short easy throw to the front. But Kay's job was to mastermind the lineout and he saw it differently.

Kay: 'Johnno said to me: "Benny, what's the 100 per cent lineout call?" I said to Johnno: "If we were Australia defending it, we'd be thinking: 'We'll hammer the middle and the front because England will be shitting themselves about going long.' So we're going to go long, to Moodos." So then we had Johnno and I with our arms round Thommo. We literally said to him: "You can throw this into Moodos's chest and there'll be no one there, just chuck it." That's what he did.'

Moody: 'It never crossed my mind, not in a million years, that the throw would be called to me at the back. Not when we had Johnno and Benny as the other options. And Thommo – who I love and had practised with so many times before – the throw to the back is not one of his best. And it was pissing it down with rain.'

Lawrence: 'Well, that's Benny for you, being a little bit more cerebral than most rugby players.'

Moody: 'Yes, smart decision. They were never going to go up and compete at the back; as long as the ball got to me, it was easy. I had no nerves. I was like, happy days. We'd practised it a million times. Thommo just had to get it to me and the rest would be easy.'

Thompson just about manages it. He doesn't hit Moody's chest; the ball arrives closer to his crotch. Yet that doesn't matter. England have possession and the zigzag dance begins. Mike Catt is the first to truck it up, but he is tackled, still about 30 yards out; the drop goal is already on, but it is still a long shot.

Then comes 'the moment'. At least that is what Johnson calls it: 'the moment' when Dawson is at the base of the ruck and every Australian is convinced the ball is going back to Wilkinson for the drop goal.

Dawson: 'I was always good at reading the opposition. At this point, they're all standing screaming: "Wilko, drop goal! Wilko, drop goal!" George Gregan is pointing at him, shouting: "Wilko, drop goal!" You've got Justin Harrison, George Smith, Phil Waugh literally in the blocks, ready to run at him. But I remember thinking: "Harrison, you're not here for me, you're here for Wilko." Harrison was literally staring past me. I'm thinking: "You're not watching me." I'm supposed to give it but as soon as I'd made the slightest movement to pass to Jonny, he was gone. That was job done.'

Johnson: 'The thing that makes me smile to myself is Daws was great at that. If you've done your homework, you know it's like when you're playing against van der Westhuizen: you've got to be so aware of him around the breakdown, so aware of him showing you the pass and going through your gap. Daws was the same. If you're the guy next to the ruck, your job is: you do not let the No. 9s go inside you. It's Justin Harrison – always makes me smile. He didn't need to take the dummy.'

Watching all this on the touchline was fellow No. 9 Andy Gomarsall, utterly astonished that Dawson would even think to pull this off. 'Genius,' he says. 'Just total genius. I would never have seen it or done it. I mean, if I was playing against Daws, I was always aware he could do it. But to do it then? At that point in the final? Absolute genius.'

Dawson darts forward; he makes around 20 yards. There is one more carry: from Johnson, taking the ball slightly more central to the posts. Wilkinson is now in the pocket and then Dawson is behind the ruck and fizzing the pass back to him.

This is how Wilkinson recounts the drop kick that would then finally kill off the game: 'Some guys in that team had been playing for 10, 12 years already, they've been through so much; everyone's put their heart and soul into it, we've all got to this point together. And it's now on you, that's you with all those worries about letting people down which will never leave you – and how could you ever live with yourself?... All this kind of stuff. I should have just frozen and crumbled. Can you imagine trying to take a moment like that where it's so on you? If I had any conscious thought process around that moment, I'd probably have fallen on the floor and just fainted. There may be a bit of fuzziness about how I'm remembering it, but I know one of the parts of the whole moment that really feels true – that it happened almost out-of-body, so I could feel it, see the ball being dropped. I don't remember any effort, any of me trying to do it. It just took care of itself.'

CHAPTER 38

WHAT WERE YOU DOING THERE, TREV?

Wilkinson's drop goal may have won the World Cup, but when the ball flies between the uprights for the winning score, the game isn't over. There are still 27 seconds left on the clock. Australia have one last opportunity and their only remaining option is to win the restart; England therefore have one remaining job, which is to stop them doing so. At this point, one last, unlikely hero steps forward.

Australia kick off short and as the ball starts to drop, it is clear that, yes, the player standing underneath it is... yes indeed it is, it definitely is... Trevor Woodman. And what is going through your mind, Trevor?

'Oh, you're just praying,' he says. 'Just catch it. You just pray you're going to catch it.'

The question here is: why Woodman? What was he doing standing there? This is a question that Clive Woodward has asked Woodman himself, albeit with a smile on his face, but the way Woodward sees it is: what on earth were you doing there? What were you doing out of position?

Woodman: 'I'm supposed to be out on the flank or standing behind Johnno or something. A prop never catches a restart. The whole set-up of a restart is to make sure your props never go anywhere near it. I've had these discussions since: when do you ever see a prop catch a restart, let alone a bloody restart in the last minute of a final?'

Because you're not supposed to be able to catch?

'Yeah. But the thing is: we used to do high-ball catching practice with Dave Alred, the kicking coach, and we used to love it. We always used to think at the time: why are we doing this? But we wouldn't complain because if we were doing catching, it meant we were getting a break from doing anything physical, scrummaging or smashing each other.'

Yet it wasn't just some random error that had Woodman standing under the ball as it dropped out of the sky.

'I just thought at the time, where are they going to kick it? The only place they'd go is short. Because if they kick it long, the ball's going to be in the air for four or five seconds and by the time we catch it and carry it in, the clock's dead. So they're going to kick it short and I thought: I'm going to go and stand there, because if I stand there, then maybe they won't see space and then maybe they won't kick it there. But what they probably saw was a prop standing there, so let's kick it on him.'

Lawrence: 'Thankfully it was a prop who could catch as well.'

Trevor: 'Yeah. That probably helped.'

Lawrence: 'You had very good hands, Trev, so it was no issue. I say to people: Trevor was completely out of position, and thank God he was too.'

So despite the Australian runners hurtling down on him, Woodman does catch it. The ball is then recycled to Mike Catt, who boots it out into the crowd. And, at last, the game is done.

CHAPTER 39

AFTERMATH

There is probably another entire book to be written on what happened over the next 48 hours, but since the finer details are predictably and impossibly blurred and only lurking in the depths beneath a haze of celebration, here are a few snapshots of what followed and that we believe to be pretty accurate.

There were the celebrations on the pitch where, amidst all the laps of honour and the champagne spraying, Mark Regan had a brief moment of clarity/inspiration and managed to whip down Simon Shaw's tracksuit bottoms.

There was the presentation ceremony, where Martin Johnson had to go and lift the trophy in the traditional, climactic way, but standing there on the podium, with their new medals round their necks, Johnson turned to Neil Back and asked if he wanted to go up and do the honours instead. 'He'd done that in a couple of Leicester's European wins,' says Back, 'where he didn't lift the trophy. Someone else did. He always sort of stood in the background.' But that wasn't going to happen this time. Back politely declined.

There is this reflection from Josh Lewsey, from that moment when the team finally quit the pitch and went back down to the dressing room – just two sentences which reveal so much, not just about that night but what had been driving him to get there: 'I eventually walked back through the tunnel in between two of the greatest leaders in English sport, Lawrence and Johnno. To be amongst that group of people, to be part of that team was the greatest of honours, and for the first time I also felt I was someone.'

Then, in the dressing room, they were joined by, amongst others, Prince Harry and John Howard, the Australian prime minister, who had just presented them with their medals. There, someone took charge of the music and out boomed The Specials' song 'Too Much Too Young', a message which Jonny Wilkinson had actually already started to think about.

Even out on the pitch, waving to the crowd, soaking up the victory, Wilkinson's mind had started to process the achievement. 'The problem with reaching the peak of your tallest mountain,' he would write in his autobiography, 'is that there is only one way to go, and that is down the other side. Here I am, celebrating the achievement of my life's goals and yet I can't stop thinking it can only be downhill from here.'

So Mike Catt's wish – that Wilkinson could now 'chill out' and enjoy himself – would go unfulfilled. Much later, back at the team hotel, when the new day had dawned and his celebrations were finally done, Catt managed to assemble his thoughts and make the last of the video recordings that he had been collecting on a small hand-held camera throughout the eight-week journey. 'Mission accomplished,' he said before turning his focus to England's match-winner. 'What a surprise that Wilko had the final say. The guy they dared to call a basket case, the guy whose frame of mind had been questioned, the guy who it was said would buckle under the pressure. Good on you, mate. You've been a genius in this tournament. Taken us to the top. I said to Jonny afterwards that he now needs to chill out, enjoy himself, have a few glasses of wine. Go and really enjoy his life. He's had five or six years of solid hard graft and he's achieved the ultimate goal. To my mind, he's probably the best player in the world. He's got nothing more to prove.'

Before that, though, there was some serious partying to be done. The party had moved from the dressing room to a reception, where they met with family and friends, and then, deep into the early hours, a nightclub on Darling Harbour called Cargo was persuaded that if it stayed open, it would sell an awful lot of alcohol. Amongst the recollections from Cargo is Mike Tindall's memory that Zara Phillips rocked up there even later than the team had done, and Clive Woodward's memory of the England team press officer coming up to him in a panic at some point later and asking if he'd seen Tindall. 'I said, "No, but why?" He said, "He's run off with Zara Phillips somewhere and the security guards are going nuts."'

Lawrence's own celebrations continued without a break well into the next day. At 4.30pm the following afternoon, he stumbled out to the main drag of Sydney's King Cross suburb with Jason Leonard, Paul Grayson, Mark Regan, Martin Corry and Mike Tindall. They agreed it was probably time to return to the team hotel in Manly. They were immediately mobbed by England fans at which point, rather conveniently, a police car pulled up.

Lawrence: 'They said, "Do you want some help?" We went, "Yeah, we do." So we got in the back of the paddy wagon and they said, "Look, we'll take you back to Manly, but you need to come back to the station and sign something for us first." So we did; we signed a few autographs at the police station and then when we were finally dropped off at the hotel, we clambered out from the back of this police van. That must have caused a few worries!'

Lawrence and Leonard then had just about enough turnaround time to make it to the official International Rugby Board dinner where, for the second consecutive evening, it seemed impossible to avoid Andre Watson. Jayne Woodward has a very precise recollection of that: 'I was sitting with Clive and I needed to leave the table. And Clive was still rather cross with Andre Watson and I'd seen Andre Watson circling the table. He was waiting for an opportunity to sit down and have a chat with Clive.'

Lawrence: 'I was at the table. I knew exactly what was going on.'

Jayne: 'Well, I should have spoken to Lawrence of course, far more reliable, but I grabbed a young Phil Vickery and I said to Phil: "OK, sit down here. Do not move. I've just got to go. I won't be long. And then I'll be back. Do not leave Woody on his own." Anyway, I should have explained why, but I didn't. I just thought, "OK, we'll be fine. He'll just sit and chat with Clive." Anyway, I remember coming out of the ladies' and I looked across the room and I did a double-take because there was Andre Watson sitting in my seat at the table next to Clive, trying to justify his decisions. I just thought: this is not going to end well. Anyway, I couldn't get across quickly enough to try and get him out of my chair. I just went and said, "Hi

Andre, do you mind if I sit down, please?" I've never moved that fast in all my life.'

The next morning, they all woke to an unexpected treat. After weeks of being bashed by the Aussie press, here, finally, was a somewhat classy and genuinely hilarious sign-off from the *Sydney Morning Herald*, which devoted its entire front page to England's victory. The main picture was Martin Johnson holding the Webb Ellis Cup, the trophy that the Aussies refer to as 'Bill'. The main headline, in upper case, just said PUBLIC NOTICE, and below it: 'To England and its sports fans. Regarding your magnificent football team's 20-17 triumph in the Rugby World Cup final, on behalf of all Australians, we would like to admit the following' and there then followed a series of bullet-point statements:

- You were not too old (though we hoped you would be when the game went to extra time).
- You were not too slow.
- You scored as many tries as we did.
- You ran the ball as much as we did.
- You entertained as much as we did.
- You are better singers than we are (and, just quietly, 'Swing Low' is growing on us, as is Jonny without an h).
- You played with class, toughness and grace.
- You were bloody superior.

There then followed more bullet points, under the sub-head: 'As a result':

- We believe Twickenham is a most fitting home for Bill, though we humbly remind you that, unlike the Ashes, you have to hand it over if you don't win next time.
- We will no longer characterise your fans as beer-swilling,

pot-bellied louts or knife-wielding hooligans and try to remember the sporting, enthusiastic supporters who did so much to make the final memorable.

- We officially remove the 215-year-old chip(s) from our weary shoulders and encourage all Australians to be nice to any person of English persuasion they come into contact with for the rest of the week... well, at least until the close of play today.

And finally there was a postscript: 'PS. Go the Wallabies who through their magnificent efforts did us proud with the magnanimous manner in which they and our fans accepted defeat at the hands of you Pommy bastards (sorry, that one slipped through the editing process).'

*   *   *

Here are three other postscripts to that incredible night in Sydney.

The first actually comes from back in London, from Brian Moore, one of Jason Leonard's front row partners from the England team that were defeated in the 1991 final, who had contacted Leonard to wish him luck second time round.

Moore: 'I couldn't get to Sydney for the final because I was working, so I watched it in Parsons Green, with a big group of people. And I was absolutely fine all the way through until John Howard put the medal around Jason Leonard's neck and then something inside me snapped and I cried. I sobbed and I sobbed. People asked me why and I kept it hidden, just said there's been a lot going on or something, but the reason was that I was jealous. That's not to take anything away from Jason, I was delighted for him, glad that he did it, but I was jealous. I thought: you lucky fucker. I'd kept my (runners-up) medal from 1991 for about 18 months, but all it did was remind me of failure and I eventually threw it into the Thames. I'd have given anything to have done what Jason did. I'd have been able to stop waking up at night thinking about it. That's why I was jealous of him, because he was the only one of us in a position to put it right.'

The second is back to Wilkinson. A while after returning home, he received a letter from Elton Flatley congratulating him on England's victory and his own central role within it. A brief correspondence was then struck up between the two. One thing that Flatley had said in that first letter was a kind of joshing 'we'll get you next time'. However, he would never get the chance to play against Wilkinson again. Wilkinson was about to endure a hellish sustained run of injuries that would keep him out of the England team for over three years and by the time he wore an England jersey again, Flatley had retired. Flatley suffered from blurred vision, following a series of concussions, and quit the game on medical advice. He was only 28.

Finally this, from Lawrence, from right back on that night of the final in Sydney, a thought that seemed to sum up so much of what had just passed and what was yet to come: 'When we got back into the changing room after the final, we closed the doors and it was incredible; I remember looking round at the room and seeing all the people and all the emotions. For me, that was the ultimate moment of joy. And I thought: You've got to treasure this because this is the absolute end of a very long journey and this team will never be the same again. From the minute we walk back out of that door, that is it; we're in a different world.'

CHAPTER 40

GOLDEN
GENERATION

As history revised itself in the days, weeks and then years that followed, different assessments started to take hold about why that England team were able to make themselves into World Cup winners. Why that team and no other? Initially, the story was that Jonny Wilkinson had won it. Then it became Clive Woodward who won it. Eventually, the honour was passed from Woodward to Martin Johnson. It was Johnno who won it. Yes, these are preposterous simplifications, but sports fans like names and easily packaged explanations.

Twenty years on, we are discussing this with some of the coaches. Why did England win it? If you took certain personnel away then, like a Jenga tower, at what point would that England team have collapsed?

Lawrence: 'Jason Robinson. You could say that he was a reason we won it. But he wasn't *the* reason. I'm not sure how you weigh the reasons. Would we have won without Jonny being the best kicker in the world at that time? Would we have won if Jonny hadn't kicked that 45-metre penalty in extra time? But Jonny had been working on his length with Dave Alred – so would we have won it without Dave?'

Andy Robinson is very self-effacing on this whole subject: 'We weren't the world's best coaches. We had the world's best team. Whatever anybody says, at least half of our players would have made it into a world team.'

That opinion helps feed a theory that was popular for a while – that Woodward was an inessential ingredient. 'In the early years,' says Dave Reddin, 'I heard people talk about that, you know: "With *that* team, anybody could have won it." Do you know what I mean? Then as that group of players grew up a bit, and some of them went into management, some of them realised that it's tougher than it looks. It ain't just about having a talented group of players.'

Lawrence has always been clear on this: 'We wouldn't have won it without Clive. People say we were a golden generation. I'm not so sure about that. I think we were maybe turned into one.'

Any reasonable assessment has to look at the whole picture: the environment that developed – and everyone contributed to that, the players and the coaches – and the circumstances at the time, and the way that Woodward led the group into the new age of professionalism.

Reddin: 'We did do it differently. That's the headline for that entire period of time. England were different. We were a different England. We were a different type of rugby team for that period of time. That's always been the stuff that's excited me. It's not just that it was an incredibly talented group of players. It was. But it was an incredibly talented group of players with the right group of management at the time.'

'We loved the game,' says Lawrence, 'and we thought a lot about it' – which might sound like a statement of the obvious, but Robinson and Dave Alred both have similar opinions.

Robinson: 'Maybe modern-day players don't love rugby as much.'

Alred: 'One thing that is overlooked is the majority of those '03 players had played when the game was amateur. And when the game was amateur, you had to take responsibility for your own stuff. No one's going to tell you to go to the gym. If you didn't go, you couldn't perform, and you'd be gone. So, they were all highly motivated and they took responsibility.'

Robinson: 'So, rugby had to mean something to them to make the sacrifices they made. Nowadays, you can win or lose and still make good money.'

Alred summarises a lot of it when he says: 'The maturity level was higher than any other England squad I've been involved in. And cerebrally, they were active and they were easier to coach. If you add in that maturity and self-management and taking responsibility and the group of teachers that was with them, you had a very potent formula to be successful – almost without the rugby.'

So, no, of course, you can't pinpoint a single reason why England won. 'There wasn't one reason,' says Lawrence. 'There were lots and lots of reasons.'

Indeed, so much had to come together for England to win. 'And as we would see from the next few months,' says Lawrence, 'when you start to pull it apart, and take things out, it is amazing how quickly the winning goes too.'

PART TWO

CHAPTER 41

STRAIGHT BACK
TO WORK

'When we returned home,' says Lawrence, 'none of us had the remotest idea what to expect.'

They touched down at Heathrow at 4.35am. When they were about to go through customs, the police informed them that they should go through in small groups. Maybe threes or fours. 'That seemed a bit tedious,' Lawrence recalls, reflecting on their blissful ignorance of the reception that was waiting for them. News stories agree that there were 'thousands' of fans waiting in the arrivals hall; the mean guestimate was about 5,000 – cheering, singing, climbing up to whatever vantage point they could find to celebrate the welcome home.

Now they had an idea.

Martin Johnson got another taste of it a week later: 'The Tuesday after we get back, I've got my book out. I go to London, I'm on Breakfast TV in the morning, I'm signing a book down Oxford Street, I get chased out of Oxford Street, we had to leave.

I'm then doing an evening signing from seven until nine, get to a quarter past nine, there's still a big queue. They're told to go but they don't. I'm still signing after 10 o'clock. I remember going to Birmingham for the book. I walked out and these teenage girls started screaming. I was wondering: "Who's coming?" And the answer was: it was me. Then Woody rings me. He says: "We're going to do this parade." I'm thinking: "Really? This is not what we're about. We're a pretty low-key team. We're not about public display.'"

The parade happened nevertheless, so did a trip to Buckingham Palace and a reception at 10 Downing Street. Yet between all the celebrations, there was the other reality: these were professional rugby players and they were therefore expected to be playing rugby. The plane carrying the team back from Sydney arrived at Heathrow early on the Tuesday morning; that coming weekend, half the team who started the World Cup final were playing again for their clubs.

Richard Hill: 'When we got back to England, I popped into the club (Saracens) on the way home to see Francois Pienaar, who was the director of rugby. He said I could have two days off, train on the Friday and play on Sunday. We were playing Rotherham; I learned the lineouts and that was it. But I was still nervous. I didn't want to mess up. You don't win a World Cup final only to then dent your reputation by playing like a prima donna, or not putting the effort in, or being seen to be above it all. In about the 50th minute of the game, I fly-hacked through to score our fourth try, the bonus-point try; I remember I looked over at the bench then, as if to say: "I am coming off!" I was absolutely hanging.'

Ben Kay: 'We landed to a text from Dean Richards [the Leicester director of rugby]: 'You're playing on Saturday, be in on Wednesday.' Johnno and I played a half each. There was no real joy to the game at all. But there was a big thing at Leicester about not being 'the international', not coming in and being treated any differently to anyone else. So, you come in, other people have been playing second row, and you are immediately under pressure for your place.'

Leicester lost the game by a point to a Bath team that included Mike Catt and Mike Tindall.

Johnson: 'That was the only time I've really struggled going back to the club, back to normality. Normally you embrace it because you want normality. And normally, you're used to coming out after games when loads of the kids want autographs, but after the World Cup, it's gone berserk, you cannot move. So, we lost this game and I knew back then you could come out of the club at the fire exit at the back of the press room, so I just went out there and went home. I hadn't realised lots of people were all waiting in the clubhouse to have some sort of reception.'

But there are some things that don't change, whatever the circumstances, and one of those is Lewis Moody – as Tindall painfully recalls. Moody was also in that Leicester team that played Bath and, at one restart, Leicester fed Moody with something that he loves, which is a kick to chase.

Tindall: 'I remember they went short, like England used to do, for Moodos. So, I've gone up to take it and Moodos has just completely wiped me out. And I just remember lying on the floor going: "Fucking hell, Moodos! I've been on the smash for a week! I did not need that!" And he's like, "Sorry, pal," gets up and just trots off.'

At Kingsholm, Gloucester beat Northampton with Trevor Woodman and Phil Vickery coming on as second-half subs.

Woodman: 'I remember the Shed singing "Swing Low, Sweet Chariot" because me and Vicks ran on at the same time to a scrum five metres from Northampton's line. We charge into the scrum and give away a penalty – so nothing's changed within a week, then. But you couldn't have scripted it any better because I remember scoring, running in from about 40 metres out to win the game. The try was ridiculous for a prop.'

Rugby players, being rugby players, just got on with the job. Wasps were playing away at Newcastle, but at least there was some enlightenment. Lawrence was given the week off, 'But I was told: everyone would like you and Jonny to parade the trophy around Kingston Park. I get that. But I think a lot of players who did play were physically and mentally exhausted. It's not exactly a surprise that some of them found it really tough.'

Clive Woodward could see that this was crazy and went straight to Twickenham to see Francis Baron, the RFU chief executive. Woodward: 'You win the World Cup and you think: right, now we're really going somewhere. But suddenly you find the players are playing the next weekend! I'm literally shouting at (Francis) Baron, in his office, about Johnno playing this weekend, Vickery playing this weekend. This is just straight out of the World Cup, we should have been celebrating. Or resting. I'm having the biggest rows ever. You've got to just fight. And I lost the battle. Baron said to me: "Well, we've had them the last three or four years; we've got to give the players back to Premiership Rugby."'

Lawrence: 'I could understand the thinking. When you are bouncing after winning the biggest game of your life, you want to leverage that and use it in a very positive way. The crowds coming through the gates want to see World Cup heroes.

You can see how that might have made sense. But would that happen today, 20 years later? No chance. And looking back now, that first weekend back was a sign of what would become increasingly apparent: that we'd put so much effort into what it took to win, but no one thought what might happen when we had done.'

CHAPTER 42

DISAFFECTED DRIFT

Not everyone had felt it such a tough demand to go back to playing club rugby. In fact, some were desperate to. Two and a half weeks after returning to their clubs, though, the whole squad were back together again for the bus parade in London. Then, before Christmas, there was another reunion at the *BBC Sports Personality of the Year* show (Jonny Wilkinson won, to his extreme discomfort) and, amongst other events, there was an excruciating evening on ITV hosted by Chris Tarrant. Yet there were some in the squad who were experiencing a rising sense of discomfort.

No one could put this any more clearly than Kyran Bracken. 'I felt a bit of a fraud celebrating the World Cup,' he said, 'because I didn't play in it.'

'But you did,' says Lawrence, 'and our hardest game was South Africa and you most certainly played in that.'

These are interesting interactions. Lawrence's nature is to

bring others along with him; the natural generosity of his spirit is such that he wishes everyone to retain the same pride and joy from the World Cup that he still feels. One point that Clive Woodward was very keen to repeat throughout and after the World Cup was that it wasn't 15 players, or 22, who won the World Cup, it was the whole squad. This is Lawrence's natural sentiment too; he doesn't feel that there is any kind of class system dividing the starters from the players on the bench and the bench from the other eight who didn't even need to wear a tracksuit on that final day in Sydney. So, he feels a sense of disappointment that some of the squad don't look at it like that and he gently tries to persuade them to see it his way, even though these are feelings that have been embedded for 20 years.

Bracken says: 'When you've not been involved in the game, you can't help feeling a bit of a fraud. You're never going be able to escape that feeling. It's just not possible. We were all there as gladiators who played for our clubs and, you know, want to play for our country and so the idea of celebrating a win that you've not played in is really hard. How do you do that?'

Bracken was actually in the matchday squad for the final, but he was one of three players, with Martin Corry and Dorian West, who were picked for the subs' bench but didn't get on. 'Twenty years later, I am over it,' he says, 'but it took a long time. I got an MBE – I didn't even play. So why have I got an MBE?'

'I've got as many memories playing with you as I have with Matt Dawson,' Lawrence says in a conciliatory tone.

'The idea of me sitting on the bench, not getting on, winning a World Cup and being happy – it just wouldn't sit well with me,' Bracken replies, unmoved, 'because that's not how I'm made up.'

Julian White was no different. His World Cup involvement was limited to two games, a start against Samoa and a sub's appearance against Uruguay; he was not on the bench for any of the three knockout rounds and he masked his disappointment with the silence that was required of the non-player role. 'I felt like a fraud,' he says. 'You feel like you are tagging along; you feel really awkward. I was the most bitter man.'

'But Whitey,' Lawrence says, 'you got over 50 caps.' For Lawrence, that is proof enough that he was no bit-part player, that he truly belonged.

'You just want to be playing,' White replies. 'I'd rather have been playing for the club side down the road. You'd get some players who were: "C'mon, boys, let's take on the water." But I was more like: "If I'm not playing, I'm not here." But you wouldn't say anything to anyone else. The thing is: I don't think you could play at the top level if you're not competitive. That's why you are where you are.'

Simon Shaw probably felt this more acutely than anyone. He had been flown out late as an injury replacement, arrived for the quarter-finals but didn't have a minute on the pitch in a single game. He effectively got a winner's medal and an MBE without touching a ball. In his autobiography, *The Hard Yards*, he says that when England finally closed out that final in Sydney, he felt like 'a competition winner'. 'All I could think is: "Why am I hugging anyone? I haven't really done anything."'

He then made a pledge to himself that, through all the celebrations, he would not lay a finger on the World Cup trophy. 'I actively didn't want to hold it because, as I hadn't touched a ball during the tournament, I thought it was hypocritical. I have a photograph with me and the World Cup, but I'm not holding it. I never picked it up.'

Danny Grewcock was not far different: 'There was an awkward moment during the bus parade when the trophy was passed around and it suddenly came to me – and you then just pass it on quickly. I have hugely fond memories of that whole period, but if you didn't play in the final, it wasn't quite your victory. And I wasn't in the final; I wasn't even in the country.'

Twenty years on, Shaw looks back on that post-World Cup, pre-Christmas celebration season as 'quite painful, almost excruciatingly so' yet he knows exactly how that sounds. 'I have to keep reminding myself that anyone else would give their right arm and probably their left arm and maybe both legs to have been in that position. But that doesn't change how you feel: as an international sportsman who has very high aspirations, you do feel completely disingenuous.'

Maybe there was a kind of kinship there between the nearly men of the squad. 'On reflection,' says Shaw, 'it's quite a strange thing that the people I still keep in contact with are Julian White, Andy Gomarsall, Ronnie, Dan Luger. The majority of the driftwood.'

Yet there is no universality of response to having not been on the pitch in Sydney that night.

This is Andy Gomarsall: 'There's no looking back from me and reflecting on anything negative. If I'm honest, I don't think I was the right guy in '03, I really don't. Would I have been able to deal with the pressure in the final or the semi-final or whatever? There are moments where I thought I would but there were other moments where I'm a human being and I thought, "No way!" It's huge, huge pressure. But it did give me a stepping stone and a life-changing moment. In the changing room after the final, I'm talking to Andy Robinson and I tell him, "In four years' time, I'm going to be starting No. 9; I'm going to be that guy." And I worked bloody hard and four years later I was. And, that time, I was ready for it.'

Frustration fuelling motivation – that was how Martin Corry saw it. 'I wanted more,' he says. 'We're all competitive people. I'm never going to settle for sitting on the bench or coming on for the odd bit. I felt in 2003 that I was part of somebody else's journey. If I wasn't there, England would still have won the World Cup. I loved it and it was great to be a part of; I look back at it as a fond time. But I came away with increased motivation.'

And this is a brief exchange with Mark Regan about the final: 'Yeah, we all had Lucozade bottles in our hand, didn't we, Lawrence?'

'And what was in those Lucozade bottles?' asks Lawrence, knowing the answer.

'Vodka, Lawrence.'

'But you were still living and breathing every single minute of it on the touchline, weren't you?'

'Of course we were, Lawrence. We wanted our 100 grand bonus.'

CHAPTER 43

RUGBY – GET ME OUT OF HERE

'The thing is,' says Lawrence, 'once you are back and up and running, it never stops. The rugby just keeps on going. And that became a huge problem.'

What he means is that the World Cup winners were like hamsters on a wheel. Within a few months, a number of them had decided to get off it. Martin Johnson (aged 33), Neil Back (turning 35), Jason Leonard (35) and Kyran Bracken (32) all retired from the international game. Add in Jonny Wilkinson and Lewis Moody, who were now both stuck in a long-term injury cycle, and that's a high turnover.

By the time the next Six Nations started, those still up and running had all played another two-plus months of club rugby. England kicked off in the Six Nations against Italy – and that was a kind of big affair: it was the return of the world champions, the start of the victory tour, however you wanted to frame it – but most of them were still playing for their clubs only the week before.

The captaincy that was then handed to Lawrence was a dubious honour: 'I immediately looked around at which of us were left and I thought, "Oh my God."'

England kept the show on the road for the first two rounds with decent victories over Italy and then Wales, but in the third round, they were finally derailed. Ireland's win at Twickenham was the first time that they had won there since 1994; it was also the first time in five years that England had lost at home. But Ireland was just the start. It was France who next claimed the scalp of the world champions. England hadn't suffered two defeats in the Championship like this for 11 years. Maybe there was an element of revenge in there for the French, though there is no lack of incentive for anyone when they are playing the world champions. 'You've got a target on your backs, haven't you?' says Lawrence. And there was plenty more and worse to come. As Lawrence puts it: 'Some stupid idiot had had an idea: Let's go on tour to New Zealand and Australia.'

Wasps won the Premiership final that summer, beating Bath in a game that included eight World Cup winners. The very day after the final, they would all board for the flight to New Zealand.

Lawrence: 'I tell you where we should have been going: we should have been going to a beach somewhere. We'd been playing rugby for almost three years solid and now we're going back to play two Tests against the All Blacks and one against Australia and I knew how pissed off both of those countries would be six months after we'd just taken the Crown Jewels back to England. I thought, "Oh my God, we're going to get massacred." Obviously, I kept that thought to myself, but I knew in my own head that we were going to get massacred and that's quite a demoralising place to be when you know that you haven't got the tools or the infantry at your disposal that can even put up a fight.'

From the relative comfort of his retirement, Martin Johnson could also see what was coming: 'The World Cup burned a lot of guys out. What the guys needed was a summer off, not to be taken down there and flogged. Then Trev got injured and couldn't play again. Benny Cohen was never the same. I remember thinking: this is madness.'

It is not as if Woodward wasn't also completely aware of how ridiculous this was. 'The Australians couldn't believe we were in the same season we'd been in at the World Cup. They'd had their off-season and they'd only just come back.'

In the first Test against the All Blacks, in Dunedin, England were beaten 36-3. 'Honestly,' says Lawrence, 'it was a disaster.' The following week, in Auckland, Simon Shaw was red-carded in the 11th minute and England were beaten 36-12. There was worse to come the following Saturday in Brisbane against the defeated World Cup finalists who certainly reaped their revenge: 51-15. For world champions, this was a humiliation.

'We got smashed to smithereens,' says Lawrence. 'I just thought: What the fuck's this all about? I've given everything and now it felt that we'd just been thrown off a cliff. No one deserves that. New Zealand and Australia psychologically ruined me.'

* * *

That feel-good factor of being world champions could hardly have faded faster. 'How do you go from being the best team in the world to that in a few months?' is how Lawrence puts it, but his intense frustration is more specific: 'Why was no one looking after us? We had just won the World Cup.

Why had no one come up with a plan for what would happen afterwards?'

The answer is that they did. 'I've got it in a drawer upstairs,' says Dave Reddin.

The problem, he explains, was that because England had just won the World Cup, the senior men at RFU allowed themselves to believe that this was proof that the system was working. 'They thought it was OK, but it wasn't OK,' Reddin says, 'it was far from OK, it was broken. We knew it was broken. This was the opportunity to fix it.'

The plan in his drawer, he explains, was all about what England required to take them forward in the fast-changing professional age. It was all about better access to players, about better coordination between clubs and country, about restructuring the season, about redeveloping their Pennyhill Park base. 'All of that stuff was in there,' says Reddin, 'and it didn't get backed. Clive and I spent endless time negotiating. Clive's position was: "Come on, this is the time you need to back me again so we can go again." Yet they chose to believe it was all fine. He genuinely felt let down.'

Dave Alred saw all this first-hand too: 'What disappointed me more than anything was when we returned from the World Cup. I remember having meetings at Pennyhill with Woody and company. We realised that we won the World Cup not actually playing very well and we were thinking: if we actually play well, wow, just think where we'd be! That was our enthusiasm – but it was just dampened by the RFU's attitude towards anything other than maximising profit from the win. They weren't interested in creating a legacy. It was a massive disappointment. I was desperate to take the World Cup learning and integrate that into the next Six Nations and beyond. But that didn't happen. We didn't have the training days we required. There wasn't the appetite.'

Lawrence: 'I don't know a team that's ever got to the top of the world and then fallen so dramatically. What I find disappointing was that everything we built was dismantled.'

It wasn't just the players who were at breaking point. According to Jayne Woodward, Clive was too. She says: 'All of these talks were happening against the backdrop of me knowing Clive was absolutely exhausted. In hindsight, we should have done that Six Nations and then had a break. Clive needed a break, you players needed a break. It needed someone in a position to say: "OK, Clive, you are taking the summer off."'

While none of that was happening, there would only be more casualties. Hardly anyone knew it at the time, but Woodward was being courted by Rupert Lowe, the chairman of Southampton FC. 'But I knew it,' Lawrence says. 'I could see it on his phone. We're on tour in New Zealand and Australia and his phone went and the name on it was Rupert Lowe. "Oh really?" I said to Clive: "Are you sure you're in the right head space for a trip like this?" I said: "Why don't you just hand in your resignation now?"'

In the end, though, the decision to walk away was one Lawrence made for himself.

Lawrence: 'You put so much in that, inevitably, something has to give. After the 2004 tour, I just concluded: enough is enough. I was thinking: no one's going to give me any time off. This game doesn't provide any players with any breathing space at all. And I was in a mess. I basically hadn't been at home for three years. I'd been missing in action as a parent, pretty much for three years solid. My marriage was in tatters and I ended up splitting up with Alice. No one realised what winning that World Cup could take out of you. I was completely burnt out. I'd given everything I could give, but everyone was just sucking you for more. I was thinking, "No one really gives a shit about me." It wasn't as if anyone sat me down and asked the question: what would you actually like to do now? Or: do you think it'd be a good idea to have a sabbatical? Shouldn't you have a couple of days off? I didn't get four weeks at the end of the season to enjoy with my wife and kids. No, I'd just gone straight off on the England tour and that cycle was only going to go on and on and on, and so I thought: I've just got to do something. And, you know, if I'd carried on, I don't think I'd be back together and married to Alice today. So I just retired from international rugby. The major part of my decision was family-driven, but I also felt angry and broken. I felt that everything I'd done had just been destroyed.'

Lawrence arranged to meet Woodward in the bar at Pennyhill Park to tell him the conclusion he had reached. But it turned out that it wasn't just him who was quitting England rugby. Woodward told him: I am leaving too.

Woodward: 'If someone had told me at the World Cup final in November, "You are going to be resigning in August," I would have gone: "What the hell have I done? What's happened?" But I just had a big fall-out with the RFU.'

Thus did the exodus from the World Cup team continue. Other players, Paul Grayson and Dorian West, retired and England had now lost two captains and a coach too.

'Why was it that everything that was built was then undone?' Lawrence asks rhetorically.

'It was unforgivable,' says Reddin. 'It was a classic corporate mistake. The organisation hadn't realised the challenges that were in place. The IP that was generated through that five-, six-year period was incredible stuff. And it just walked out of the door.'

CHAPTER 44

TREVOR, ONLY 22 CAPS

When we drive away from Trevor Woodman's house, Lawrence sucks in the air between his teeth and says, as if slightly stunned: 'Wow! That was really something. I wasn't expecting that!'

Woodman lives in a Cotswold village, a reasonable commute from Gloucester, where he is on the coaching staff. His is another family home where you wouldn't know that there is a World Cup winner living there. The trophy cabinet is non-existent, though that may be because it still hurts him that he feels robbed of the opportunity to fill one with more.

The reason is apparent from the moment Lawrence asks him how many caps he won. His answer is 'Only 22.' He mentions this a few times, the word 'only' always appended. He is genuinely delighted to see Lawrence and they quickly rewind to the good times, to Sydney 2003, to the final and to their victory party afterwards.

'We were in the Cargo bar,' Woodman recalls with a throaty

laugh. 'I had it on my camera: you, Loll, were up on stage, on the drums. Then there was some bloke, quite a nice bloke, a ginger-headed bloke called Harry.'

'That would be Prince Harry.'

'Cracking guy, wasn't he?' says Woodman. 'Yeah. He was up there as well, playing the drums too.'

At that point in his career, anyone would have thought that there would be more of these good times for Woodman. He was 27 years old, but due to the stiffness of the competition and still being relatively young, he had gone to the World Cup with only ten caps and, of those, he'd had only three starts. He also had a bad injury record; his career was supposed to get a kick-start on the South Africa tour in 2000, but his tour only lasted three days and he then spent six months recovering from a bulging disc. So, at that World Cup, he was early in his career, one of the best modern-day ball-handling props in the world and just coming into his prime. And yet, as he says, he won 'only 22 caps'. Only seven months after that glorious Sydney night, he would play for England for the last time.

His last game for England was against the All Blacks on that doomed 2004 tour. Woodman then came back, switched clubs from Gloucester to Sale and played six games before injury struck again. His last game for Sale was in October 2004; that was the end.

The final, career-ending injury was to the lower back and, as always, he raged against it, refusing to accept what it was telling him. In Gloucester, he would consult Mike Teague, a British and Irish Lion and an icon of the club 15 years ahead of him. 'I remember sitting there with Teaguey because I trained a lot with him; he was a great mentor for me. It was 2004 going into 2005 and there was a Lions tour coming. The next step is a Lions tour, isn't it? You want to get on the Lions tour because that's where you can prove yourself and show you're the best in Europe. So I said, "I want the same jersey you've got." He said, "But I want the medal you got," and then he said, "You can't have everything in life" – because he lost a World Cup final in 1991 against Australia and that haunts him still to this day.'

Yet Teague could produce no miracle for his friend. For over half a year, Woodman remained hopeful of another return but by the time the Lions tour came round, he was at his absolute worst: 'Literally, after 15 minutes of walking, I was just in constant pain. I watched the whole of the Tour de France that year, just lying there after trying to go for a walk, just lying there on the floor watching it because I was just in that much pain.' The following month, he declared: that's it, rugby career officially over.

In those days, there wasn't anyone to catch you when you fell. There wasn't really much awareness that retired rugby players might need catching. There certainly wasn't advice or a structure to help you into a post-playing career and Woodman is quite upfront about the extent to which he felt buffeted, often lost and inadequate.

'The one thing I was very comfortable being or doing was being on a rugby field. All the other bits that go with being an international rugby player – the dinners, whatever, some people love that side of it – but the one place I was completely comfortable was on the field. You know that's where you can excel and that's where you feel that that's almost who you are. So when you can't do that, it does hit you mentally. Everything that you are good at is gone. And, of course, you're going to dark places because it's not just a matter of what you're doing next, it's what's been taken away. That's why I always say "only 22" because in my head I wanted more. Your mind's still going, "I can do this," but your body's gone. At the same time, you're fighting insurance companies [for an early career-ending claim]; they are great at taking your money and crap at giving anything back. So, you've got that all in the background. And you don't know what you can do physically. So how can I know what I am going to go and do next?

'I remember going to watch my first game at Gloucester. I'd moved back down from Sale because I had my house here, went to the first game and absolutely wrote myself off drunk. You're seeing the shirt, you're seeing Gloucester winning, you're seeing the fun the players are having on the field. I just wrote myself off. I remember a few years later, James Forrester, [a great young England player who also had an early career-ending injury], he said to me: "I'm going to go down to watch Gloucester play this afternoon, do you want to come?" I said: "Bud, is that your first game since you retired?" He went, "Yeah." I said, "Mate, I'll leave you to it. But just give me a ring later tonight. Let me know you're OK." Later, when I asked: "How did you get on?" He went: "Oh, I absolutely ruined myself." I said, "It's painful, isn't it?" And it is – when you're so good at something and you then no longer can do it, it can be difficult.'

For Woodman, the lack of direction eventually became too much and he decided to escape as far as possible. 'I was fed up with people asking: "What are you doing now? What are you doing now?" When you don't have an answer, you then pile that pressure on yourself as well. Because you're going: well, I should be having an answer to this. But I didn't. And finally, I'm just like: "Right, I'll go to Australia." I didn't come back for three and a half years.'

For Lawrence, Woodman's is a story of its time: the young professional game putting athletes' bodies through unprecedented physical stress without knowing where the limits lay, with the front-rowers the worst off, regularly over-training on scrummaging machines with huge forces going through backs and necks. Lawrence, being Lawrence, tries to empathise; he starts telling Woodman about his own nine-month struggle with an ACL injury – 'I was thinking about whether I'll ever play again' – but he quickly reins it in. His travails just don't compare and he concedes: 'Whoever wrote my script was definitely looking after me.'

Woodman knows Lawrence is right; yes, he was a victim of his time. As a modern scrum coach, he would never put players through the physical over-stressing to which he himself was subjected. But, even stuck on 'only 22', he finds no target for blame. 'You didn't know any different back then, did you?' he says. 'I know you can look back and you could say, "If only we had what the players today have now." But no one knew. The strength and conditioning guys didn't really know what they were doing.'

Lawrence: 'You could be feeling sorry for yourself.'

Woodman: 'I could. Or I could go: "Actually, we were better off than the Mike Teague era."'

Lawrence: 'They didn't have a clue what they were doing either. But they didn't train full-time.'

Woodman: 'Yeah. But they were still asked to do the same things probably and they weren't getting paid to do it. So at least we were getting paid to do something we would've done seven years before for nothing.'

At least Australia worked for him. He found an anonymity there that he welcomed and that gave him a chance to reassess.

He then found his way into coaching and discovered that there was something else that he was good at.

One of his first coaching jobs was with Sydney University, who would always invite in alumni before each game to present the matchday jerseys. One occasion, they had John Howard, the recently retired prime minister, who had presented the trophy at the 2003 World Cup final. 'I just went over to him,' says Woodman, 'and I said: "The last time you and I met, you had to put a medal over my head." He had no idea who I was.'

* * *

There is one episode in Woodman's story that still preys on minds. His first game in the starting England XV was in the 2002 autumn, against the All Blacks. Phil Keith-Roach, the scrum guru, recalls it like it was yesterday: 'He played the most fantastic game, in open field and in the scrum. He completely out-scrummaged Kees Meeuws [the tighthead opposite him]. Suddenly he was everyone's No. 1.'

What Woodman remembers, specifically, was only two days later being back on the scrummaging machine at Pennyhill. 'We hit the machine,' he says, 'and "Bang", it's like someone just stabbed me in the back. I then waited three weeks for surgery, couldn't lift up my hand, lost all strength and control of that hand. So they just sliced the disc off. You let it repair. And then I came back for the end of the Six Nations.'

'You were quick,' says Lawrence.

'Well, it had to be quick, didn't it? You are running out of time, aren't you?' says Woodman, in reference to the selection battle and the World Cup on the horizon. 'Self-preservation is not something that you are really thinking about. It's: I just want to do everything I can do because I want to get out at

Twickenham and play for my country. So you don't really think about what you're doing and what the risks are.'

When we speak to Phil Keith-Roach, he brings all this up himself unprompted. Twenty years on and he still has that scrummaging training session in his head. 'To this day I regret it,' he says. 'Maybe it was a day too soon.'

He also feels a burden because of what Woodman said in a book, published nine years ago. The book, *Behind the Rose*, is an aural history of the England rugby team. In it, Woodman says of that single scrummaging session: 'If health and safety actually looked in, they would have stopped it.' It was this that weighed long and heavy on Keith-Roach's mind.

The respect and bond between the England front-rowers and Keith-Roach remains deep, right to this day. Woodman makes this clear. And as he says: he never meant to point the finger, and certainly not at Keith-Roach.

'Over time,' he says, 'we've learned that you do not play on Saturday and then do scrummage training on a Monday. You just don't. When I'm coaching, I don't really use scrummaging machines much any more. But for me – was that session a day too early? Would I have done the injury the following day? You don't know. I don't blame anyone. And I have called Roachie; I hated it that I had affected him like that. I told him: "It's certainly not on you." And anyway, it wasn't the injury that retired me.'

*   *   *

We drive away from Woodman's home with his story stuck in our heads, asking ourselves questions that can never be answered about what it took to play in that England team and the resulting collateral damage.

'The system was not designed to look after players,'

says Lawrence. 'It's still not really now. We were playing huge amounts of rugby. And unless someone says, "Stop," you just carry on going.'

The point about Woodman, though, was he never wanted to stop. 'Only 22,' were his words. 'Fifty was the benchmark, wasn't it? God, I wish I'd got 50 caps. I wish I'd kept doing it.'

And what represents satisfaction? What is enough? What is a good career? Lawrence rewinds to our conversation with Julian White: 'It feels like Trevor's career is not defined by the World Cup but by the fact that he didn't win 51 caps like Julian White. So Julian White wanted to be Trevor Woodman and Trevor Woodman wanted to be Julian White.'

Lawrence then pauses before arriving at a typically Lawrence conclusion: 'They should both be so proud of what they achieved. They both won the World Cup.'

CHAPTER 45

SEARCHING FOR ANOTHER SUMMIT

The further time moved on beyond 2003, the more the squad and its culture moved on too. Winning in 2003 was always going to affect what happened next, but no one could foresee how it would affect motivation and desire, how it would leave players with broken bodies, how the special formula in that 2003 World Cup squad could not just be topped up with fresh new personnel. When you've reached the pinnacle once, it's a very different process trying to do it again; for a start, you have a frame of comparison, you know how it felt to be the best in the world and you are painfully aware when that isn't where you are any more.

Thirteen of the 2003 World Cup squad would make it to the next World Cup in France four years later, where England's campaign started with an unconvincing 28-10 win over the United States followed by a 36-0 hammering by South Africa. Ben Kay described that first fortnight in France as 'horrific' and 'the lowest part of my whole career'. But he was disillusioned long before they had even got to France. Part of their training camp, before that World Cup, was held in Bath and Kay says: 'I nearly didn't come back one week. We'd just had our first baby. I was away loads. And I just hated the environment. Cozza [Martin Corry] and I were driving away one week, and I said: "I'm not sure I'm coming back on Monday."'

Lawrence was back in the fold again by 2007; his international retirement had lasted a year. 'But at no point did I find a squad or an environment that was even close to what we had in that room in 2003,' he says. 'And you can look back and reflect and go, "Well, is that my fault? Is that the RFU's fault? Whose fault is it?" And the reality is it's probably a mixture of everything really.'

Different players have a different take on where those years of drift between World Cups took them.

This is Mike Tindall: 'Hand on heart, the environment at England would never be as good again. I just think of '03: perfect coaches, perfect players, perfect set-up, perfect timing. Obviously, my role within England changed. In '03, I was a young kid and I was just flying, sitting in people's slipstreams for the majority of it, trying to get better, but following some of the greats of England rugby around the field and learning from them. And then, as you go on, with some guys having left, you move further to the top so you are sort of trying to replace what you've lost. But then, you look down and... Well, when you looked up at Loll, when you looked up at Johnno, they'd do anything to win – and so then I'd do anything to win. I learned off them. But then, as you look down, you'd sometimes go, "I don't think he'd do anything to win."'

'But what also made it hard as well for me, having played

with Will [Greenwood], was then having to find a new centre partnership. There was a load of time where the centres were the biggest problems, changing constantly. And then nothing you could ever do was right. That was a shit time, mainly because, yes, you're not winning, but it just always seemed to me that centres were the problem.'

This is Dan Luger, who returned from the World Cup and moved straight to play for Perpignan in France: 'I'd always wanted to go to France. I'd nearly gone to France once before. Then, the year before the World Cup, I decided I'd go after it, whatever happens. That was always my kind of goal. Then, in that summer of 2004, there was that tour to New Zealand and Australia and Clive called me and said, "Do you want to come? I'd like you to come." And I was like: "I'm in the French championships semi-final. We're probably going to be in the final. So, no. I'm going to take the summer off." And I think that was it. I was still only 29. I mean, it would've been nice to play for England again, and I'd loved my time, but my body wasn't up to it any more.'

This is Iain Balshaw: 'I got a lot of injuries after '03. Quite a lot of us did. When you put your bodies through that level of physical and mental intensity, something's going to give. But then I tried to rush back, because I wanted to keep getting into the England team and that then just caused more injuries. And I probably didn't look after myself as I should have done. I was 23 at the time and unless you win it a second time, you've already hit the pinnacle of life in rugby, really. If I'd been 33, it would've been a bit different. But there was a period where, for a couple of years, you become a little bit complacent. So the next two, three years was a difficult time. You just want to replicate what we'd done before, don't you? You want to be involved in the next thing, go to the next World Cup final. You've tasted what it's like to smash teams by 40 points, 50 points, go down to the southern hemisphere and beat them in their own backyard, and go to the World Cup, have a huge amount of England supporters cheering you on. You want to emulate that. That's all I was thinking about. All I wanted to do was get in the England team and be part of the next World Cup-winning squad. You're thinking about the result rather than: right, how the hell are we going to get there? You're already thinking about experiencing the highs, but to do so, you've got four years to prepare. And I definitely didn't think of it like that. I thought I could just turn up: well, I've done it once, let's crack on and do it again. But it takes shitloads of hard work and dedication to get back to the physical peak that we were on. And there was a mental side of it as well.'

Lawrence: 'When did you leave Bath, Balsh?'

Balshaw: 'I moved to Leeds in 2004.'

Lawrence: 'Did you lose a card game, or what?'

Balshaw: 'Basically!'

What Balshaw means is that he felt that Bath messed him around with his contract negotiations, so in a 'knee-jerk reaction', he left and accepted an offer from Leeds. 'Was it a good idea? I don't think it was. Look, I did enjoy my time at Leeds. But rugby-wise, was it the right idea? Probably not.'

When the 2007 World Cup came round, he didn't make the squad. And he doesn't even suggest that he was hard done by or that the selectors made a duff decision; in fact, due to form and his injury record, he says it was the right one. 'Did I want to go to the next World Cup, get to the final and potentially win it? Fuck, yes, of course. But that's just the way life is, isn't it? I can't dwell on it too much. Yes, I do regret not being more professional at the time, but it's not something I lie awake at night pondering.'

This is Mark Regan: 'Unfortunately, I made a few mistakes upsetting certain coaches, saying the wrong things, and not being politically correct.'

What he means is that in 2004, he won the starting No. 2 shirt outright off Steve Thompson. However, when Andy Robinson took over as head coach from Clive Woodward, he told him that he was not starting any more and wasn't even on the bench – and Regan didn't take that very well. 'I said some really disgusting words to him, to some effect that you can imagine, Lawrence. And I also said, "Stuff it," and "I want to be on the next flight home."'

So Regan didn't play for England again until Brian Ashton took over from Robinson as head coach in 2007. 'Brian rang me and said, "Right, you're playing well enough. Do you fancy playing for England again?" I said, "Does a one-legged swan swim in circles, Brian?" And he said, "OK then, I'll see you Monday." So that was it. Back in the team. Played the World Cup final later that year.'

This is interesting. While some of the 2003 team struggled to maintain their level through to 2007, there was a significant element of 'the drift' who did. It wasn't just Regan who started that final, but Simon Shaw and Andy Gomarsall plus Joe Worsley, who was on the bench, plus Martin Corry, who didn't get on the pitch in the 2003 final but started in 2007. This was no coincidence, at least not according to Shaw: 'It was good to be able to prove something to the world in 2007, who judged us to be second to other players in 2003. Not that I felt that I needed proof myself, but it does go back to 2003 and that element of unfinished business.'

After that 2007 World Cup, Balshaw did get back into the England team. He played full-back throughout the 2008 Six Nations, but that summer, even though he was still only 30, he made the decision to move to France. And, he says, he did so knowing that that would probably bring an end to his international career: 'When I left the UK, I was sick of it, sick of the Premiership, really, the rugby was getting a bit stale and boring and it felt that there was a lot of negativity around it. It was a time when, from my side, I felt lots of criticism. Every rugby player is trying to do their best on the field, right? You're not trying to make mistakes; you're not trying to make a cock-up. But all I felt was that either I was being criticised by club coaches or the press were coming down on you. Just negative press. You eventually go, "I've been here for a while now. My England chances are probably limited. Why don't you have a crack somewhere else?" So I joined Biarritz, who were one of the top teams in Europe, and had been for quite some time. I went from very professional club rugby in England to Biarritz, where nine of the French international players at the club were tabbing and having espressos at seven o'clock in the morning. It was a bit of an eye-opener. And when I arrived, the first thing that Serge Blanco, the club president, said to me was: "Look, we don't mind if you make mistakes. You've been brought here to run with the ball, to go rogue." I was like, "Holy shit!" But that's all you needed, just confidence, backing. I think I then played some of the best rugby of my career.'

CHAPTER 46

ROYAL WEDDING

When we talk to Iain Balshaw, there is one subject that Lawrence Dallaglio is desperate to get into. 'Balsh,' he says, 'please tell us about Mike Tindall's wedding.'

Balshaw was always a breezy spirit, never keen to take himself too seriously. He doesn't mind telling a story against himself – and so he does.

He and Tindall were both best man at each other's weddings. They go back together to their teens when they played county rugby against each other, Tindall for Yorkshire, Balshaw for Lancashire. At under-16s level, they were united in the same England team and then graduated to a celebrated England under-18s team, who had a certain Jonny Wilkinson playing inside centre and whose achievements culminated in an unbeaten tour of Australia.

After that tour, Balshaw and Tindall both joined Bath as new recruits in the club academy. They shared a flat with another of that England under-18s team, the hooker Lee Mears,

251

who would go on to win 42 caps for England and one for the British and Irish Lions. But Mears moved out of their flat after a few weeks, according to Tindall, 'because Balsh's missus worked in a bar in town and she gave us free beer, so we went out pretty much every night'. Tindall and Balshaw remained housemates for four years and, says Tindall, 'We stayed best mates after that.'

As for being best man, Tindall's wedding wasn't an everyday wedding. It was a royal wedding. So there must have been some pressure on the best man's speech.

'Well, there was,' says Lawrence, 'after you turned up from Biarritz, looking like the elephant man.'

Balshaw: 'Yes. That's the accident on the scooter. I'd like to call it a motorbike, but it was actually a 50cc scooter.'

The crash he was in occurred on his way back home from a Biarritz home game.

Lawrence: 'You might have been slightly over-refreshed, but that's all par for the course in France. Isn't it?'

Maybe. But he was fortunate that he didn't turn up to the wedding with any limbs in plaster.

Balshaw: 'Well, I didn't have anything broken, because I was so relaxed when I fell! Yeah, I had 20-odd stitches in my face, and my face was all swollen. Not ideal.'

And how was that received by the royal family?

Balshaw: 'Prince Philip sort of capped it when he called me "the moron who fell off his motorcycle".'

CHAPTER 47

JOHNNO BACK IN CHARGE

In the years of struggle and disappointment that followed 2003, one of the most undignified episodes was the fate that befell Martin Johnson. Like most supporters of the England team, Lawrence has become long-suffering in his disappointment, but what happened to Johnson just makes him plain angry.

We are on the motorway back down to London from seeing Johnson in Leicester when Lawrence launches into one of his monologues. 'It is baffling how it was allowed to happen,' is his way into it. 'Classic RFU... Why would you invest all that time in Johnno and then sack it off? And then make the relationship so bad that he wants nothing to do with the game any more... I find that really tragic.' And so on.

Johnson's own take on it is comparatively philosophical and unflustered. He actually seems a little uncomfortable with the fact that anyone should still be talking about him and his second coming as England's supposed saviour. He certainly doesn't welcome any pity. He'd just rather that this unfortunate piece of England rugby history remained filed away, gathering dust. But it doesn't. Twelve years on, it still provokes a reaction. Especially if you're Johnson's mate; particularly if you're an emotional human being like Lawrence. But the same probably goes for pretty much anyone with England rugby at their heart too.

The short history is this: after Clive Woodward, Andy Robinson was given the top job; when that didn't work, Brian Ashton was given the top job; and when that wasn't perceived to be a success, even though England reached a World Cup final under him, the smart people at the RFU scratched their heads and, instead of finding another highly qualified, experienced coach to take over, they decided instead to offer the job to someone who actually had zero coaching experience. This was Johnson. That is apparently what comes with being an intelligent World Cup-winning captain who commands soaring levels of respect: it is decided that because you have won the World Cup as a player, you can now do it with a tracksuit on too.

Lawrence: 'I did say to him: "What do you think?" He said: "I think I'm going to take it." I said: "Have you done any coaching? Maybe you should go and coach your son's or your daughter's team first." But I did feel for him a bit because if I was offered the job, I'd have probably accepted it as well – it's such a hard job to turn down because of the natural pull and your love affair with England rugby.'

Some other old teammates, like Neil Back, had already got stuck into their coaching careers and had been learning the trade the traditional way – by actually doing coaching. 'When he phoned me,' says Back, 'and asked: "Should I take the job?"

I said: "You're never gonna get the opportunity again. Go for it." But also: "You've not had any management experience in work or a club. What you need is a figure with experience that you can sit on and learn from to do that job.'"

But that is exactly what Johnson didn't get.

When you ask Johnson about his three years as England manager, he challenges the perception that it was a serial disaster: 'We won the Six Nations in 2011. We beat Australia away in 2010. We brought in a lot of the guys who went on to have successful careers.'

It was the 2011 World Cup that was his downfall. 'What happened in 2011 was more off the field than actually on the field. We got beaten in a quarter-final by the team [France] that possibly could have gone on to win the World Cup. Could we have beaten them? Yeah, we could. Did we get things wrong at times? Of course we did. Would we have possibly been better four years later? Yeah. But, in the home World Cup four years later, England didn't even qualify through the group.'

A lot had changed in the eight years since Johnson lifted the World Cup. Commercial rewards for players had risen, as had their sense of their own value. Probably the most significant change of all – at least for his story – was that mobile phones now had cameras; this played a massive part in England's downfall. What used to stay on tour was now shared on social media, particularly given that Tindall was now a member of the royal family, and England went from being a rugby team to a frat house soap opera.

The infamous episode that dragged them down was when a few of the players were drunk at a bar in Queenstown that was staging a dwarf-throwing contest. The pictures of Tindall certainly weren't great and the news media revelled in it.

Johnson attempted to dismiss it all with a one-liner – 'Rugby player drinks beer, shocker' – but he couldn't kill it off.

Tindall concedes that 'yes, it was stupid on my behalf, having got married three months earlier into the royal family.' He also says that 'I'm a product of my past environments that I've been in and what I've done at other World Cups,' which is to say that the odd night out in 2011 was not significantly different to 2003 apart from the presence of camera phones.

The world changes, attitudes change; clearly the tapestry of personalities in the squad had changed. Thus Lawrence asks rhetorically: 'Was it naive of Johnno to think: you go away with a group of players in 2011 and expect it to be the same as eight years previously?'

Tindall sketches a fascinating portrait of Johnson as the team manager: 'There were all the young kids in the squad looking up at this guy going, "Fuck, he's Martin Johnson." But Johnno just didn't really open up, as Johnno doesn't. He didn't really let people in, so no one really got to know him. You got sort of bits of it because in training he'd always get a tackle pad and he'd get in the middle of a mauling session. But then he just wouldn't share any of his character. But by the time that we went to New Zealand for the World Cup, I just really thought we were just starting to get him; Johnno was really settling into the role and he was, I mean, he was just growing and getting better at it. And then he got shafted.'

In other words, a man who was completely inexperienced and new to a job didn't hit the ground running but gradually worked out how to do it. Nevertheless, the fallout from the World Cup was so great that Johnson resigned. There cannot have been anyone in English rugby who didn't feel a little crushed by the World Cup captain's public humiliation.

What happened next? He closed the door on rugby and did not come back out. Quite soon, it seemed that he had done a vanishing act. The perception was that he was licking his wounds. Whenever Leicester were looking for a new coach, the speculation inevitably involved his name yet he remained silent. At some point it became apparent that he was out on the roads cycling a lot. Then, in 2018, when he joined the BBC's punditry team for the Six Nations, it was strange because there he was again and he looked and sounded the same.

How does Johnson make a living today? He is involved with a few businesses, mainly property. You wouldn't be the tenant not paying his rent. His name and his record still command so much respect that he also still gets brand ambassador gigs. Plus, there's the TV work.

And he seems genuinely extremely content. 'People say: "Oh, you've disappeared."' He says, 'I've not disappeared. I did a job for three years and then I didn't. No, I don't have a huge social media presence or media presence, but come train with me on a Sunday morning with my kids' team. Just because I'm not in the professional game doesn't mean I've disappeared from the game. I did the England job, then got chucked out of the England job. It wasn't great. It wasn't great for the game. It wasn't a nice experience, but I didn't fall out of love with the game. You have good things happen to you, you have not so good things happen to you. I've had loads of incredibly good things happen to me in the game and very few bad things happen to me in the game. You get into it because you enjoy playing it. Managing it or coaching – it's a different thing. My choices after doing the job were: to get back in or not to. And I decided no, I don't want it. You can't be half in, half out. You've got to be fully enough in. Do I want to be fully in? No, I don't.'

And that is why Lawrence is pounding the steering wheel en route home: 'Even now, if he was sitting above the England coach as an external selector, he would still be adding value. The reality is that when you make an appointment, you've got to look at it and ask: does that go far enough? We've appointed one of the best rugby players England and the world has ever had, but a player who has never coached at any level. So should we not support him with an infrastructure that allows him to flourish? I don't know any top coaching job in the world where you get it on the basis that you've never done any coaching before. I can't imagine the All Blacks or the Springboks ever appointing anyone without doing a bit of due diligence, like asking: have you ever actually coached before? I was bewildered. When you then allow that person to jump in the deep end and then watch them drown without giving them any support whatsoever and then no one accepts any responsibility for the appointment in the first place – it's completely baffling. I'm sure that if Johnno had his time again, maybe he'd have made some different decisions. But having invested in him, to then just cut him loose?! Why would you invest time, effort and money into someone like that and then bin it? It's a waste of time, effort and energy and a waste of one of the greatest rugby men we've ever had.'

CHAPTER 48

MOODY'S LAST STAND

The 2011 World Cup quarter-final was the end of the end; it was the last time that any of the 2003 world champions would wear the England shirt again. That defeat by France had Wilkinson at No. 10 for the last time, likewise Steve Thompson at hooker and Simon Shaw coming off the bench. Mike Tindall had already been dropped from the team. Lewis Moody was its captain that day, also for the last time, and was in the process of making an exit from the game that would prove painfully sad.

As the captain of a team whose World Cup failures were both chaotic and very public, he knew he had to shoulder some responsibility. 'That's what you have to do as a skipper and a manager, right?' he says. 'So that fell on me and Johnno. When you accept that role as captain, you accept all the shit that comes with it as well. Sport's the journey – right? – the highs and the lows, and I feel privileged that I got a chance or that Johnno asked me to be captain. As a leader you think you're doing all you can to get it right, you think you're saying the right things. And when that's not working, you have to be accountable and I was. But that's why I say I don't think I was a particularly good captain. I clearly wasn't the right person for that team at that time. But it's frustrating and, yeah, it was a tough time and it's more challenging when you feel your family are coming under the cosh as well. You have to develop rhino-thick skin and you can either hide away or you can confront it.'

Moody's natural response was to find an outlet and every rugby player's natural outlet is to play rugby again. Prove yourself again. 'I just wanted to go out and perform. I'd retired from internationals and I wanted to spend a couple of years playing club rugby and just enjoying it. I was captain of Bath. Ultimately I wanted to prove to myself and everyone else that I was still a decent player and a decent captain.'

His second game back after the World Cup was in the Premiership against Worcester Warriors, away at Sixways. He describes it as 'probably my worst game ever': 'I got knocked out twice, tried to stay on, played even worse and, after about 35 minutes, fucked up my shoulder. Stephen Donald was our fly-half and I remember him walking over, going, "Mate, are you going to play in the second half?" I was like, "Of course I'm going to fucking play in the second half." And it just went progressively worse. The final string to my body capitulating was a tap tackle. I tried to tap tackle the Worcester full-back, completely missed it and landed awkwardly on my other shoulder. That was it, I was done.'

Indeed he was. The shoulder required surgery; three months later, he announced his retirement. 'So that Worcester game was my last ever game of rugby.'

Yet the greatest injury he suffered that day was not his

shoulder or the concussions. It was what was said on the TV commentary.

Moody: 'It was Austin [Healey] that said it. He talked about me being driven by money. Now, for me, playing the game as I think I've tried to – I was all about the team. I loved it. I loved doing what I could to support the team. That didn't mean there's not a small part of you that plays the game because we're professionals earning money, but I was never driven by that. I know Austin well, I get on with Austin, and it was probably something he just said as a flippant statement that he thinks nothing about. But at the time it fucking cut me deep. And I just remember being in my room upstairs at home feeling like the world's against you, feeling like everyone knows, that everyone thinks you're a dickhead, that everyone thinks you're driven by money. I felt like everything I'd played the game for was being undermined. It was like my whole character was being called into question.'

After 71 England caps, 34 games for Bath and 223 for Leicester Tigers, this was Moody's exit from the game: upstairs at home in tears. 'I was in tears because I felt I had no control over what was happening,' he says. 'And, in my whole career, it was the only time that I ever had tears. That was how my career ended.'

CHAPTER 49

HIDDEN TRUTHS

Sometimes on this journey, there are moments that really stop you in your tracks, when you realise how much was going on that you couldn't possibly guess at. And it is only with the safety of hindsight and retirement and a slightly more forgiving world that old teammates can finally open up about it.

Here is Kyran Bracken.

Bracken: 'I read somewhere if you get eight hours' sleep, that's perfect peak performance for a sportsman. So, then I'd go to bed and try and sleep and I couldn't. But in reality, I was suffering from anxiety. And then I got a bit addicted to sleeping tablets to try and sleep. That's not good. Sometimes I'd have about four hours' sleep before a Test match. In 2001, I was feeling quite sick, went to the doctor and they checked me and said I had a viral stomach infection. So I had treatment for that. But I still felt sick, really sick. Plus, I was having this anxiety and having palpitations. And I couldn't stop thinking about going to the toilet. I felt I needed the toilet because at night I'd want the last drop out – so then I could sleep. And then I was going to the toilet 40/50 times in the night. Then it started taking over during the day too. Needing the toilet – it was on my mind all the time, and I'm trying to prepare for a game and play South Africa or whoever. With OCD, a thought comes into your head and you try and nullify it. It's called Pure O [purely obsessional], which is much harder to treat. No one else knew, of course. I was playing great rugby as well. I was going through all this and scoring tries, captaining Saracens. It was just a really weird time; stressful. OCD is horrific. I was in quite a bad way really. At the time, I'd have been mortified if someone had found out: they're going to think I'm weak.'

When you ask him what might have caused it, he says that, of course, you'll never really know, but he does suggest that being in a selection dogfight for the No. 9 jersey for an entire decade can't have helped.

Bracken: 'It was a culmination of everything and probably built up over a period of time. I don't know if it was anything to do with the amount of concussions I had. Anxiety, depression are related. But also, my career was a proper bumper ride: I had 51 caps, I started 38 times and I came on for the rest and there were periods when I wasn't selected at all. I don't know if that was related to the OCD.'

Lawrence: 'You didn't talk to any teammates about all this?'

Bracken: 'No, too embarrassed. What: "I'm having these palpitations and I've got anxiety?" You know, man up.'

Lawrence: 'It wouldn't have been like that. We were all quite sensitive people.'

Bracken: 'Not at that time, not 2001–03. No chance. It was my dirty little secret. You just think: you're a man. You're never going to admit a mental weakness. It took about ten years to do that.'

Lawrence: 'We all had different things going on. Everyone has demons. Everyone has doubt. I used to go back to my room, asking myself all these questions. Then as soon as you walk out of the room, you put on your full-on armour again.'

Bracken: 'Well, I imagined that every other player was like a Trojan and would never have a problem.'

His road to recovery started when he went to Simon Kemp, the England team doctor, who immediately identified what he was dealing with.

Bracken: 'The biggest achievement in my career has been recovering from that, not winning a World Cup. Recovering from all that was a much bigger battle: getting the right drugs, getting the right therapist, working out what was going on. It's not that you are cured and then suddenly never have it again. It's keeping on top of it. I'm still on tablets for the anxiety, have been for years. I've tried to come off the tablets, but every time I come off them, it's come back. So, I'll be on them for life.'

Which begs the question: was it all worth it?

Bracken: 'That's a really good question. Would I do it all again? Rugby has given me too much to say I wouldn't. And we'll never know if it was the rugby that gave me the anxiety – we'll just never know. The answer is: in the middle of my worst point, not in a million years. If you asked me when I was struggling, I would just say: "Let me stack shelves rather than go through this." But now I'm out of it, I would say the opposite.'

But when you were right in the worst of it, couldn't you have just walked away?

Bracken: 'That's very hard to say. It's your career, your living. So, in a way you can't.'

* * *

When Mark Regan announces that he is deaf, Lawrence thinks that he is joking. Regan is always joking.

'You used to have a crack at absolutely everyone,' Lawrence says.

'Yes,' says Regan. 'But I think that was just part of my defence mechanism, Lawrence. No one knew that I was severely deaf at the time. It's because I had measles as a kid.'

'OK,' Lawrence is now listening intently.

'At two years of age.'

'And how much could you hear?'

'Eighty. That is 80 per cent gone. I was left with 20 per cent. Yes, I'm severely deaf. Not profoundly deaf.' He then twists his head, proudly revealing his hearing aids.

Lawrence says: 'I had no idea.'

Regan then explains his problem with lineout calls. As the hooker, it was essential that he could hear the lineout calls. 'I can't say: "Sorry, missed that." I can't ask, "What did you say?" Not with 100,000 people in the crowd, Lawrence.' That, he says, is why he'd so often run to the huddle to check the call.

Like Bracken, he never told anyone.

'Why would I tell anyone? I didn't tell anyone. Only my parents knew. Even when I was at school, the school didn't know; they just put me in the back of the class. I used to go to a comprehensive school; I got no help at all. Mum and Dad pulled me out of that, put me through a private school. But they did exactly the same – they still put me in the back of the class.'

Lawrence: 'And does this explain why you speak so loudly?'

Regan: 'Laugh loudly, speak loudly. Yeah, definitely, Lawrence. It's because I can't hear myself speak.'

Lawrence: 'So you would never even have told Phil Keith-Roach, or Simon Hardy, the lineout coach, about this?'

Regan: 'No one. Didn't trust anyone.'

Lawrence: 'Because it was a danger that they thought...'

Regan: '... yes, Lawrence, exactly.'

His fear was completely understandable: in a world where there is relentless competition for places, why lodge in anyone's mind a reason not to pick him, the idea that he might mess up the lineout because he had a disability.

* * *

For Lawrence, this is all both extraordinary and yet somehow entirely understandable. He'd known Regan since they were both playing age-grade representative rugby aged 16. He remembers Bracken from the trials for England under-18s, the ones where he didn't get selected: 'I was crying my eyes out on my own at the bus stop. And Kyran pulled over at the side of the road and said, "Look, just for what it's worth, I think you're a brilliant player. You should have been picked; don't be so upset." I've never forgotten that.'

So, by 2003, he'd known them both for well over a decade yet had no inkling of what they were masking. At the same time, even though no one actually discussed it, he knew what was required to be accepted in that England squad, the behaviours that were demanded and that were probably no different to any other professional rugby team. Rugby was an environment where anxiety or deafness might have been considered weaknesses. Twenty years on, it probably hasn't changed an awful lot.

Lawrence: 'Am I surprised that one or two of those individuals wouldn't have talked about it? No, not really because they probably felt it wouldn't have been understood – which I don't think is true. And so they just didn't want to expose themselves, because you're in a very alpha environment. We were in quite a macho world then. It's about not showing any weakness, isn't it really? Whether it's with your own teammates or your opponents, your perception is that if you show any vulnerability, it could be exploited and exposed. Yet at the same time, every player, every person I've met in rugby is no different. What I mean is that there's going to be external factors for everyone that might be impacting on your professional career; there's loads of things that we don't know about. It's only human to have vulnerabilities and challenges.

'I'm fascinated by these conversations. It's been very, very, very interesting, because we've spoken to nearly everyone and they have, all in different ways, expressed how challenging that time was for all of them.'

CHAPTER 50

AFTER THE ROAR

In September 2022, Brian O'Driscoll fronted a documentary on BT Sport entitled *After the Roar*. The taster clip hinted at some deep soul-bearing from him. 'When the crowd stops roaring,' he intones, 'the silence can be deafening.' Trevor Woodman watched it and he knew exactly what O'Driscoll meant. When you've stopped being a rugby player, who, actually, are you?

O'Driscoll calls it 'the rediscovery of yourself'. In the documentary, Woodman was particularly struck by the interview with AP McCoy, the jockey, where McCoy declares that sportspeople die twice. 'It's like you live one life,' Woodman says, 'and luckily, I achieved the pinnacle. But it's almost like you've reached your Everest and then you've got the second part of your life. When you are so comfortable being a player, being on the field is where you are at your most confident, that's where you know you can really shine. But when that's all done and dusted and finished, what's next?

What's going to replicate that feeling of what you achieved as a player in your twenties? How are you going to get that again? You probably never will.'

No doubt every member of the squad has had to deal with this identity crisis in some shape or form. Woodman says he reckons 'everyone has dark moments'.

'When I finished,' says Phil Vickery, 'I struggled like everyone does. It's not just not knowing what you're doing, it's not being in that environment. That's the hard thing. It's not the fame and certainly not the rugby, it's the people and the relationships and the guys that you've done things with.' Vickery refers, then, to the ups and downs of mental health he says he has experienced too. 'I think we all have, if we are honest with ourselves. I don't know if it's all down to rugby. Forget the fact that we are hugely passionate people, which I don't think helps sometimes. But you go lights on to lights off; I'm sure that the extremes that we've lived haven't helped.'

Lawrence nods like he knows exactly what Vickery is talking about. 'No one gives you any manual about how to behave or how to decompress from being a professional rugby player,' he says. 'It's not until you take a couple of years away that you actually start to rediscover the person that you are, that actually existed long before you played rugby. Because to survive at the top level of sport, you've got to be something very different. You've got to have this kind of outer casing of toughness, which takes a bit of desensitising. And then you sort of take a step back and you realise, actually, that I haven't got to be that person. And then it takes a couple of years to realise who that person actually is.'

Yes, the sun can go in on even the brightest of characters in the squad. This is Iain Balshaw, still in Biarritz, reassessing the perception that his new life post-rugby was set to be one long sandy beach: 'It's just like "Shit, what do I do now?" because no one's actually telling me where I need to be, what colour jersey I need to wear every day. Seriously, after 18 years' rugby with that structure around you where you've been basically told what to do, when to do it and what to wear every day, one of the hardest things for me stepping away was that suddenly it's like, "It's all your lifestyle now, crack on." For a two-to-three-year period, that was very, very difficult.'

Then he laughs at himself and explains further. 'Actually, the first six or eight weeks were great. You've got no pre-season, you're basically boozing and partying, doing everything you normally do on the weekend but you're doing it over a two-/three-month period. But then, after that, when all my mates were going back to pre-season, when I called – "Do you fancy a coffee? Do you fancy golf?" – it's like, "Well, we've got training. We've got this, we've got that." That's when loneliness is another problem that comes in. And I'm not sure what it's like in the UK, I hope now it's better, but with the French, you are literally a commodity.'

'No,' says Lawrence. 'No different here.'

To many people, Lawrence would be the last person whose mental health would suffer. At least that is what Woodman says later on a phone call when Lawrence is not on the line. Woodman's point is that Lawrence just seems so together, doesn't he? He explains: 'Someone said to me the other day, very randomly: "Do you think Lawrence is all right?" I said: "What do you mean?" He goes: "I just worry about him." Then I'm thinking: "Worried about Lawrence? From the outside in, he's got everything." I almost laughed because, I mean, what could Lawrence have wrong with him? But then you go: well, you don't know, you don't know what's going on with someone's life. We all put on brave faces, don't we?'

When this is relayed to Lawrence his reaction is instant: 'He thinks I'm not all right? Of course I'm not completely all right. But who is? If you lose your sister at the age of 16, of course you're not all right.'

A little later, Lawrence reflects on all this, this life after the roar: 'Part of the good thing about professional sport is you've always got the next game, but at the same time, one of the real dangers is that it doesn't give you time to stop and analyse beyond the superficial things. It becomes relentless. When you play sport, there's always a purpose to what you're doing and you're pointing in that direction. So, I guess afterwards, it's just about finding purpose, isn't it? I've been retired now for 15 years, and there's been no lack of energy, but I'm still not quite sure, sometimes, which direction to point in. I mean, what's the exam question now? Because the exam question always used to be an easy one, it was: can you win at the weekend? You've got to win. You've got to win. But what's the exam question now?'

* * *

There is probably no member of the '03 squad who pursued the answer to Lawrence's question with more determination than Josh Lewsey. When he was a rugby player, he was simultaneously a soldier. When he retired, he had already studied law and finance and has since worked in investment banking, professional services, was a trained lawyer who worked in finance, then in rugby administration and he is now the Asia-Pacific CEO of a financial consultancy. His mission has been to take himself beyond the identity that being a World Cup winner gave him.

Lewsey: 'Most normal people don't play a Centre Court final, they don't lift trophies and we were used to doing that, doing it every single week of your career when you have a high or a low and it's very addictive. Most careers aren't like that. So, when you finish that, you have to get yourself comfortable with not having quite as high highs and not quite as low lows but people still seek that adrenaline and seek that dopamine. Of course, emotionally your body still craves those moments and the feeling of walking out into a Test match, but if you endlessly try and seek those highs, if you only feel that your best days are behind you, I think you can get yourself on to a sticky wicket.'

He has got to the point where he would rather not be introduced as 'World Cup winner'.

'I don't mind but I'd really prefer not to be as that's not only who I am, and people do definitely pigeonhole you and immediately put barriers around their perception of you and what you're capable of. You don't want it to define you. You have different chapters in your life; you don't want to be defined by just that one.'

Martin Corry gets that completely: 'When I stopped playing, I knew I didn't want to be in rugby. Rugby was the best time ever and I absolutely loved it. But I wanted to have something else. I didn't always want to be "ex-rugby player".'

Lewsey certainly never wields his 2003 credentials in business: 'I've deliberately distanced myself and not associated with it. What works far better is if you are working with CEOs and after a few months, they then find out what you did, back in the past. There's then a far deeper respect. It's then a nice thing.'

The good news is Balshaw cracked the code eventually too.

He works on the sales side of investment management and loves the way that now pieces together around his life in Biarritz.

'My children have all been fully integrated into the French schooling system,' he says. 'We're outdoors probably 70 per cent of the year, we live a couple of kilometres from the beach; you surf, play padel tennis, there's loads. Honestly, the lifestyle's fantastic.'

CHAPTER 51

THE PELOTON

Twenty years on, if there is one place where you will be reassured that Martin Johnson is still kind of captain, it is on the road when rugby players are reunited in a peloton. Johnson used to lead from the front and, on two wheels, he still does.

The subject of cycling with Johnson makes Martin Corry sigh. They still live near enough to each other, but Johnno says that Corry is too busy to ride with him any more. Corry sighs again. He now works as the sales director for the northern Europe arm of Alteryx, a tech company. 'Yeah. This is me now, in the corporate world. I'm working five days a week; I'm doing what normal people do.' Then he pauses and gives it to you straight: 'Truth be told, Johnno's of a level where I need to be going out all the time to keep up with him. He's annoyingly good on a bike. And there's nothing worse than being dropped off the back of a group with Johnno in it. He's a mate and you never want to lose out to your mates.

Plus, he's one of these people who takes pride in breaking people. And I don't want to be in any walk of life giving him that satisfaction!'

What does a World Cup winner do after the roar? One answer, as Johnson and Corry can testify, is: a lot of cycling. Lawrence is a case in point. Every other year, he sets off on a two-wheeled charity ride; in six trips to date, he has clocked up 12,445 kilometres; that's like riding from London to the Falkland Islands. Lots of the 2003 squad ride, even if Martin Corry is often too busy. Even Jason Leonard, not an obvious partner for a road bike, started recently too. Though he did fall off. But Johnson is their yellow jersey.

We are sitting overlooking the beautiful cricket ground at Clifton School in Bristol and discussing this very matter with one of the schoolmasters, the 2003 England lock forward, Danny Grewcock. It is hardly surprising that World Cup winners would find themselves searching for an adrenaline replacement, but what Grewcock soon realised was that it wasn't actually the rugby that he missed. What he felt he still needed was 'that anxiety, that matchday feeling. And I did need it, but I just didn't need it every Saturday.'

So, he started setting himself challenges, the first of which was the Bath half-marathon. 'That was my Everest,' he says. He was delighted to discover that his knees were up to the job. So, he then began signing up to a different endurance event every one or two years.

Lawrence gets this completely. 'There's a muscle memory that you always find,' he says. 'There's a switch in you that goes, "Yeah. There is something quite good and masochistic about this." You just go into machine mode.'

Grewcock agrees: 'Yeah, you're nearly killing yourself,

whether you're cycling or running or whatever, and there is that old Neanderthal in you going: "Yup, still got it."'

Amongst Grewcock's endurance challenges was a trip to the North Pole, which he did with Lewis Moody and Josh Lewsey. Moody seems to be making a collection of these endurance events, which he does for his own charity; he has done the South Pole as well as the North. Will Greenwood is the same; he has done the North Pole, Kilimanjaro and, in 2022, a coast-to-coast 275km crossing of Costa Rica by foot, bike, kayak and raft.

Greenwood: 'I keep giving myself things in two years' time, three years' time, that athletically I can focus on before I've run out of time and my legs stop working. It's the same for Tuesday and Thursday nights when I'm still down at rugby training. People laugh at this: "Oh, are you reliving your youth?" No, I'm just doing what I was born to do and love doing.'

Grewcock's main focus in 2022 was a 24km race up, down and back again over Pen y Fan, the highest peak in the Brecon Beacons. He did it with some of the Clifton boys and beat them all comprehensively.

Annoyingly, he says, when he got back, he had to get a train straight up to Uttoxeter, where he was a late arrival joining a 750km 'Road to Twickenham' bike ride organised by Wooden Spoon, the leading rugby charity. Amongst others on this ride were Jack Clifford, the recently retired England international, and Nathan Hines, the former Scotland international. And Martin Johnson.

Grewcock had missed the first two days. His good fortune was that Johnson had only signed up to those first two days because he then had to leave to go and join a 25-year anniversary reunion of the 1997 Lions squad. What Grewcock found made him laugh: 'These boys were like, "Oh, my God, days one and two have been horrendous."' That was a reference to the pace Johnson was setting. 'He's a proper endurance athlete. I think no one dared say, "Could you rein it in, Johnno, and slow down?"'

Lawrence has seen this first-hand himself. 'When Johnno's at the front, no one wants to go past him,' he says. 'They're all a bit terrified. Still.'

CHAPTER 52

WHAT DO WE DO NOW?

Ten years ago, when there was last a reunion of the 2003 squad, Lewis Moody took the opportunity to pin down Will Greenwood. It was two years since Moody had quit rugby and he still wasn't really sure in which direction to go next with his professional life. In Greenwood, he had identified a success story, someone who had cracked it; in other words, someone who could give him some advice. What he saw in Greenwood was 'all the broadcasting stuff... the great relationship at Sky he'd created... a brilliant job.' Moody didn't, however, get quite the answers he was hoping for.

Moody: 'I was like, "Mate, you've set yourself up pretty well. You've got a career." But he was like, "No, mate, no, no, no, this isn't a career. I don't really know what I want to do yet." And that really amused me because I was like, "Well, I've just retired. I have no idea what I want to do or what I'm going to do." So, it was really eye-opening to hear him say he still didn't know what he wanted to do because in my eyes he'd already figured it out. But I suppose that's the journey we all go on. Maybe we never quite know.'

Maybe you don't. Paul Grayson retired a year before Greenwood, went straight into coaching and broadcasting yet he says: 'I still don't know what I want to do when I grow up really. That's where I am at 51.'

Another ten years on, has Greenwood worked it out? Not by the sounds of things: 'I still continually wonder what I'm going to be doing in five years' time. I do remember having those thoughts with Lewis ten years ago. I also remember harbouring them myself in 2008, two years after retiring. I still have them now, but less frequently: "Shoot, what am I going to do in five years' time?" Actually, why am I worried about five years' time?'

In the 17 years since he stopped playing, Greenwood has, amongst many things, been a broadcaster, a newspaper columnist and a schoolteacher. His main occupation, now, is as chief customer officer for Afiniti, a data and artificial intelligence company. He says he loves it. He also says he still doesn't know long-term what he wants to do and that maybe he'll never really answer that question: 'The reality is, absolutely there have been times when I've been questioning: what on earth am I doing? And: should I be doing something else? The reality is probably what I was good at had a particular shelf life. And that's why sportsmen struggle.'

Lawrence gets that completely. When you're not a rugby player any more, you're trying to work out who it is that you are now, as well as what it is that you are going to do next: 'In your rugby career, there's very little time to focus on yourself. Life in professional rugby moves at such a pace that you don't have time to sit down and think about what's going on within yourself individually. That's what I found. It's just 100 miles an hour and you're often trying to be something that you're not anyway. Then you've got to pick up the pieces and push them back together again. And part of that is understanding your own identity within the world. And it's not always what you think it is. When you are playing, you are going week to week, game to game and you are in a bubble. You adopt a mechanism to get yourself into character; but that is not the person you are; you very rarely get to be the real you. And I am now 15 years post-retirement and I am still on that journey of discovering who that is. I am still trying to unpack it. I know I'm not that nasty aggressive person you saw on the pitch. I'm actually the opposite; I'm quite nice, I think.'

*   *   *

It is also really hard, even with 'World Cup winner' by your name – at least that has been the experience of Phil Vickery. All those wonderful supporters who told you how great you were – where were they when you were trying to find your way and needed some help?

Vickery has had an extraordinarily varied career post-rugby. It started before he had even been capped by England – when he was 21 years old and had been selected to play tighthead in a scratch 'England' invitation team to play the All Blacks' midweek team on their autumn tour in 1997. That scratch team contained one other significant uncapped up-and-comer (Joe Worsley), but no one was sure how Vickery would fare against Mark Allen, the Kiwi loosehead, who was nine years his senior, had got his first All Blacks cap four years previously, was a player of real swagger –

at least by a prop's standards – and was nicknamed 'Bull' Allen. Yet when Clive Woodward was asked how this young farmer's boy would stand up against the Bull, Woodward replied that Vickery was a bit of a 'raging bull' himself. Thereafter, the nickname never left him.

So when Vickery started a modest clothing line, making kids' sports kit, the brand name was 'Raging Bull'. In 2004, he decided to push the boundaries: 'I said in 2004: "We need to go lifestyle." People said: "You can't do it, it won't work." But we launched that in 05/06. We keep pushing. Blood, sweat and tears. Now we are quietly going along.' Quietly? Raging Bull is in John Lewis and Next. Vickery's next target: M&S.

Yet that is just a part of Vickery's new world. He also runs the restaurant. He is deeply involved, too, in a food wholesale business, Creed Foodservice. 'I am the chief brand officer,' he says. 'I find makers and growers. I am passionate about that.'

Yet for all his success, one of his most striking observations was how little the rugby world and all its satellite hangers-on had been prepared to help him. 'You expected some of the doors to be open,' he said, 'from a business point of view – with sponsors, guidance and help. But I was amazed at how many people just drifted away.'

* * *

Back to Moody. He eventually found his way, but it certainly took him time. When he had finished his England career, he was the England captain and he listened to all those well-meaning people who had told him what that would do for him: 'People go, "Wow, you're going to be doing all sorts. There's the leadership stuff. And you've got all these leadership skills." So, I felt like I should be doing something like that.'

With retrospect, he now recognises that what he was actually feeling was 'I should be doing something that fitted me as an ex-England captain rather than something that fitted my actual skill set and actually the person that I was.' And when he then gets really honest, he becomes very disparaging of his own qualities, admits to suffering from a bad dose of 'imposter syndrome' and says: 'In all fairness, I never thought I was a particularly good England captain anyway. I was just the person who got the role at that time.'

He also says that 'one of my flaws as a player was that I thought I could do everything, that I knew everything and maybe didn't ask enough questions' and that this filtered into his search for the next thing after retirement. 'It meant that I completely ignored the shit that I needed to deal with' – which is largely a reference to the failures of the 2011 World Cup. 'That screwed me mentally for a little while.' Finally, he had a kind of epiphany. 'It's only when you sit down and chat to someone who asks the right questions that you realise, "Actually I'm in the shit. I need a proper conversation."'

That someone was a life coach. Moody says his influence was completely transformative. Around the same time, Moody was also so moved by a young man, Joss Rowley Stark, who died of a brain tumour, that he decided to dedicate his life to his cause. So, he and Annie, his wife, set up a charitable foundation. 'The purpose of my entire existence, until that point, had been being a rugby player. That had gone. My new purpose became supporting people with brain tumours.'

He doesn't earn from the charity, though. His income is from another business that he set up, bringing rugby into schools. This combination appears to have brought him fulfilment and real contentment. He got there, he says, 'because I realised what my natural skill sets were, which were working with other people, supporting other people, all the soft skills.'

So, has he found the answer to that question: what are you going to do next? He pauses and smiles. 'To a degree you're always trying to work it out, right? Whatever role you're in. I think there's always part of you thinking, "Should I be doing this, or should I be doing something else? Maybe I should be selling jet ski rental rides on a beach in Bali."'

CHAPTER 53

THE REAL WORLD – IT'S DIFFERENT, ISN'T IT?

The more that Josh Lewsey worked outside rugby, the more he realised that winning behaviours from the England team weren't necessarily the same behaviours that would translate into success outside of the game. You might be a World Cup winner in rugby, but don't assume that you can carry on operating the same way beyond it. People are wired differently in that place they call 'the real world'. They communicate differently. You have one option, which is to understand and adapt.

That was the conclusion that he reached. So too Iain Balshaw. So too Lawrence. They share furrowed brows at the dawning of their new post-rugby new reality.

This is Lawrence: 'It's quite hard, because we've all been involved in a sport where it's all been about results. It's all been about delivering and performing at your best. And then you join the workplace. And I've been in lots of different roles since

I retired, and you can't understand why people don't share that same mentality. It's like, "Well, what do you mean?"'

Balshaw agrees: 'That was one of the most bizarre things for me. In rugby, everyone is invested in the same outcome, everyone's got the same goal and vision. We're all striving to win the league, win the Heineken Cup, win the World Cup, Six Nations. So, there was no mincing of words and it wasn't personal. If you weren't pulling your socks up, you got told. One of the things I found bizarre is that that's not necessarily how it works in the workplace. You can't tell anybody how it is, because you get reported to HR!'

In other words, you have to make that adjustment from an elite environment to an everyday one. This is Lewsey, who has learned about that adjustment as well as anyone: 'When you're in sport, or the military, you have a clear, simple purpose, a very fast feedback loop and a presumption that people around you also want to be as good as they can be and want the same thing. There's just a presumption and understanding that everyone has the same aim and motivation, which is to make the boat go faster, or whatever it is you are trying to achieve, and that's just ingrained as part of the culture and DNA. Which means that you can be very honest with people, as long as it's with the right sentiment of actually, "I still care about you because ultimately what we all care about is getting the job done." Whereas, when you're in large multinational organisations, there isn't that clarity of purpose, because people have different motivations, the measure of success is also far more opaque and people are different. People are from different backgrounds, they maybe have different key performance indicators, which basically creates this very complex web of cultures and motivations. Therefore, your presumption that everyone wants to achieve the same thing is naive. But this is one of both the blessings and curses of coming out of high-performance environments – you just presume everyone's made like you. High-performance environments prepare you well to lead or deal with pressure, but I don't think they necessarily equip you well for relationships or normal life. You have a level of honesty, which most other people would find direct and uncomfortably rude. Most people don't work in a small special forces unit or an international sports team, which can be quite brutal environments because there's no room for weakness or mistakes. So, becoming kinder, more patient and empathetic to other people who aren't from that environment has probably been a learning experience for a lot of us. You also don't say things that you would do in a sports team; you wouldn't use the same type of language. Just toning down that highly tuned, critical mentality is important to be able to operate in normal life and also, quite possibly, key to becoming a happier and more balanced human.'

CHAPTER 54

NEIL BACK – ALL-IN AND ALL OUT

Neil Back looks great. Healthy, trim, fit. And being Neil Back, he can give you the fitness stats. After retiring as a player, he continued training like one – which is a very Neil Back way to carry on – but after five years, he stopped and asked himself what on earth he was doing. He didn't stop training, he just trained differently and started reconditioning from a rugby player into a more everyday athlete. He is now 6 to 7 kilos down on his World Cup weight and has 4 to 5 per cent more body fat. 'I couldn't wear normal clothes before because my upper torso was too big,' he says. 'It was ridiculous.' He dug out his 2005 Lions blazer the other day, for a charity auction, and tried it on. 'It was like an overcoat.'

Lawrence has an expression for people like Back. He calls them 'all-in' people. Lawrence was an all-in person when he was a player. All of the 2003 squad were. But Back was the most all-in of the lot. Back's all-in commitment was part of what defined him.

In 1996, Back was given a six-month ban for pushing a referee. 'That could have broken me,' he says. Instead, he went so all-in for his rugby career that he hired a personal trainer and a nutritionist for the six months hiatus and trained so hard twice a day, six days a week that, he says, he 'never looked back'.

He had started coaching even before he stopped playing. His last two seasons at Leicester Tigers were as a player-coach. That is a typically all-in approach. Naturally, he had big ambitions: 'I thought: "If I've done it playing, I can do it as a coach."'

So probably the least Neil Back thing you would ever expect Neil Back to do, then, was to say: that's it, I'm out, I've had enough. But after ten years in coaching, that was his decision.

He tells a story about the World Cup final celebrations. People who recall the pictures of that triumphant night in Stadium Australia may remember Back with his four-year-old daughter, Olivia, in his arms. What he himself remembers was before that, when he went over to the crowd to where his family were sitting and he took Olivia from his wife, Ali – because when he then went to take her younger brother, 14-month-old Fin, he wouldn't come. The reason, says Back, was 'because he didn't have a clue who I was'.

That didn't slow him down, though. He did those two years as a Leicester player-coach, then three years as a full-time coach, then three years at Leeds, one year at Rugby Lions, which was a disaster, and then one year at Edinburgh. When he was at Leeds and Edinburgh, he lived where he worked and commuted home. For the last four years of his coaching career, he reckons he was home 30 days a year and for many of those, he says, 'I wasn't really there because my head was somewhere else.' Those were the years when Fin and Olivia were between seven and 11 and nine and 13 respectively. 'Basically,' he says, 'I was never there.'

In the end, Back, the most all-in man in the squad, decided that he was finally all out. 'It had been all about me for the previous 25 years,' he says. 'Then, for the only time in my life, I prioritised my family. I put them first.'

And he looks good on it.

And everything he says, every single word, Lawrence completely and utterly understands. Winning the World Cup was their almighty achievement, but there was untold collateral damage along the way.

Lawrence: 'The biggest regret I have is the guilt. Because it's all about you. When you win, it's all about you. And when you lose, it's all about you too. It's very hard to be a selfish, single-minded rugby player and be a father and a husband. People like Matt Dawson say to me now, "How did you do that? How could you have kids at the age of 24 and do all the shit that we had to go through as well?" And the answer is: I didn't really. That's the biggest regret I have in my rugby career – it's not about being injured at certain times or this, that and the other, it's remorse really and regret at not being able to finish my career and then have kids afterwards. If I didn't invest all of that selfishness in myself, would I have been a better human being at the time? Too right. Would I have been a better father? I mean, I have a relationship with my children, my girls and my son. But if I hadn't played rugby and I hadn't been such a selfish shit, I'd have been such a better father.

'I became very selfish as a sportsman and that was my way of dealing with winning. I realised if I wanted to win, I was going to have to be very, very ruthless and selfish to myself, in the sense I was having to give up friendships. I didn't have enough time for them. I mean, there's no time to be anyone's friend because you're obsessed and you're training and you're working and when you're not doing that, you're resting. So, unfortunately, normal friendships go out of the window. You can't interact and socialise with people in the way that you would like to if you had a normal job because you can't go out on a Friday night or a Thursday night, and then on a Saturday, you've had the shit kicked out of you.

'That's selfish to your family as well, because mentally, physically and emotionally you're away for long periods of the time. I mean, everything happened a bit by destiny: I met Alice on a bus and then we were together and we had our first child at 24 and we weren't married; there was no structure to what happened. And I went away on my first Lions tour in 1997 when my daughter was only a couple of months old. I didn't even think about not going. And still everyone else had to play to my tune. Alice had to live where I wanted to live because I needed to be close to the training ground; she had to stay in London because I wanted to play for Wasps, who were based there. Your family's whole life has to be shaped and changed to accommodate you. It's not normal, and it's all about you.

'So I knew I wasn't going to go into coaching, not because I wasn't a student of the game, or I didn't love the attraction, but I just thought: if I carry on doing this, it's going to be bad for me. It's going to be bad for everyone else around me. All I've ever done for the last 20 years is be obsessed with winning, and playing rugby, and going from week to week, to week. If I continue to do that for another 20 years, I'll either be dead, divorced or both. I thought to myself: I'd played the selfish card long enough. I'd had enough of being disconnected in that way. And I felt that if I do this for another ten years and I end up coaching, then my kids are going to grow up and I'm not really going to know them and they're not going to know me.'

*   *   *

The Neil Back of today no doubt has other passions that he is all-in for. He loves his cars. Maybe that's it. But it isn't any longer as if he is under a magic spell; he isn't a man possessed, determined to prove himself, identifying the top as the only place worth shooting for.

Today, he works mainly with two businesses; one in insurance, the other in retail and construction branding. He represents them in whatever way is required, often ambassadorial, often talking about sport. All in, he speaks at about 30–40 events a year. 'I love what I do now,' he says. Meanwhile, his son Fin is now a professional footballer, on the books at Nottingham Forest and out on loan to Carlisle United for the 2022–2023 season. And Back can go and watch pretty much every match.

And Lawrence was not allowed to forget the sight of Back in those World Cup final celebrations with the four-year-old Olivia on his shoulders. It was not as if his own daughter back home hadn't clocked it: why wasn't I invited, Dad? So, a few weeks later, Lawrence rocked up at Twickenham with a plan to put that right.

'I said to the security guard, "I'm going to take the World Cup," and he said, "No, you can't do that," and I said, "I certainly can." He then said, "You can't," and I said, "Last time I looked, you didn't have any involvement in winning it. I played every minute of every game, so I'm taking it. I'm taking it down to my daughter's school, which is two miles away, and we're going to do 'Show and Tell' in her class." I said to him: "You don't have to tell a soul about this. This will be back here in a few hours, but it's coming with me." And it did.'

CHAPTER 55

BROKEN BODIES

At the back of Matt Dawson's autobiography, there is the kind of career statistics section which you often find in sports books. What is unusual about his stats section is that it includes two pages under the headline 'Career Injuries'. It says that he had 53 of them over ten years, hamstrings and shoulders mainly, though neck and back creep in towards the end. But the book was published two years before his career ended, so we can assume there were a whole load more and yet you don't even think about Dawson as a particularly injury-plagued player.

The cost of a rugby career on a player's body is high and the painful reality is that you never stop paying the price. Body parts carry on giving up on you long after you have given up the game. Like all his teammates, this is what Dawson is coming to terms with. 'I can't run,' he says. 'My calf and hamstrings – even when I am playing football with the boys in the garden, I am dead and buried. No chance.'

He is not alone. Josh Lewsey can't run. Stuart Abbott can

run a bit but only in straight lines. His boys will never see his sidestep. Richard Hill has had a knee replacement and can just about run on it, but he knows he shouldn't. And Dorian West is jealous; he also needs a new knee. These are retired players whose average age is around 50.

'One of my knees needs doing too,' says Jason Robinson. 'The worst thing for me is my neck, which is knackered. I've hardly got any movement. It's always sore.'

Dawson has had heart surgery, though that was due to contracting Lyme disease, one issue that cannot be put at rugby's door. Dan Luger also had heart surgery in 2022, though that was due to a bicuspid heart valve; again, not a rugby matter. Not that rugby didn't come back to haunt him. 'I've had many operations since I stopped,' he says. 'I had my back operated on 18 months ago. I had a laminectomy, where they took some bone out because I lost all the feeling in my left leg and the strength went. It was just from old back injuries. My neck and my back are pretty fucked.'

'I just can't run,' Lewsey says. 'I mean, running is basically a nightmare for my Achilles and ankles and the impact's pretty bad on my back. So, I avoid running and just do regular, lower-impact exercise. Hong Kong is a great place to stay active as it's mostly rainforest and has many beaches. However, I do miss team sports; I miss being part of a team and competing. I miss the camaraderie so I'm trying to get a bit into the sailing here. I also love my surfing, which is my absolute favourite form of exercise but the waves are seldom very good here in Hong Kong.'

After the World Cup, Abbott never got a run of luck. He was only 25 at the World Cup, but a few weeks later, a bad ankle injury put him out for the 2004 Six Nations. He was fit again for the following summer when a shoulder injury, in the second Test against the All Blacks, then kept him out until nearly the end of the year. Then, after only a few weeks back, in a Heineken Cup game against Biarritz, he broke his leg. Thereafter, the niggles kept recurring; he played for most of 2006–07 on an injured knee, but in the last game of the season, another shoulder injury brought the curtain down on his career for good. Unlucky? Yes. An unusual career history? Not really.

Yet, as with so many of Abbott's teammates, there is a hangover. Neither the knee nor the shoulder ever recovered. 'Unfortunately,' he says, 'the injured shoulder is half the size of my other one. It's got really wasted away. And I have no feeling in it; that's the whole deltoid muscle.'

He is clinging on to the remnants of an athletic life. 'I still play the odd game of golf,' he says, 'though the shoulder's still a bit sore. But surfing's good.' This is a man who is 45.

Yet maybe the worst hit of the lot is Hill. He did the ACL in his left knee in October 2004 and then re-tore the same ligament on the Lions tour the following summer. In the process of the second knee reconstruction surgery, he picked up an infection and had to return to hospital for two weeks for three knee clear-outs. When he went in for another clear-out after he retired, the scar tissue was greater than expected, the scalpel snapped and the surgeon informed him that, if he wished, he was in a position to sue the hospital.

'A year later,' he says, 'it was so painful, I went to see the surgeon again and said: "I wish you could just chop my knee off."' He may be losing count, but he believes he's now had 14 knee operations. One of which was to give him an artificial knee. That is the one that he shouldn't be running on.

'The thing is,' says Kyran Bracken, 'we can't get health

insurance.' Bracken still plays tennis and five-a-side football and actually considers his limbs to be working quite well. 'They go: "What's your history?" And I go: "Three back ops, three groin ops, three shoulder ops." I was going skiing and they said, "Any prior operations or injuries?" and I listed them and they said: "Sorry, mate." So, no, I can't get insurance.'

And here is the point. You might be a World Cup winner, but like any professional rugby player, that price that you are still paying is a bill that you are footing yourself.

'I just think that is fundamentally wrong, it's so bad, it's unacceptable,' says Phil Vickery. Vickery managed to push his career through four major back and neck operations, but it was another neck injury that finally did for him and he retired, declaring that it would require 'a lifetime of maintenance'. But now, he says, the business of looking after retired players is 'down to charities, to individuals or groups like the Wasps Legends group to rally round and pull together' and it is this that he finds unacceptable. 'I don't know how the people who run our game can look themselves in the mirror sometimes,' he says. 'We had the best treatment at the time. Wouldn't it be good to have a provision for people now?'

And Lawrence? He got dealt the same hand as everyone else: 'I had 13 operations when I played, I'm probably going to need about another seven or eight before I die, and there's no one that's going to pay for that. I've got an arthritic thumb that bends around in every direction and I'm probably going to have to have a new knee in a few years' time. But there's no duty of care. There's no one saying: you've given 20 years of your body mentally and physically, perhaps we should look after you for the next 20 years. Who is going to pay to look after you? There's only one answer and that is you.'

CHAPTER 56

CONCUSSION

Lewis Moody had warned that Steve Thompson probably wouldn't want to meet up for an interview for this book and it was no surprise to find that he was right. 'I totally understand,' says Lawrence, 'that he doesn't want to speak to me because he's consumed by whatever. I certainly don't take that personally.'

Moody is one of the two players from the '03 squad with whom Thompson keeps a regular line of communication: Moody, who was his roommate at Pennyhill, and Ben Cohen, who was his old teammate at Northampton.

Moody and Cohen both made appearances with Thompson on a BBC documentary in 2022 entitled *Head On: Rugby, Dementia and Me*, a really chilling hour of television which would segue straight from happy family footage of Thompson with his young children to Thompson with his therapist, discussing his suicidal thoughts. And that wasn't a one-off. In 2022, in an appearance at the Hay Festival of Literature with Clive Woodward, Thompson told a heaving audience:

'Have I tried to commit suicide in the last few months? Yes, I have.'

Thompson was at Hay to talk about his autobiography, *Unforgettable*. There are a couple of sentences in there which tell you exactly what he thinks of the game of rugby: 'If I could hitch a ride in the TARDIS and return to my teenage years, I'd much rather not have laid eyes on a rugby ball.'

Of all the collateral damage caused by the World Cup – or by the game – Thompson is the player who has suffered the most. Three years ago, he was diagnosed with early onset dementia. At the time of writing, he is 45; he is already forgetting the names of his children. It is a terrible price to pay. His old teammates hardly know how to summon a response and some are wondering, sometimes worrying, what might be in store for them. Kyran Bracken and Simon Shaw have both reported significant memory loss problems of their own. But almost everyone in the squad can look back on what they put themselves through on the rugby pitch and then, with hindsight, arrive at an understanding of why this has impacted Thompson in this way.

Lawrence: 'I had many, many incidents where I got hit either legally or illegally and I'd have these luminous yellow flashes going off in my head, like Belisha beacons. And I'm looking around thinking: floodlights are flashing in your head? That's not right? And by the time the medic comes on, they've gone. The medic goes: "You OK?" And you go: "Yeah, OK." They go: "OK, that's fine." But if that happened today, you'd obviously go: "No, I'm not OK," and you'd come off.'

Bracken: 'I remember I got knocked out at university a couple of times and I woke up in hospital. I got knocked out quite a few times. I'd say seven or eight times. For one of them, at Saracens, they made me carry on playing. I couldn't see out of one eye. I was being sick at half-time and they were still making me play. I was clearly concussed. What a nightmare.'

Trevor Woodman: 'I had plenty of head collisions. At times I couldn't see anything, as in I didn't have any peripheral vision. I could only see what was in front of me on the playing field. Everything out the sides was flickery. Sometimes after a game, I'd sit in my living room and it had to be pitch-black because any bright light and my head would be killing me.'

Andy Gomarsall still feels haunted by an incident from the 2007 World Cup, when England played Tonga and Moody was allowed to play on even though he had clearly been knocked out not once but twice. The incident sticks in Gomarsall's mind partly because of how bad it was, but also because we know now, 16 years on, how serious these incidents are and how dangerous it is to play on after not just one but two blows. Back then, Gomarsall simply didn't know what was the appropriate response. 'He was out cold twice,' he says. 'It was fucking horrific. And I wasn't strong enough, I didn't know, I was like, "We need Moodos." You know what I mean? But now you think that would never ever get to that stage.'

Lawrence has another anecdote to chuck back at Gomarsall, a 2004 European Cup quarter-final, Wasps versus Gloucester, when they were on opposing sides: 'It was ten minutes in, the score was 0-0, and I clashed heads with my teammate, Paul Volley, and the pair of us were out cold. Now, concussion protocols were rather different back in 2004. When I eventually came round, I then argued with the doctor on duty that there was no way I was coming off the field and convinced him that I was fit to carry on. That wasn't out of any sense of bravado but more out of necessity and the win-at-all-costs mentality. When

I got down the tunnel at half-time, I didn't know the score or, more worryingly, that I had scored a try from a driving maul only minutes earlier. I did go back out for the second half but thankfully I got yellow-carded soon afterwards and, with the game already won, didn't have to come back on.'

What we know now is that incidents like these were dangerous and, in some cases, will have had a long-term impact. Twenty years ago, every player understood that professional rugby might eventually take its toll on their knees most likely, or their backs or their shoulders, or whatever particular limb of theirs was most susceptible, but no one knew that all these impacts might also be long-term bad news for their brain.

This is how Bracken came to understand what was happening to him: 'About four or five years ago, I noticed a little bit of a slur in my speech. I noticed a couple of other things: I was forgetting the names of the in-laws. Then I couldn't get into my house. There was a key code on the outside – and we've been living there a year – and I couldn't remember the code. We're talking just four numbers. And that was not right. I then had psychometric testing for memory stuff. And they're saying: "We need to monitor you over the next few years." So I'm sort of waiting to see. And I also don't know if this is because I had head knocks or was I always going have memory loss? I don't know. If there is anything wrong, it's probably something that is going to be manageable, because I haven't had a decline that I've heard some other people are having. I'm able to do business. I'm able to speak at events. In ten years' time, it may well become a problem. I don't know. But I'm not worried about it because hopefully medicine will be advanced and there'll be more help in ten to fifteen years' time.'

The first time that Bracken talked about this publicly was in an interview in the *Guardian* in 2021. Of the many responses to it were other rugby players getting in touch to ask him more about it. 'There were quite a few,' he says. 'A few from this [2003] group. I won't say who they were. They were saying: "I'm struggling. What do I do?" I said: "Here's a number, just get in touch with them. Go get yourself tested."'

Thompson went public with his memory-loss problems at the end of 2020. Thereafter, other players started sharing similar problems. Bracken was one. Shaw, too, shared the following in an interview in the *Sunday Times*: 'I have my moments. Forgetfulness has always been part of me. And I fob it off as that. There have been occasions where I have forgotten a day and that has concerned me quite a bit. Generally, it's when I'm really tired. Not so long ago we holidayed in Sardinia. Travelled from Toulon on a ferry. I didn't get much sleep. First night at the hotel, sleep wasn't great. We've been to this place a few times and we like to hire a speedboat and go to beaches that can't be accessed by road. After a few days I suggested we spend a day at the beach near the hotel because we hadn't done that. The whole family stopped: "What are you talking about? We spent our first day on the beach near the hotel." I was adamant we hadn't. That day had vanished.'

Yet Shaw rejects the idea that this can be pinned on his rugby career. It is now two years since that initial interview and he says that he hasn't noticed any slow degeneration thereafter: 'I've always been incredibly forgetful. I was the kid that left to go to sport without their trainers. I can't remember where I left my keys. But then to attribute that to what I did for 20 years, I think is just the wrong thing to do. In periods when I've been travelling a lot, I'm not great with sleep. And sleep deprivation is a massive cause of memory loss and cognitive impairment.

For instance, my French is infinitely worse if I'm fatigued and then on other days, I'll almost be bilingual. So, I just don't think when you hit a certain age you can say this is all to do with the sport you've been playing for 25 years.'

Yet it's not as if Shaw has decided that rugby doesn't need help or that concussion doesn't need to be better addressed. Quite the opposite; he has pretty much dedicated himself to the cause.

* * *

Thompson's own relationship with rugby is completely contradictory, as he acknowledges in his autobiography. At one point he writes: 'Rugby was the making of me. But at the same time it destroyed me.' And another: 'The sport that had become my saviour would also be my downfall.'

The backstory here is his tough upbringing in Northampton, where his mother and stepfather chucked him out of the home when he was still a teenager. He hasn't seen them since. He is a classic case of how sport can provide a lifeline. Rugby became his family. His teammates' parents would take him in. The father figure in his life, he says, was one of his rugby coaches from those earlier days. And the game gave him identity, motivation and a sense of self-value.

As a young player breaking into the professional ranks, he was a back-rower. However, he then became a Clive Woodward project: Woodward believed he could be a hooker. Hookers were traditionally small, squat and masters of their art in the scrum and lineout, but Woodward wanted to reinvent the position. He wanted to retain all that set-piece excellence – that was non-negotiable – but he couldn't see why a hooker shouldn't be a ball-carrier too. This was classic Woodward; Woodward the disruptor. In his mind's eye, he had a different kind of hooker. Thompson, it turned out, was exactly whom he was thinking of.

'I thought we had great players all over the pitch,' says Woodward, 'but the one position I didn't think we were really world class on was hooker.'

Woodward then put Thompson to work with Simon Hardy, the England lineout coach. 'I knew he was the right coach,' he says. Hardy babysat Thompson until he was fit for purpose for the international game and the final product was outstanding.

'He was one of England's greatest ever hookers,' says Lawrence, 'and one of England's greatest ever players. A guy that changed the game, really. And I don't think there's been anything quite like him for England since.'

Sitting together at the Hay Festival, Woodward chose to tell the audience about how crucial Thompson was to England by talking them through the lineout throw at the start of the zigzag move in extra time in the World Cup final, the one that led to the Wilkinson drop goal. He told them about the lineout call that Ben Kay made, about his decision to throw to Lewis Moody at the back of the lineout and how that was the harder call and how it was the last thing that Thompson would have wanted to hear: 'I said at the time: "If we win this lineout, we win the World Cup." This is massive pressure. The obvious call, the easy call, is to throw to the front where Martin Johnson is; that's where the Australians thought it was going to go. The tough call, the pressure call, is to throw to the back where Lewis Moody is fundamentally unmarked. When I hear the call, I've gone: "That's a gutsy call." But bosh, away you go: Thommo hits Lewis Moody, we win the World Cup.'

That Hay Festival appearance is a strange thing to watch. On the one hand, they are celebrating Thompson's career and the World Cup triumph; on the other, Thompson is talking about what he believes the game has done to him. And now he is involved in the multimillion-pound legal claim that a large number of players are making against the game's administrators.

From speaking to his old 2003 teammates, you are struck by two reactions to his terrible situation. One is the universal concern, the sense of extreme pity, the recognition that it is one of 'them' and a feeling of helplessness about being unable to remedy the situation. When Lawrence says the following – 'I feel enormously sad that any player is in that situation. I can't begin to imagine what that must be like to deal with day to day. It's incredibly tough. We were all doing the same thing; we were all getting our faces smashed in every week and we were blissfully ignorant of what has turned out to be one of the consequences. So, I am also very aware that that could have been me' – he is repeating sentences that could have come from almost anyone and everyone in this squad.

The other is the fact that though this is a group of players who are now stretched far and wide and rarely united, their bonds are still strong and they will be only too happy to do a favour for each other, to make a charity appearance, attend a fundraising dinner or the like. The time they will give to each other's charities is invariably generous. As Lawrence says: 'The rugby world, I think more than any other world, comes together very quickly to help.' Yet if that is the case, why has there been no 2003 World Cup winners' fundraiser for Thompson?

Even Lawrence himself is not sure why. 'I don't know,' he says. 'Maybe it will happen pretty soon.' He also says: 'Maybe it's not been positioned in the right way yet.'

That last comment might be the point. There are some players who say that they wouldn't have pursued the legal case that Thompson has. There is this middle ground where Lawrence stands. 'I've got no issues with him suing the game,' he says. 'I mean, if that's what he wants to do, that's what he wants to do. Maybe if I was in the situation that he finds himself in, maybe my attitude would be that I would blame other people, but I'm not sure that I would. However, I do think that there is a duty of care, that a club has or the game has, to players after they finish.'

There are also the differing positions held by Bracken and Shaw. Bracken is a member of Progressive Rugby, a group (mainly) of medics and retired players lobbying for quicker and more far-reaching changes to the game to better protect players and then give them aftercare post-retirement. Like Bracken, Thompson is a member of Progressive Rugby, but unlike Thompson, Bracken is not pursuing the legal case against the game.

Meanwhile, Shaw is president of another pressure group called Love of the Game. Shaw had his epiphany when he started thinking about two injuries he suffered, both fractured cheekbones, one in 1997, the other in 2011: same injury, same treatment, same lack of concern for the possibility of a brain injury. And these were 14 years apart. He knew how much treatment for knee injuries, for instance, had improved in that time. 'How had that advanced so much,' he asked himself, 'and yet concussion has basically stood still?' He then considered his work in helping to spread the word of the game and asked himself another question: 'How can I be promoting a sport in these communities around the world that potentially could be dangerous to the people playing it?'

His mission with Love of the Game is not to change the way the game is played. He says: 'My greater purpose for this is absolutely not to dissuade parents from getting their kids into sport.' Instead, he is pushing for a faster pursuit of the science and technology that he believes is required to prevent, diagnose and treat brain injuries. He says: 'I think we're only seeing piecemeal efforts, bit by bit, slowly drip-fed in. The movement should be far more extreme than that, because there's an absolute wealth of knowledge out there.'

Yet his position puts him in a different place to Thompson. 'I've spoken to Thommo a couple of times,' he says. 'I've always got on fine with him. But he probably doesn't think that what I'm doing is the right course, actually, and he probably wants me alongside him, fighting that fight, but I just don't think, from an overall perspective, that does anything for the game, not just our game, for any game.'

So there is no unanimity on this. There is no collective sense of purpose or direction. There are just a lot of teammates knowing that solutions are needed, disagreeing on where to find them but agreeing firmly on one point, as Lawrence puts it, that 'one story, like Steve Thompson's, is one too many, right?'

CHAPTER 57

LEGACY, WHAT LEGACY?

There is another rather more revealing question than 'where are they now?' which is 'where are they *not*?' Because there is a pretty clear answer to that. They are *not* in the system. They are *not* in the RFU. They are *not* with the England team.

Only one of the 31 World Cup winners is permanently employed by the RFU and that is Richard Hill. He is team manager of the England team. Jonny Wilkinson also works as a consultant to the England kickers and Martin Corry sits on the RFU Council. The other 28 World Cup winners have nothing to do with England at all. Previously, Jason Leonard was president of the RFU for a year. Martin Johnson took the team to the 2011 World Cup, was then spat out and that was that. Mike Catt was one of the England coaches in the 2015 World Cup campaign and was also sacked thereafter – which may not have been the smartest use of his intellectual property, because he is now one of the Ireland coaches and, yes, that is the Ireland team who are going into the 2023 World Cup as Grand-Slamming Six Nations champions and the number one ranked team in the world.

Why on earth aren't more of the 2003 squad of 31 involved with England?

That, at least, is a question that Lawrence asks – and he is infuriated by the fact that there is no answer: 'The last time I checked, only one England team has ever won the Rugby World Cup and that was us. Only one group of people know how it was done. So, it might have been smart to ask those 31 people a bit about it. But none of us were ever encouraged to reintegrate back into the fold. There was not even a download after the tournament: 'What do you know that we don't?' It was very strange. It's like: thanks for coming, see you later. Most successful organisations, what they do when they become successful, they come in and they look at the reasons why they're successful and they keep those things in place and they build and add on to that. Not here, not with us.'

It is not that Lawrence is looking for love or attention. 'This isn't about me,' he says. 'It's only about me being very passionate about England rugby. It's me asking: why haven't England won another World Cup? And it's me asking: how can England have produced Martin Johnson, one of the best rugby brains I've ever known, and not found a way to use him? And it's not just Johnno; it's almost an entire squad.'

And it is certainly not that Lawrence is alone in this. It's Neil Back who says: 'I am literally amazed.' Or it's Jason Robinson who says: 'There is a lot of frustration. It's almost so obvious.' Or it is Back asking why Will Greenwood, the brains of the England backline, was never asked to be the England attack coach. Or it's Clive Woodward, who kept on knocking on the door of the RFU and asking to return as director of rugby, who says to Lawrence: 'If I had been there as director of rugby – not as England coach, but director of rugby – all the top people from 2003 would have been involved, because I knew your skill set. And I wasn't scared of any of you. And I saw the opportunities to bring these really talented people into all sorts of varieties of jobs. I'd love to see you guys back involved in really senior positions, where we're using all that knowledge that you had as players. But we just haven't used it.'

It's not as if old England warriors are asking for jobs either. That time has probably largely gone. It's asking what might have been and whether, 20 years on, there isn't still some IP that might be worth tapping into.

'I am amazed they don't set up a mentoring club,' Back says. 'Imagine having Loll as the mentor to the current England No. 8s. He would pass on some gems.'

And imagine using Jason Robinson, the first black player to captain England in a sport that has notoriously struggled with its diversity. Imagine using him as your poster boy, the face of the future. Robinson has certainly imagined that but no one ever asked. 'There are lots of opportunities that constantly get missed,' Robinson says. 'But it's not just the missed opportunity with me, it's the missed opportunity with the whole team – because there is so much knowledge within that team.'

'What they should have done,' Lawrence replies to Robinson, 'is grabbed a number of players, probably you, Martin, Jonny and just said: "Look, you guys really shaped the way that this game has gone, let's use you to drive growth to the game in so many different ways." And they didn't do that because they just sat back and thought it would all just happen. And of course, it didn't happen. It actually came apart much quicker than it took to put it together.'

'From that one World Cup,' Dave Reddin says, 'there should have been a legacy of winning three or four more.'

'What we did,' says Lawrence, 'is we dismantled everything that we built and it was like we went backwards 12 years. For me, it was not so much that we were pushed away. It was almost that everything that we achieved we saw slowly being pulled apart. What we achieved shouldn't have been the peak of success for England rugby, it should have been the start of it.'

CHAPTER 58

WHERE WERE YOU WHEN IT HAPPENED?

Kids are into F1 these days, so in 2022 Lawrence conceded to the pressure from his daughter and took her to the British Grand Prix at Silverstone. When they were there, he knew that her eyes were rolling when people who spotted him stopped and asked him for his autograph. 'But what am I supposed to do? Say no? I never want to say no.'

Then he saw that Jason Robinson was there too, not far from where he was sitting. Same deal. Similarly famous face. And they shared a familiar smile of acknowledgement: here we are, it is 19 years since Jonny's drop goal, and still people want to thank them for it.

For Lawrence, this still happens pretty much every day. Robinson too. Robinson says that you can pretty much see them coming: 'They don't have to speak, I just know. Then they shake your hand and they say thank you. And you know what that is for. And that, for me, is kind of priceless.'

Many won't leave it at that. Robinson: 'They want to tell you where they were that morning. That continues to this day, where people will go back in the blink of an eye, in a split second, to that moment in 2003.'

Lawrence: 'I still smile when people say to me: "You're the only person who's got me drinking in my local pub at eight in the morning."'

That moment, that drop goal, that England victory, absorbed on TVs all around the country early on a late November morning – it was one of those 'Where were you when it happened?' moments. On the road with Lawrence, we've come to something of an understanding of what it took, of what it required those boys of winter to put into it to achieve it and also what it took out of them in return. But nothing will alter the most basic of currency which is the unadulterated joy it brought. England rugby was rich with joy on the back of it and that is why joyful England fans still thank the players for a result they delivered in Sydney 20 years ago.

Lawrence reckons he didn't have to pay for a London taxi for about the next five years.

'People would come up to you everywhere, supermarkets, anywhere,' says Robinson. 'I never paid for anything for a while. It was: "No, no, it's on me."'

For the players, clearly, it opened doors to a different future. Five months after Wilkinson's drop goal, for instance, Matt Dawson was asked to make an appearance as a guest captain on *A Question of Sport*. Seventeen years later, he was still there. And if Jonny had missed? 'There is not a chance that I would be where I am now,' he says. 'Not a chance!'

Ben Kay had always fancied doing TV commentary. When he was at school, for a project in classical studies, he did a commentary to the ancient Olympics in Greece. That was maybe an early indication of how well one of the finer brains in the squad was developing. And he did go on to get his big spot on BT Sport and ITV, and he is excellent at it, but 'absolutely,' he says, that was another prize the World Cup delivered him.

This is all a little sliding doors. Mark Regan didn't get on the pitch that day in Sydney 2003. Four years later, though, he did, as starting hooker for the England team in the 2007 World Cup final against South Africa, when England came up nine points short of a repeat victory. 'If we'd won that,' he tells Lawrence, 'I'd be doing your job on BT Sport.' He is only joking, but he isn't completely wrong either.

Likewise, if Jonny had missed, Jason Leonard might never have become RFU president, Kyran Bracken probably wouldn't have been invited on *Dancing on Ice*, let alone won it, and Phil Vickery probably wouldn't have won *MasterChef* and the knock-on then is that he probably wouldn't have opened his own restaurant either.

'It's not changed us,' says Woodward. 'It's just given us different opportunities.' The whole Woodward family have long recognised that and found a way of celebrating it in a family tradition which still makes them laugh. At the start of a meal out together, they'll raise a glass and share the toast: 'Well done, Jonny Wilkinson!'

CHAPTER 59

SHOW US YOUR MEDALS

If you walked into most of these players' homes, you would do well to spot that a rugby player lived there, let alone a World Cup winner. They tend not to live in rugby memorabilia galleries or in museums of their own personal achievements. Most don't even have a framed shirt on the wall. Mark Regan has what comes closest to a trophy cabinet, but he is the exception.

'I've got a picture of Paul Weller on my wall,' says Martin Johnson, 'and a Stranglers gold disc they gave us, because they're your heroes. I've got a picture of Kenny Dalglish on my wall. And someone gave me a lovely Ray Clemence picture. But I don't want to see pictures of me, it's not a particularly nice sight.'

What you won't see is a World Cup winner's medal. Most of the players aren't exactly sure where their medal is. Some, it seems, are in sock drawers. Some are in storage. Some are at the houses of the players' parents (Dan Luger, Jonny Wilkinson) because they thought they would treasure them more. Indeed, there is only one that we see out on show and, actually, you would hardly call it 'on show'. Mike Tindall's World Cup winner's medal dangles in amongst his wife Zara's bountiful medal collection and is completely dwarfed, particularly by her Olympic silver medal.

Olympic medals tend to be proper big trophies, like small saucers but weighty. Yet as Lawrence says: 'I thought the Australians were good at mining – but you wouldn't have known it by what they put round our necks.'

Phil Vickery's medal actually got stolen. He took it to an event he was attending and showed it around – which is standard practice – but when he next tried to find it, it was gone. It remains a mystery to him.

Matt Dawson thought that his was lost too. He kept it in a bank safety deposit box, but after a couple of years, when he went to collect it, it was gone. The bank was flustered and attempted to find it and eventually worked out that somehow the Dawson deposit box had been getting mixed up with Jason Leonard's. Initially Leonard had kept his medal at home, anyway, but he only moved it to the bank, he explains, when he came home one day and found his two young boys trying to flush it down the toilet. But then Leonard was far more active with his medal (which turned out to be Dawson's medal), taking it to schools, sponsors events and other such occasions. 'So when I eventually go to pick it up,' says Dawson, 'it falls apart. The front comes off, the back comes off. It is a shit medal.'

Danny Grewcock didn't get a medal in Australia for the obvious reason that he was back home in Bath by then. It was then over a year before he did get one – not that he particularly minded – and that was only because of a campaign, waged by the journalist Ian Stafford in the *Mail on Sunday*, which made medal-less Grewcock into a kind of cause célèbre. 'I probably wouldn't have got one otherwise,' he says. 'I certainly wouldn't have chased it. I just left it. And probably didn't come across as wildly grateful to Ian.' Indeed, he didn't. When Stafford rang him with the exciting breaking news that the campaign had been successful, that he had righted the wrong and that Grewcock was finally to receive his medal, he tried to organise a day for the big medal presentation. To which Grewcock responded: 'Thanks, but can't you just bung it in the post?'

*   *   *

The coaches and staff are not quite as phlegmatic about their medals as the players, maybe because some of them knew that they wouldn't get one. Clive Woodward had informed them, even before they left for Australia, that there was only a certain number of 'official' staff that could be named in their World Cup delegation and they were half a dozen over that official number. If they were to win, therefore, those six would not be honoured at the medal presentation.

They were OK with that. But they were a tight group and they weren't so happy when a kind of class system was imposed on them. They were all invited to the BBC 'Sports Personality' night, for instance, to find that some were seated with the players in the audience and some were not. That didn't go down well.

To this day, they remain a tight group. They meet for a reunion dinner every year, taking turns to organise it.

And Woodward was not one to allow a class system to develop. On his return from the World Cup, he organised for replica World Cup winners' medals to be cut for the six who hadn't received them in Australia. 'I put it on my RFU credit card,' he says. 'They cost a fortune.' You get the impression he quite enjoyed the cost aspect and who was paying for it.

The medals were then presented at Pennyhill Park. 'And,' says Woodward, 'it was all quite emotional.'

*　　*　　*

Well, maybe the players do care about their medals after all. In February 2023, Vickery was asked to do an appearance at Gloucester RFC and he was sitting on a stool in front of an audience when Lance Bradley, the club's chief executive, announced: 'We've lured you here under slightly false pretences.'

Bradley then explained that, together with the RFU, they had been trying to see if there was anything they could do about his missing World Cup medal. And Vickery was then presented with another freshly-cut replica World Cup winner's medal.

Vickery was genuinely overwhelmed and warned his audience that he was 'a big old soppy bugger' and likely to get emotional. When he finally pulled himself together, he said this: 'It was 20 years ago, one of the most special moments of my life. And it still goes on today, people stopping me and mentioning it. That moment was one which will be with me forever. To have the medal back – thank you. I will look after this one, I won't be taking it out and showing it to anybody any more.'

CHAPTER 60

JONNY: I'M BETTER THAN EVER

One of the more extraordinary answers to any question asked on this tour of 2003 was when Lawrence asked Jonny Wilkinson when he last did any kicking and the reply that came back was 'Almost every night.' And then, in response to Lawrence's considerable look of surprise, Wilkinson clarified that, yes, he still kicks every day that he possibly can. This is a guy who retired nine years ago.

This requires further explanation. For most of those years since retirement, Wilkinson has lived outside Ascot, which is near Pennyhill. Every evening that he can make it, in that time, he has been back at Pennyhill, back at the heart of this story, kicking for maybe 20 minutes and sometimes shooting basketball hoops for 20 minutes in the gym. He does it, he says, because it is his 'spiritual practice' and then he points out the significant distinction between then and now. The reason he still does it, he says, 'is because I absolutely love it. Not because

I have to. It's part of me exploring who I am. It's no longer a part of me trying to achieve something.'

Still, this was registering some surprise with Lawrence. 'So much has changed,' Wilkinson says, 'and yet so little has changed.'

Indeed, it is quite something that goal-kicking, the skill that tormented and obsessed him, is now his form of therapy. His happy place.

It is quite something, too, when he says that 'I'm better than I ever was.' Again, another Lawrence double-take. 'Of course I am,' Wilkinson says. 'Of course I am.'

'You must have lost a bit of distance?' asks Lawrence.

'No,' comes the reply. 'When you relax, your limbs lengthen, loosen and lengthen.'

It would be nice to report here that the Wilkinson we meet today has found some peace – and that statement would be largely true, though the workings of this complicated mind defy any such straightforward summary. His professional life these days is multi-stranded: there is the bit that the public sees which is the broadcasting, plus he does some coaching with the England team kickers, and added to that there is some work, through his foundation, with businesses and teachers, certain other business involvements, plus his own podcast series, which is about psychology and philosophy. However, there is probably always going to be an outlet for his obsessiveness and it's not going to be something every day like a hobby – his garden, for instance, or snowboarding. It is deeper and more philosophical than that, as he says: 'I'm obsessed with understanding who I am and what life's about. It's an endless journey.'

At least this journey, now, is not controlled, as he says it used to be, 'through anger and fear'. Now, he says, 'it's one that works around things like acceptance, love, compassion. So it's the opposite of the one I was in before.' Which has to be a good thing.

CHAPTER 61

END OF THE ROAD

We are at the end of the road now. But it isn't quite all over.

Just occasionally, on a Saturday afternoon, at Minchin-hampton RFC, you might see a 2003 World Cup winner still at it. The division that Minchinhampton play in is Gloucester 2 North, which is effectively level ten. Yet Mike Tindall doesn't care, in fact he prefers it that way. And he'll sometimes turn out for the veterans' team too.

It helps that 'Minch' is not much more than a mile from his home. What doesn't help them so much is how his contribution has changed. 'I'm so slow,' he says, before asking rhetorically: 'Why am I so slow?!' The solution is he sometimes plays back row, now, instead of centre. But he's done shifts at No. 10 too, when required.

One of the biggest dramas of the matchday now, for him, is when he gets to the changing room. 'That's when I know whether we'll win or lose because you see how many people have come back from university, how many young kids we've got. If you walk in one day and you can see we're all 35-plus, you're like, "We're going to get hammered today."'

That is quite some mind shift from the changing room in Sydney. Yet he is still loving it.

Tindall is the last show on the road, though last season Phil Vickery managed one more game of real significance. As a young boy in Cornwall, his dreams stretched as far as playing for Bude RFC: maybe one day. But he left the club before he ever got to wear the first team jersey. Then the chance came up last year: a charity game against the Bolingey Barbarians, a pub team formed by the Bolingey Inn in Perranporth. Would Vickery consider playing? Of course he would. And he swapped shirts at half-time to play for the Barbarians. There was one particular man who was the reason that Vickery jumped so quickly at the invitation. 'He was a local legend there,' he explains. 'He inspired me when I was a kid because I wanted to be like him. And when I went back, I made sure I told him: "Thank you for what you did for me."'

Will Greenwood is also still inspired by the sheer love of it. 'If I hadn't gone up through the ranks,' he says, 'I'd have been with Preston Grasshoppers till I was 35. For me, it was never about England, really. I just loved the sport. That's why I'm still running around now, occasionally putting a tackle suit on and trying to stay alive.' Those occasions tend to be Tuesday nights when he is coaching his local Maidenhead RFC, who play in the London and South-East Premier Division, which is level five. 'I tell you,' he says, 'I can still run a line at 49. I score a hat-trick most Tuesdays.'

Martin Corry has long been planning his last game. He was waiting for son, Ned, to turn 17 so that they could play in a senior game together. Ned, he says, 'can't really be arsed, but

I'm asking him: just one game.' So that will be for his junior club, Tunbridge Wells, probably around Boxing Day 2023. 'The standard needs to be so shit,' says Corry. Yet he is so keen to play, he put himself through a trial run in a vets' game last season, just to see if he could still survive. 'I was awful,' he says, 'pulled my hammy, but I still did it.'

Lawrence rolls his eyes. 'I can only think about the pain in the physio room afterwards,' he says, but he likes the idea that there are still some 2003 warriors out there, still having a go. He likes it, too, that there is still so much love for the game that united them all 20 years ago.

Yet that is just one perspective. They were united by that one achievement on that magical night in Sydney; the story that has unravelled on the road is how many different perspectives there are.

Here, at the end of the road, Lawrence looks back at a story that is now told so many different ways. It is more layered, now, than tale of triumph and it didn't just end with a drop goal on a magical Sydney night: 'I do, now, reflect more than I ever did at the time that we all had a slightly different experience. This journey has reinforced the love, respect and admiration I have for all of those people, because of the unifying feeling of doing something together. Yet to listen to different versions of the same event and to hear about what was truly going on in the minds of different people is quite fascinating. I thought I knew everything, but you don't, do you? What I realise now are things that I didn't understand about other people and they didn't understand about me. We all knew there was a lot going on in the background, but never exactly what.

'I thought everyone was feeling as joyous and happy as I was – but then that's the way I am, I suppose, or that's the way I want people to be.' This journey has challenged his assumptions. 'I didn't realise the torturous anxieties that some people were having to deal with. And when you go back through it again all these years later, a lot of us have reflected on our own selves and thought: 'I could have been better, I could have been more compassionate.' We look back now and see ourselves as we were then: so completely wired up to doing what we did that we didn't know how to be any other way.'

Everyone has repackaged 2003 in different ways. 'Certain individuals have chosen to forget certain things, because it suits them to do that – and that's OK. As a sportsman, you have to reinterpret events the way it suits you to. What became very apparent is the World Cup meant different things to different people.'

What is also abundantly clear, he says, is that it came at a different cost to different people too: 'Winning is a good thing, but it's complicated.' He then pauses for a different reflection altogether: what if the drop goal hadn't gone over? 'None of us have ever thought about what it would have been like if we hadn't won. What would losing have felt like? I've sometimes joked that we'd have had to go and hide on an island somewhere, but mentally, I'd still be on that island 20 years later.'

But there is a bottom line to all this. As Lawrence says: 'Yes, everyone remembers it differently. Some people wish it had gone better for them; some people are happy just being part of it; but none of it would have been achieved without all of us.'

Here is one final thought. Four World Cups have passed since 2003; at the time of writing, the fifth is just about to commence. That 2003 team remain the only England team to have won the Rugby World Cup, the only northern hemisphere team to do it. As Iain Balshaw says, from the warmth of his

Biarritz home, where he is now a fully-fledged Frenchman with a passport to show for it: people tell him he is still the only Frenchman ever to have won the World Cup. But that doesn't make Lawrence happy. Not the French joke; no, the subsequent failures of generations of England players.

Lawrence: 'There is a part of me that is a bit sad that 20 years later, I am writing a book about something that we did 20 years ago because it's not been done again. Don't, for one minute, think that I wouldn't be really proud if it was done again. If I could finish the book my way, I'd be setting up the winning drop goal in the Stade de France this autumn and England would be winning the next World Cup. Having tasted a small amount of success in my life, I'd want nothing more than for other people to have that. I am not someone who just wants to have it for myself, I want other England players to know what it feels like to win the World Cup. I want other supporters to be able to say: "I was there," or "I was watching you, pissed in the pub at eight o'clock in the morning."'

ACKNOWLEDGEMENTS

This book is about a famous victory, so clearly it wouldn't have happened without everyone who helped England become world champions in 2003. This was one massive team. A lot of those people then spoke to us for the book; we are hugely grateful to everyone for sharing their time, often their hospitality, their recollections and their truths.

This book would also never have happened without David Luxton, who came up with the idea and proposed this book to us. It is fair to say that, initially, we took some persuading! Huge thanks also to Matt Phillips, our editor at Bonnier, who has been smart, encouraging and impeccably patient. We have loved working with the whole Bonnier team.

Lawrence would also like to thank all the husbands, wives, relatives and close family and friends of all the England squad and management. Elite sport can be a selfish business – without your sacrifice and suffering we would never have been able to achieve our goals. Owen would also like to thank Keith

Blackmore and David Chappell: my first *The Times* sports editors, it was you who sent me to Australia for eight weeks to follow this team.

INDEX

INDEX